World Economic Situation and Prospects 2014

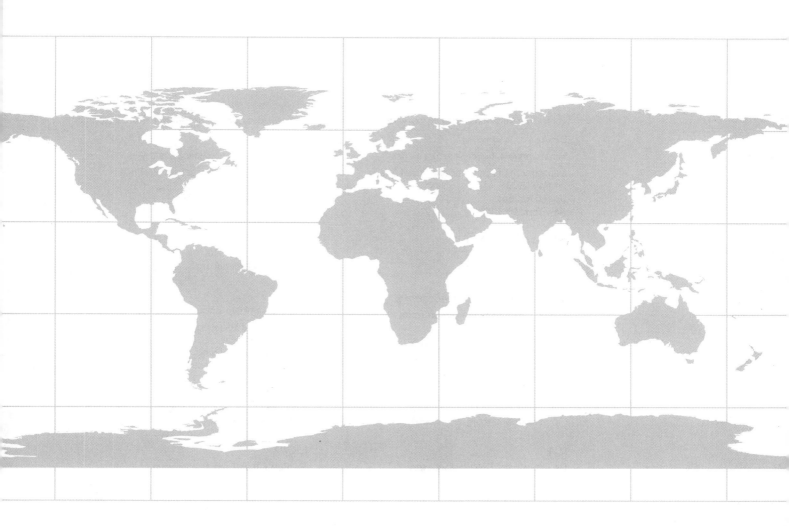

United Nations
New York, 2014

The report is a joint product of the United Nations Department of Economic and Social Affairs (UN/DESA), the United Nations Conference on Trade and Development (UNCTAD) and the five United Nations regional commissions (Economic Commission for Africa (ECA), Economic Commission for Europe (ECE), Economic Commission for Latin America and the Caribbean (ECLAC), Economic and Social Commission for Asia and the Pacific (ESCAP) and Economic and Social Commission for Western Asia (ESCWA).

For further information, see http://www.un.org/en/development/desa/policy/wesp/index.shtml or contact:

DESA

Mr. Wu Hongbo, *Under-Secretary-General*

Department of Economic and Social Affairs
Room S-2922
United Nations
New York, NY 10017
USA

☎ +1-212-9635958
✉ wuh@un.org

UNCTAD

Dr. Mukhisa Kituyi, *Secretary-General*

United Nations Conference on Trade
and Development
Room E-9042
Palais de Nations, 8-14
Av. de la Paix, 1211
Geneva 10
Switzerland

☎ +41-22-9171234
✉ sgo@unctad.org

ECA

Dr. Carlos Lopes, *Executive Secretary*

United Nations Economic Commission for Africa
Menelik II Avenue
P.O. Box 3001
Addis Ababa
Ethiopia

☎ +251-11-5511231
✉ ecainfo@uneca.org

ECE

Mr. Sven Alkalaj, *Executive Secretary*

United Nations Economic Commission for Europe
Palais des Nations, CH-1211
Geneva 10
Switzerland

☎ +41-22-9174444
✉ info.ece@unece.org

ECLAC

Ms. Alicia Bárcena, *Executive Secretary*

Economic Commission for Latin America
and the Caribbean
Av. Dag Hammarskjöld 3477
Vitacura
Santiago de Chile
Chile

☎ +56-2-22102000
✉ secepal@cepal.org

ESCAP

Ms. Noeleen Heyzer, *Executive Secretary*

Economic and Social Commission for Asia
and the Pacific
United Nations Building
Rajadamnern Nok Avenue
Bangkok 10200
Thailand

☎ +66-2-2881234
✉ unescap@unescap.org

ESCWA

Ms. Rima Khalaf, *Executive Secretary*

Economic and Social Commission for Western Asia
P.O. Box 11-8575
Riad el-Solh Square, Beirut
Lebanon

☎ +961-1-981301
@ http://www.escwa.un.org/main/contact.asp

Acknowledgements

For the preparation of the global outlook, inputs were received from the national centres of Project LINK and from the participants at the annual LINK meeting held in New York from 21 to 23 October 2013. The cooperation and support received through Project LINK are gratefully acknowledged.

The report was prepared under the coordination of Pingfan Hong, Acting Director of the Development Policy and Analysis Division (DPAD) in UN/DESA. Overall guidance was provided by Shamshad Akhtar, Assistant Secretary-General for Economic Development.

We gratefully acknowledge the team at **UN/DESA**: Grigor Agabekian, Clive Altshuler, Rachel Babruskinas, Ian Cox, Ann D'Lima, Cordelia Gow, Matthias Kempf, Leah C. Kennedy, Pierre Kohler, Mary Lee Kortes, Hung-yi Li, Nitisha Pandey, Mariangela Parra-Lancourt, Ingo Pitterle, Daniel Platz, Hamid Rashid, Benu Schneider, Oliver Schwank, Krishnan Sharma, Benjamin Singer, Shari Spiegel, Alex Trepelkov, Sebastian Vergara, Sergio P. Vieira and John Winkel; at **ECA**: Hopestone Chavula, Adam Elhiraika, Michael Mbate and John Robert Sloan; at **ECE**: José Palacín and Robert Shelburne; at **ECLAC**: Juan Alberto Fuentes, Michael Hanni, Sandra Manuelito, Ricardo Martner and Jurgen Weller; at **ESCAP**: Shuvojit Banerjee, Sudip Ranjan Basu, Anisuzzaman Chowdhury, Yejin Ha, Matthew Hammill, Aynul Hasan, Daniel Jeongdae Lee, Nagesh Kumar, Muhammad Hussain Malik, Oliver Paddison, Rakesh Raman, Vatcharin Sirimaneetham and Sutinee Yeamkitpibul; at **ESCWA**: Abdallah Al Dardari, Mohamed Hedi Bchir, Sandra El-Saghir Sinno and Yasuhisa Yamamoto; at **UNCTAD**: Christina Bodouroglou, Alfredo Calcagno, Rajan Dhanjee, Pilar Fajarnes, Marco Fugazza, Masataka Fujita, Samuel Gayi, Jan Hoffmann, Taisuke Ito, Alex Izurieta, Alexandra Laurent, Mina Mashayekhi, Jörg Mayer, Nicolas Maystre, Alessandro Nicita, Janvier Nkurunziza, Victor Ognivtsev, Jose Rubiato, Mesut Saygili, Astrit Sulstarova, Komi Tsowou, Vincent Valentine, Jan-Willem Vanhoogenhuizen, and Yan Zhang; and at **UNWTO**: Michel Julian, John Kester and Javier Ruescas.

Explanatory notes

The following symbols have been used in the tables throughout the report:

..	Two dots indicate that data are not available or are not separately reported.		.	A full stop is used to indicate decimals.
–	A dash indicates that the amount is nil or negligible.		/	A slash between years indicates a crop year or financial year, for example, 2013/14.
-	A hyphen indicates that the item is not applicable.		-	Use of a hyphen between years, for example, 2013-2014, signifies the full period involved, including the beginning and end years.
–	A minus sign indicates deficit or decrease, except as indicated.			

Reference to "dollars" ($) indicates United States dollars, unless otherwise stated.

Reference to "billions" indicates one thousand million.

Reference to "tons" indicates metric tons, unless otherwise stated.

Annual rates of growth or change, unless otherwise stated, refer to annual compound rates.

Details and percentages in tables do not necessarily add to totals, because of rounding.

Project LINK is an international collaborative research group for econometric modelling, coordinated jointly by the Development Policy and Analysis Division of UN/DESA and the University of Toronto.

For country classifications, see statistical annex.

Data presented in this publication incorporate information available as at 30 November 2013.

The following abbreviations have been used:

bpd	barrels per day		LDCs	least developed countries
BIS	Bank for International Settlements		LLDCs	landlocked developing countries
CIS	Commonwealth of Independent States		LTROs	long-term refinancing operations
CPI	consumer price index		MDGs	Millennium Development Goals
DAC	Development Assistance Committee (of the Organization for Economic Cooperation and Development)		MDRI	Multilateral Debt Relief Initiative
			MFN	most favoured nation
DFQF	duty-free quota-free		ODA	official development assistance
ECB	European Central Bank		OECD	Organization for Economic Cooperation and Development
EU	European Union			
FDI	foreign direct investment		OMT	outright monetary transaction
Fed	Federal Reserve of the United States		pb	per barrel
FSB	Financial Stability Board		QE	quantitative easing
G20	Group of Twenty		RTAs	regional trade agreements
GCC	Gulf Corporation Council		SEC	United States Securities and Exchange Commission
GDP	gross domestic product		SIDS	small island developing States
GNI	gross national income		SMEs	small- and medium-sized enterprises
GVCs	global value chains		UN/DESA	Department of Economic and Social Affairs of the United Nations Secretariat
HIPC	heavily indebted poor countries			
IDA	International Development Association		UNCTAD	United Nations Conference on Trade and Development
IIF	Institute of International Finance		UNFCCC	United Nations Framework Convention on Climate Change
IMF	International Monetary Fund		WGP	world gross product
IT	information technology		WTO	World Trade Organization

Executive summary

Prospects for global macroeconomic development

Global growth underperformed in 2013, but is expected to improve in 2014-2015

The world economy reached only subdued growth of 2.1 per cent in 2013. While most developed economies continued to grapple with the challenge of taking appropriate fiscal and monetary policy actions in the aftermath of the financial crisis, a number of emerging economies, which had already experienced a notable slowdown in the past two years, encountered new domestic and international headwinds during 2013.

Some signs of improvement have emerged more recently. The euro area has finally come out of a protracted recession, with gross domestic product (GDP) for the region as a whole starting to grow again; the economy of the United States of America continues to recover; and a few large emerging economies, including China, seem to have at least stopped a further slowdown or will see accelerating growth. World gross product (WGP) is forecast to grow at a pace of 3.0 and 3.3 per cent in 2014 and 2015, respectively.

Inflation outlook remains benign

Inflation remains tame worldwide, partly reflecting excess capacity, high unemployment, fiscal austerity and a continued financial deleveraging in major developed economies. Among developed economies, deflationary concerns are rising in the euro area while Japan has managed to end its decade-long deflation. Among developing countries and economies in transition, inflation rates are above 10 per cent in only about a dozen economies scattered across different regions, particularly in South Asia and Africa.

High unemployment remains a key challenge

The global employment situation remains dire, as long-lasting effects from the financial crisis continue to weigh on labour markets in many countries and regions. Among developed economies, the most challenging situation is found in the euro area, in which the unemployment rates have reached as high as 27 per cent in Greece and Spain, with youth unemployment rates surging to more than 50 per cent. The unemployment rate has declined in the United States, but remains elevated. In developing countries and economies in transition, the unemployment situation is mixed, with extremely high structural unemployment in North Africa and Western Asia, particularly among youth. High rates of informal employment as well as pronounced gender gaps in employment continue to characterize labour markets in numerous developing countries.

A number of countries are making concerted efforts to improve employment conditions, such as aligning macroeconomic policies appropriately with domestic conditions and taking steps to induce advances in productivity and innovation. However, further public investment in skills training and upgrading will be necessary to integrate those groups that have been excluded.

International trade and financing for development

Moderate rise in trade growth is anticipated along with flattening commodity prices

Growth of world merchandise trade weakened further in 2013, dragged down by slow global growth. Sluggish demand in many developed countries and faltering growth in developing countries led to a decline in world export volume growth from 3.1 per cent in 2012 to only 2.3 per cent in 2013—well below the trend prior to the financial crisis. The prospects for world trade are expected to improve, driven by a modest increase in demand in Europe, further recovery in the United States and a return to more dynamic trade in East Asia. Growth of world exports is projected to be 4.6 per cent in 2014 and 5.1 per cent in 2015. Trade in services, which appears to be recovering faster than merchandise trade, is expected to continue growing over the forecast period after a noticeable improvement in mid-2013.

Commodity prices have displayed divergent trends over the course of 2013 in the midst of an overall moderation. Food prices have gradually declined, owing to better than expected harvests of major crops. Soft demand, ample supply and high stock levels all contributed to declines in base metals prices. Oil prices have seen significant fluctuations over the course of the year as a result of various geopolitical issues. Commodity prices are expected to remain relatively flat on average across the forecast horizon.

Multilateral trade negotiations reach limited agreement while regional trade agreements boom

There have been some limited agreements in Doha Round negotiations in three areas: agriculture, development and trade facilitation. The economic effect of these changes is unclear at this point and is unlikely to affect trade in the forecast period. The international trading system has become more fragmented, and considerable uncertainty about particular forthcoming decisions remains.

Regional trade agreements (RTAs) continue to boom, with 379 already in force. There are currently two large RTAs being negotiated—the Trans-Atlantic Trade and Investment Partnership between the United States and the European Union and the Trans-Pacific Partnership, involving 12 countries including Japan and the United States. These agreements would cover a majority of world trade and are seen by some as a less ambitious, alternative version of the Doha Round. There is some concern about the potential effects on developing countries that are not a part of these RTAs, such as marginalization or impacts on their competitiveness. Steps to further South-South regional integration are being explored, including efforts by the African Union to fast-track the initiation of a Continental Free Trade Area by 2017.

Volatility of capital inflows and risk premium to emerging economies have increased

Capital inflows to a number of developing countries and economies in transition have shown a measurable decline during 2013, along with significantly increased volatility in the financial markets of emerging economies, featuring equity markets sell-offs and sharp depreciations of local currencies. This was partly triggered by the United States Federal Reserve announcement that it may begin tapering the amount of its monthly purchases of long-term assets later in the year. Waning growth prospects for emerging economies have also played a role in triggering the decline of capital inflows.

Long-term financing is essential for promoting sustainable development

Discussions on the post-2015 development agenda have highlighted the enormous needs for financing the social, economic and environmental dimensions of sustainable development. Long-term financing will be essential for raising the resources required for a transition to a green economy and for promoting sustainable development. Yet, to date, the international financial system has failed to adequately allocate resources for long-term sustainable development needs. There has been insufficient investment in a number of critical areas: infrastructure; health, education and sanitation services for the world's poor; small- and medium-sized enterprises and financial services for all; and the green technologies necessary to address climate change in both developed and developing countries.

Uncertainties and risks

A bumpy exit of quantitative easing measures poses significant risks for the world economy

Great uncertainties and risks for global economic growth and the financial stability of the world in the coming years are inextricably associated with the unconventional monetary policies, such as quantitative easing (QE), adopted in major developed countries. Uncertainty and risk come into play particularly when the central banks of these countries start to change their stances on these policies. A bumpy exit from QE could lead to a series of disruptive events, such as: a surge in long-term interest rates, not only in developed economies but also in developing countries; a sell-off in global equity markets; a sharp decline of capital inflows to emerging economies; and a spike in the risk premia for external financing in emerging economies. Those first-round shocks in international financial markets could transmit quickly to the domestic real economic sectors of both developed and developing countries.

Many large developing countries, including Brazil, China, India and the Russian Federation, saw a significant deceleration in GDP growth in the past two years, owing to a combination of challenging external conditions and domestic impediments. In the baseline outlook discussed earlier, growth in these economies is expected to strengthen in some cases, such as Brazil, India and the Russian Federation, and to stabilize in others, such as China. Risks remain, however, for a further slowdown for some of these economies.

The systemic risks in the euro area have abated significantly, but fragilities remain in both the financial sector and the real economy. Uncertainties associated with the political wrangling in the United States over budget issues and the debt ceiling continue to loom. Moreover, beyond economic risks, geopolitical tensions might spiral out of control. These and other risk factors, unfolding unexpectedly, could derail the world economy far away from the projections outlined in the baseline forecast.

Policy challenges

Policymakers in major developed countries should work to harness a smooth process for the changes in QE coming over the next few years. Central banks in these countries should develop a clear communication strategy to articulate the timing and the targets of the policy action. A premature unwinding may risk choking off the economic recovery, but a delayed unwinding could risk creating financial bubbles. Efforts are needed to enhance the supervision, regulation and surveillance of financial markets in order to identify and mitigate financial risks and vulnerabilities.

For developing countries and emerging economies, the challenge is to forefend themselves against the spillover effects of the QE unwinding. These economies should address external and internal imbalances and build policy space. Supervision and regulation should also be strengthened to prevent a build-up of mismatches in foreign currency funding on bank balance sheets. Prudential oversight should be tightened, particularly for shadow banking activity.

In addition to macroeconomic policies, many countries, both developed and developing, have undertaken various institutional reforms, including reforms in social security, income distribution, financial sector, taxation, energy, transportation, education and health care. These reforms are crucial to the rebalancing of economic structure, removal of supply-side constraints, mobilization of resources for long-run investment, and improvement of macroeconomic management and financial regulation.

The globally concerted policy actions should be focused on a stronger recovery

The multiple and complex challenges in the world economy call for strengthening of international policy coordination. The primary focus of the globally concerted and coherent policy actions should be on a stronger recovery—particularly the recovery of jobs—and increasing attention should be given to mitigating the spillover effects emanating from the QE exit.

International policy cooperation and coordination are needed to advance the reforms of the international financial system on several fronts. Progress in financial regulatory reform has been slow, encountering growing resistance from the financial industry. Some progress has been made in amending the global financial safety standards for the banking sector. More forceful efforts are needed to address the issues of international tax avoidance and evasion, particularly through tax havens.

International policy cooperation should ensure that sufficient resources are made available to least developed countries

International policy cooperation should ensure that sufficient resources are made available to developing countries, especially least developed countries and countries that possess limited fiscal space and face large financing needs for sustainable development and poverty reduction. The decline in official development assistance flows over the past two years should be reversed. As the target date for the United Nations Millennium Development Goals (MDGs) is approaching, international donors should redouble their efforts to deliver on existing commitments. These resources are badly needed in order for developing countries to accelerate progress towards the achievement of the MDGs, and for all countries to build a solid foundation for long-run sustainable development beyond 2015.

Table of contents

Statistical annex
Country classification

Tables

Page

Annex tables

Chapter I
Global economic outlook

Prospects for the world economy in 2014-2015

Global growth continues to face headwinds

The world economy has experienced subdued growth for another year in 2013, unable to meet even the modest projections many institutional forecasters made earlier, including the *World Economic Situation and Prospects (WESP) 2013*. According to the information available in November, world gross product (WGP) is estimated to have grown by 2.1 per cent in 2013, lower than the baseline forecast of 2.4 per cent published in *WESP 2013*, but still better than the alternative pessimistic scenario presented in that report.[1]

Underperformance in the world economy was observed across almost all regions and major economic groups. Most developed economies continued struggling in an uphill battle against the lingering effects of the financial crisis, grappling in particular with the challenges of taking appropriate fiscal and monetary policy actions. A number of emerging economies, which had already experienced a notable slowdown in the past two years, encountered new headwinds during 2013 on both international and domestic fronts.

The world economy underperformed across almost all regions in 2013

Some signs of improvements have shown up more recently: the euro area has finally come out of a protracted recession, with gross domestic product (GDP) for the region as a whole returning to growth; a few large emerging economies, including China, seem to have backstopped a further slowdown and are poised to strengthen. Premised on a set of assumptions (box I.1), WGP is forecast to grow at a pace of 3.0 and 3.3 per cent for 2014 and 2015, respectively (table I.1, figure I.1). Again, this baseline forecast is made in the context of a number of uncertainties and risks emanating from possible policy missteps and factors beyond the economic domain.

Despite the notable differentials in the growth rates among different groups of countries, cyclical movements in growth remain synchronized (figure I.2). While the average growth of middle-income countries continues to be the highest, growth for the least developed countries (LDCs) is expected to strengthen in 2014-2015 (box I.2).

Cyclical movements in growth remain synchronized among world economies

Among developed countries,[2] the United States of America is estimated to grow at a meagre pace of 1.6 per cent in 2013, significantly lower than the 2.8 per cent growth of the previous year. Fiscal tightening and a series of political gridlocks over budgetary issues during the year have weighed heavily on growth. Monetary policy has been extremely accommodative, but it has had greater effect on boosting equity prices than

Political wrangling over budgetary issues lingers in the United States

---

1 *World Economic Situation and Prospects 2013* (United Nations publication, Sales No. E.13.II.C.2), available from http://www.un.org/en/development/desa/policy/wesp/wesp_current/wesp2013.pdf.

2 Chapter IV contains a more detailed discussion on the economic outlook for different regions and countries.

Table I.1
Growth of world output, 2007-2015

Annual percentage change	2007-2010[a]	2011	2012[b]	2013[c]	2014[c]	2015[c]	Change from WESP 2013 forecast[d] 2013	Change from WESP 2013 forecast[d] 2014
World	1.8	2.8	2.4	2.1	3.0	3.3	-0.3	-0.2
Developed economies	0.3	1.5	1.3	1.0	1.9	2.4	-0.1	-0.1
United States of America	0.3	1.8	2.8	1.6	2.5	3.2	-0.1	-0.2
Japan	0.0	-0.6	1.9	1.9	1.5	1.2	1.3	0.7
European Union	0.2	1.7	-0.4	-0.1	1.4	1.9	-0.7	-0.3
EU-15	0.1	1.5	-0.5	-0.1	1.4	1.8	-0.6	-0.2
New EU members	2.0	3.0	0.6	0.5	2.1	2.7	-1.5	-0.8
Euro area	0.2	1.6	-0.7	-0.5	1.1	1.6	-0.8	-0.3
Other European countries	1.1	1.6	1.9	1.7	2.6	2.9	0.2	0.7
Other developed countries	1.6	2.4	2.5	2.0	2.6	2.9	0.0	-0.4
Economies in transition	2.9	4.6	3.2	2.0	3.3	4.0	-1.6	-0.9
South-Eastern Europe	2.6	1.9	-0.9	1.8	2.6	3.1	0.6	0.0
Commonwealth of Independent States and Georgia	2.9	4.8	3.4	2.0	3.4	4.1	-1.8	-1.0
Russian Federation	2.4	4.3	3.4	1.5	2.9	3.6	-2.1	-1.3
Developing economies	5.9	5.9	4.7	4.6	5.1	5.3	-0.5	-0.5
Africa	4.8	0.8	5.7	4.0	4.7	5.0	-0.8	-0.4
North Africa	4.6	-6.1	7.2	2.3	3.3	4.3	-	-
East Africa	6.5	6.5	6.0	6.0	6.4	6.4	-	-
Central Africa	4.8	3.9	5.8	4.2	4.8	4.1	-	-
West Africa	6.0	6.1	6.7	6.7	6.9	6.8	-	-
Nigeria	6.9	6.8	6.5	6.5	6.9	6.7	-0.3	-0.3
Southern Africa	3.9	4.0	3.5	3.6	4.2	4.4	-	-
South Africa	2.6	3.5	2.5	2.7	3.3	3.7	-0.4	-0.5
East and South Asia	7.6	7.0	5.5	5.6	5.8	6.0	-0.4	-0.5
East Asia	7.7	7.1	5.9	6.0	6.1	6.1	-0.2	-0.4
China	10.8	9.3	7.7	7.7	7.5	7.3	-0.2	-0.5
South Asia	6.9	6.4	4.2	3.9	4.6	5.1	-1.1	-1.1
India	8.1	7.3	5.1	4.8	5.3	5.7	-1.3	-1.2
Western Asia	4.0	6.9	3.9	3.6	4.3	3.9	0.3	0.2
Latin America and the Caribbean	3.4	4.4	3.0	2.6	3.6	4.1	-1.3	-0.8
South America	4.5	4.6	2.5	3.2	3.4	4.1	-0.8	-1.0
Brazil	4.6	2.7	0.9	2.5	3.0	4.2	-1.5	-1.4
Mexico and Central America	1.4	4.1	4.0	1.5	4.0	4.2	-2.4	-0.6
Mexico	1.2	4.0	3.9	1.2	4.0	4.2	-2.6	-0.6
Caribbean	3.5	2.7	2.8	2.4	3.3	3.8	-1.3	-0.5
By level of development								
High-income countries	0.6	1.7	1.5	1.2	2.1	2.5	-0.1	-0.1
Upper-middle-income countries	5.9	5.9	5.1	4.6	5.3	5.4	-0.8	-0.5
Lower-middle-income countries	6.1	5.8	4.4	4.7	5.0	5.4	-0.8	-1.0
Low-income countries	6.1	6.2	6.0	5.7	6.1	6.1	-0.2	0.2
Least developed countries	6.9	3.6	4.9	5.4	5.7	5.7	-0.3	0.2
Memorandum items								
World trade[e]	3.0	6.7	2.9	2.3	4.7	5.2	-2.0	-0.2
World output growth with PPP-based weights	3.0	3.7	3.0	2.9	3.6	4.0	-0.4	-0.4

Source: UN/DESA.

a Average percentage change.

b Actual or most recent estimates.

c Forecast, based in part on Project LINK and baseline projections of the UN/DESA World Economic Forecasting Model.

d See *World Economic Situation and Prospects 2013* (United Nations publication, Sales No. E.13.II.C.2).

e Includes goods and services.

Figure I.1
Growth of world gross product, 2007-2015[a]

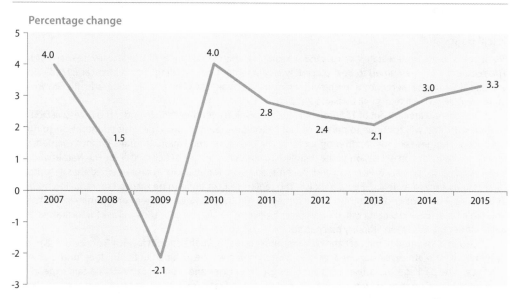

Percentage change

Source: UN/DESA.
a Growth rate for 2013 is partially estimated; rates for 2014 and 2015 are forecast.

Box I.1.
Major assumptions for the baseline forecast

This box summarizes key assumptions underlying the baseline forecast, including monetary and fiscal policies for major economies, exchange rates for major currencies, international prices of oil and other primary commodities. Policy assumptions for other countries can be found in the text of chapter IV.

Monetary policy

The United States Federal Reserve (Fed) is expected to continue its accommodative stance in the outlook for 2014-2015. In accordance with the forward monetary policy guidance of the Fed, it is assumed that in the forecasting period of 2014-2015 the federal funds interest rate will remain within the range of 0.0 to 0.25 per cent until mid-2015, followed by a gradual increase starting in the third quarter of 2015. The adjustment of long-term assets on the Fed balance sheet will be implemented in three phases: the Fed will taper the amount of its purchases beginning in December of 2013, from the current level of $85 billion per month, and gradually reach zero by mid-2014; assets will be held on its balance sheet for the period until mid-2015; assets will then be unloaded gradually, beginning in the third quarter of 2015.

The European Central Bank is assumed not to cut its policy interest rates further, but to keep policy rates at the current levels through the end of 2015, followed by a gradual path of increases. The outright monetary transaction programme will remain in place and refinancing operations will continue to meet the needs of the banking sector.

The Bank of Japan (BoJ) is assumed to continue its Quantitative and Qualitative Monetary Easing programme as it was originally designed until the end of 2014. The policy rate for BoJ is also assumed to stay within the range of 0.0 to 0.1 per cent through the end of 2015, to accommodate the second hike of the consumption tax rate that is assumed to be implemented in October 2015.

The People's Bank of China is expected to maintain its prudent monetary policy stance, while making some adjustments to ensure a balance between growth and economic restructuring. Interest rates are likely to remain unchanged over the next few quarters. Money supply growth is expected to moderate slightly in 2014-2015. Meanwhile, continued financial reform—especially further liberalization of interest rates—and increased regulations in the shadow banking sector will have significant impacts on the liquidity conditions in the economy, on top of conventional monetary policy.

Box I.1.
Major assumptions for the baseline forecast (*continued*)

Fiscal policy

Fiscal policy in the United States is expected to remain restrictive in 2014-2015, but less severe than 2013. The sequestration is assumed to be replaced by an agreement on spending cuts in Medicare, Medicaid and Social Security. Emergency unemployment insurance benefits will be phased out gradually. Government spending in real terms will be flat in 2014-2015.

In the euro area, 12 out of 17 European Monitory Union countries remain under the Excessive Deficit Procedure and will continue to pursue consolidation programmes, with the crisis countries pursuing even more stringent consolidation programmes. The Economic and Financial Affairs Council granted a number of countries an extension of the deadline to correct excessive deficits: 2014 for the Netherlands and Poland; 2015 for France, Portugal and Slovenia; and 2016 for Spain. They also deemed that Italy has corrected its excessive deficit. Fiscal policy in the region will continue to be focused on reducing fiscal imbalances. The debt crisis countries are assumed to continue their adjustment programmes, but the timetable for achieving targets will in some cases be extended, and no countries will ask for formal assistance, under the European Stability Mechanism.

Japan is assumed to increase the consumption tax rate from the current level of 5 per cent to 8 per cent in April 2014. An expansionary package of 5 trillion yen will be included in the budget for the 2014 fiscal year. The package will consist of lower rates for other taxes and higher outlays for certain expenditure categories. The second increase in the consumption tax rate, from 8 per cent to 10 per cent, will be implemented in October 2015.

China is expected to maintain a proactive, mildly expansionary fiscal policy stance. Public spending will continue to increase in the areas of education, health care and other forms of social expenditures. The general government budget deficit is expected to rise slightly to 2.0 per cent of gross domestic product in 2013 and 2014.

Exchange rates among major currencies

The dollar-to-euro exchange rate is forecast to fluctuate around its current level, averaging 1.32 dollars per euro in the rest of 2013, with the dollar appreciating gradually, resulting in a full-year average of 1.27 dollars per euro in 2014, and 1.21 in 2015.

The yen-to-dollar exchange rate will average 102.5 and 104.5 for 2014 and 2015, respectively.

The renminbi-to-dollar exchange rate is expected to average 6.07 CNY per dollar in 2014 and 6.03 CNY per dollar in 2015, following an estimated 6.15 CNY/dollar in 2013.

Oil price

Source: UN/DESA.   The Brent oil price is expected to be about $108 per barrel for 2014-2015.

on stimulating the real economy. Expectations arising in mid-2013 about the possible tapering of the quantitative easing programme caused some jitters in financial markets, pushing up long-term interest rates. A moderate improvement earlier in 2013 in such areas as housing and employment lost momentum towards the end of the year. In the outlook, assuming that the future unwinding of the monetary easing will be smooth, GDP is expected to increase 2.5 and 3.2 per cent for 2014 and 2015, respectively. Risks remain on the downside, however, particularly because political wrangling over the budget may linger for several years.

Europe has emerged from recession, but just barely

Western Europe emerged from recession in the second quarter of 2013, led by net exports and, to a lesser extent, private and public consumption, but investment remained weak and unemployment stood elevated. GDP is expected to grow by 1.5 and 1.9 per cent in 2014 and 2015, respectively. Growth remains weak due to a number of factors: fiscal austerity programmes, while reduced in intensity, remain a drag; intraregional demand is

Figure I.2
Growth of per capita GDP by level of development, 2000-2015[a]

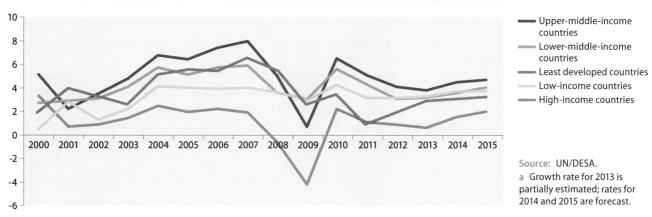

Legend:
— Upper-middle-income countries
— Lower-middle-income countries
— Least developed countries
— Low-income countries
— High-income countries

Source: UN/DESA.
a Growth rate for 2013 is partially estimated; rates for 2014 and 2015 are forecast.

Box I.2
Prospects for the least developed countries

The economies of the least developed countries (LDCs) will continue to expand at a solid rate, with growth forecast at 5.7 per cent in 2014 and 2015 following growth of 5.4 per cent in 2013. However, per capita GDP is expected to increase at only 3.2 per cent in 2014 and 2015, which, in many LDCs, will have only a limited impact on living standards, given the widespread levels of poverty. Major obstacles for stronger economic and social development include institutional deficits, a lack of infrastructure, and political instability.

Performance is diverse among individual countries in the LDCs. In numerous African LDCs, such as Angola, Liberia, Sierra Leone, the United Republic of Tanzania, and Zambia, investment in the natural resource sector will drive growth in 2014. However, the challenge lies in achieving a more comprehensive and lasting impact on development. Infrastructure improvements, for example, should not be tailored exclusively towards natural resource projects, but also towards the broad needs of the population. Moreover, the positive impact on growth from natural resources can prove short-lived, given their finite nature and the exposure to volatile global commodity prices. Consequently, countries face the challenge of using the proceeds from natural resources to promote other sectors in the economy. For example, higher-value-added processing of natural resources should have a positive impact on employment opportunities. Such diversification could also help rebalance the external trade accounts of many LDCs, which are running trade deficits as net food and energy importers.

Numerous LDCs are still coping with the fallout from past natural catastrophes or remain vulnerable to new ones, such as the exposure of harvests to drought risks in the Horn of Africa and the Sahel. A case in point for the accumulation of effects from natural catastrophes is Haiti, where economic activity is expected to have recovered only moderately to 3.5 per cent in 2013 from 2.8 per cent in 2012. This pace of growth is too slow in the light of the destruction wreaked by hurricane Sandy in 2012, which in turn came on the heels of the catastrophic earthquake in 2010. Economic growth remains constrained by a weak agricultural sector damaged by hurricane Sandy and continuing institutional inefficiencies. On a positive note, the industrial sector has improved, stimulated by external demand, for textiles in particular. Although the Haitian economy is expected to perform relatively better in 2014, driven by higher government spending in infrastructure, a revival in the agricultural sector and stronger private consumption supported by aid inflows and remittances, the country remains extremely vulnerable to natural and external economic shocks.

Employment conditions, both in the formal and even more so in the informal labour market, are a further challenge in many LDCs. In Bangladesh, for example, a factory building collapse in April 2013 that killed more than 1,100 workers sparked a debate over employment conditions in the garment industry, triggering a wave of protests. This led to the adoption of a new labour law in July 2013 that strengthens worker rights, including the formation of trade unions. Awaiting approval by the Ministry of Labour, a proposal has been made to raise the minimum wage for garment industry workers by 77 per cent to 5,300 taka (about $67) per month.

Source: UN/DESA.

still exceptionally low; and extraregional demand has slowed. Lending conditions remain tight for some countries, particularly for small- and medium-sized enterprises (SMEs). Considerable diversity is found across countries, with the United Kingdom of Great Britain and Northern Ireland showing relatively strong growth, followed by Germany, while the crisis countries remain in very weak positions, with Cyprus, Greece and Portugal expected to stay in recession in 2014.

Many of the new European Union (EU) members in Eastern Europe remained in a sustained recession in the first half of 2013, but the situation improved in the second half of the year, with business sentiment and household confidence strengthening in response to the return to growth in Western Europe. For example, the automotive industry in Central Europe showed signs of an upturn and retail sales also increased in the Czech Republic and Poland. The aggregate GDP growth for the region is estimated to be 0.5 per cent in 2013, and is forecast to strengthen moderately to 2.1 per cent in 2014 and further to 2.7 per cent in 2015.

Japan is estimated to grow by 1.9 per cent in 2013, boosted by a set of expansionary policy packages, including fiscal stimulus and large-scale purchases of assets by the central bank. Fixed investment has been a key driver of growth, as a number of public construction projects have been financed by the supplemental budget. The Government is also expected to introduce another package targeting structural reforms soon, but the effects are not certain. Meanwhile, the anticipated increase in the consumption tax rate over the next two years is expected to curb growth. GDP is forecast to moderate to 1.5 per cent in 2014.

Regarding other developed countries, GDP in Canada is estimated to grow at 1.6 per cent in 2013, and is expected to grow by 2.4 and 2.8 per cent for 2014 and 2015, respectively. Residential construction was a positive contributor to GDP growth in 2013, but the pace of construction is near a maximum. GDP in Australia is estimated to grow by 2.6 per cent in 2013 and is forecast to grow by 2.8 per cent in 2014. While export growth will remain solid, investment in the mining sector is expected to peak in 2014. Growth in government consumption and public investment will decelerate. GDP in New Zealand is estimated to grow by 2.6 per cent in 2013 and is forecast to grow by 2.8 per cent in 2014, driven by growth of exports to Asian markets.

Among developing countries, growth prospects in Africa remain relatively robust. After an estimated growth of 4.0 per cent in 2013, GDP is projected to accelerate to 4.7 per cent in 2014. Growth prospects are expected to be supported by improvements in the global economic and regional business environment, relatively high commodity prices, easing infrastructural constraints, and increasing trade and investment ties with emerging economies. Other important factors for Africa's medium-term growth prospects include increasing domestic demand—especially from a growing class of new consumers associated with urbanization and rising incomes—and improvements in economic governance and management. A moderate growth recovery in 2014 in emerging and developing countries, led by China, and projected improvement in major developed economies should also stimulate growth in Africa, through increased trade, investment and capital flows.

After a notable slowdown in 2011-2012, economic growth in East Asia stabilized at a moderate level in 2013. The region continues to be adversely affected by relatively weak external demand from developed economies, as well as an adjustment to slower growth in China. The average growth of the region is estimated to average 6.0 per cent in 2013, almost the same pace as 2012. A moderate pickup to 6.1 per cent is forecast for 2014 and 2015, mainly driven by a gradual recovery in export growth amid improving conditions in

Growth prospects in Africa remain relatively robust

Growth in Asia stabilized at a moderate level

developed countries. In most East Asian economies, private consumption and investment will continue to expand at a solid pace, supported by stable labour market conditions, low inflation and fairly accommodative monetary policies. Fiscal policies will remain moderately expansionary and continue to provide support for growth.

Growth in South Asia remains lacklustre as a combination of internal and external factors hamper activity, particularly in the region's largest economies, such as India, the Islamic Republic of Iran and Pakistan. Growth is estimated to be 3.9 per cent in 2013, nearly the slowest pace in two decades. Growth is forecast to pick up moderately to 4.6 per cent in 2014 and 5.1 per cent in 2015, supported by a gradual recovery in domestic demand in India, an end to the recession in the Islamic Republic of Iran and an upturn in external demand. However, in most economies, growth will likely remain well below the level prior to the global financial crisis. Private consumption and investment are held back by a wide range of factors, including energy and transport constraints, volatile security conditions and macroeconomic imbalances.

Western Asia is estimated to grow by 3.6 per cent in 2013, and will accelerate to 4.3 per cent in 2014. While the member countries of the Gulf Cooperation Council (GCC) have been on a stable recovery path, continuing political instability, social unrest, security incidents and geopolitical tensions have hampered a number of other economies in the region. The Syrian crisis has been impacting the neighbouring countries in a multifaceted way. The subdued cross-border economic activities—including trade, investment and tourism—between GCC countries and the rest of Western Asia continued to fail to bring intraregional positive spillover effects. The stagnation of private capital inflows put Jordan, Lebanon and Yemen under moderate foreign-exchange constraints. Turkey continued to face financial pressures, with its currency depreciating and interbank interest rates rising as a result of the decline in international capital inflows.

Growth in Latin America and the Caribbean decelerated in 2013, to a pace of 2.6 per cent, but is forecast to improve to 3.6 and 4.1 per cent in 2014 and 2015, respectively. In South America, Brazil is still growing at a subdued pace, curbed by weak external demand, volatility in international capital flows and tightening monetary policy. The expected improvement in the outlook will depend on strengthening global demand. Private consumption has been supportive of growth in many South American economies. Growth in Mexico and Central America is expected to accelerate in 2014-2015, supported by better performance of manufacturing exports and stable domestic demand, as well as structural adjustment. Growth in the Caribbean has been hampered by weak external demand—for the tourism sector in particular—and weaker commodity prices, but is expected to strengthen in the outlook.

Growth in Latin America and the Caribbean is forecast to pick up slightly

Among economies in transition, growth in most economies of the Commonwealth of Independent States (CIS) decelerated in 2013, curbed by weak exports and external financing constraints, supply-side bottlenecks, and weak consumer and business confidence. Growth in the Russian Federation weakened further in the first half of 2013, as industrial output remained weak and investment became a drag on growth. The economic slowdown eventually affected previously resilient consumer confidence and led to weakening retail sales growth. The weakness in the Russian Federation has had a negative impact on its neighbours in the CIS through trade, investment and remittance channels. In the outlook, structural problems such as sluggish energy sector expansion, capacity constraints and weak investment will prevent an acceleration of growth to pre-crisis levels.

CIS is constrained by structural problems

Growth in South-Eastern Europe has improved in 2013, but growth is expected to remain marginal in the near term, fluctuating between 1 and 2 per cent, which is insufficient to address the region's long-standing needs for reindustrialization, increased labour force participation and reduction of excessively high unemployment rates. In the outlook, the external environment for those countries is expected to improve, including the terms of access to external finance. With easing credit conditions, investment is set to recover gradually in 2014-2015, along with strengthening private consumption. GDP growth is projected to accelerate to 2.6 per cent in 2014 and 3.1 per cent in 2015.

Inflation outlook remains benign

Inflation remains tame worldwide

Inflation remains tame worldwide, partly reflecting output gaps, high unemployment and a continued financial deleveraging in major developed economies. Among developed economies, inflation decelerated in the United States during 2013 and is expected to remain below 2 per cent in 2014 and 2015. Inflation has similarly decelerated in the euro area, but has dipped below 1.0 per cent, which has raised some deflationary concerns. In Japan, the large expansionary policies aiming to reflate the economy managed to end the decade-long deflation in 2013, as the consumer price index (CPI) is estimated to increase by 0.3 per cent, and is forecast to hit the target of 2.0 per cent in 2014.

Among developing countries and economies in transition, inflation rates are above 10 per cent in only about a dozen economies scattered throughout different regions. Several economies in South Asia and Africa, plus a few in the CIS, will continue to face high inflation rates, mainly owing to elevated inflationary expectations, rapid credit growth, localized food price pressures and structural bottlenecks such as energy shortages. On the other hand, most economies in East Asia continue to face benign inflation.

High unemployment remains a key challenge

Long-lasting effects from the financial crisis continue to weigh on labour markets

The global employment situation remains challenging, as long-lasting effects from the financial crisis continue to weigh on labour markets in many countries and regions. How much of the unemployment is structural and how much is cyclical is still under debate. The answer appears to differ by region, with some countries, such as the United States facing mainly cyclical unemployment, whereas others, such as Spain, face more structural issues.[3]

Among developed countries, the unemployment rate in the United States has continued its slow decline, down to 7.0 per cent in late 2013, from a peak of 10 per cent in 2010 (figure I.3). A significant portion of this decline, however, is owing to a retreat in labour force participation. The unemployment rate is expected to decline further and reach the United States Federal Reserve's (Fed) critical threshold of 6.5 per cent sometime in mid-2015. Unemployment in the euro area appears to have stabilized during 2013, at the historical high of 12.2 per cent. In the euro area, while the unemployment rate in Germany is near historical lows of about 5 per cent, Greece and Spain are facing extraordinarily high unemployment rates of about 27 per cent, with the youth unemployment at twice this rate. These high rates in the euro area are expected to come down only slightly, as GDP growth will not be strong enough to make significant progress over the forecast period.

---

3   Estimates for Spain's structural unemployment rate are somewhat controversial as they also tend to be procyclical—meaning they will overestimate the rate during times of already high unemployment—but they are still below the current unemployment rate with room for improvement.

Figure I.3
Unemployment rates in selected countries, January 2007-September 2013

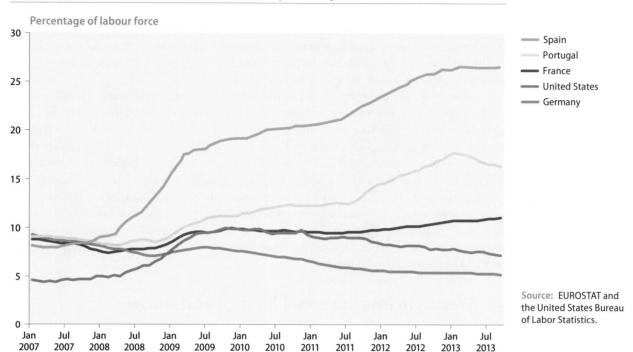

Source: EUROSTAT and the United States Bureau of Labor Statistics.

In addition, there will be lasting damage to the labour market from discouraged workers who have been unemployed for significant periods of time. The unemployment rate in Japan is relatively low, while the labour force participation rate continues to decline as the working-age population shrinks.

The unemployment situation is mixed across developing countries and economies in transition, with extremely high structural unemployment in North Africa and Western Asia, particularly among youth.

The unemployment rates remain low across much of East Asia, estimated at below 3 per cent in Malaysia, Singapore, Thailand and Viet Nam. In the outlook period, little change is expected, based on the comparatively modest growth forecast for the coming two years. Slowing growth in South Asia appears to have had a considerable adverse impact on employment. Reported unemployment still remains relatively low in India, but has deteriorated somewhat over the past fiscal year. In some of these economies, changes in employment due to structural issues have affected women to a greater degree, aggravating already significant gender gaps, with high female unemployment rates in Pakistan and low female participation in Bangladesh. Modest growth in the outlook period combined with population pressures is likely to exacerbate pressures on the labour market. Positive growth in many African countries has had a limited impact on employment; the informal sector is still large and opportunities remain limited for many of those seeking to enter the labour market, as manifested in high youth unemployment rates and wide gender disparities in earnings. In addition, continual pressure on labour markets from a steady stream of new entrants has meant that even solid GDP growth rates have not been sufficient to make measurable impacts. Even as growth slowed down in major economies in South America, such as Brazil and Mexico, unemployment remained at about 6 per cent or below. Labour market indicators are likely to remain solid over the remainder of the year for the region; however, there may be no further improvement in the near future, despite improvements in growth, due to the fact that unemployment growth is barely equal to the growth of the labour force for a number of countries. The unemployment rate remains at historical lows in the Russian Federation, between 5 and 6 per cent, despite a noticeable slowdown and in-migration from surrounding countries in the CIS.

More concerted efforts are needed to address labour market issues

A number of countries are making concerted efforts at addressing labour market issues, such as aligning macroeconomic policies appropriately with domestic conditions, promoting training for youth and other excluded segments of the labour force, and taking steps to induce advances in productivity and innovation.[4] The expectation is that these measures will be enacted through a coordinated and integrated policy framework that will balance labour demand and labour supply, with sufficient efforts to ensure sustainable social protection. This also includes promoting an environment that is conducive to job creation with access to finance, necessary infrastructure, and support for SMEs. Further steps to activate labour through skills training and upgrading will be necessary to integrate those groups that have been excluded or that have been forced to subsist through intermittent and vulnerable employment.

Trends in international finance and trade

Capital inflows to emerging economies declining

Net private capital inflows to emerging markets,[5] a subgroup of developing countries, and the economies in transition have shown a measurable decline during 2013. At the same time, volatility in the financial markets of emerging economies has increased significantly, featuring equity market sell-offs and sharp depreciations of local currencies—both partly triggered by the Fed announcement that it might taper the amount of its monthly purchases of long-term assets later in the year. Waning growth prospects for emerging economies have also played a role in triggering the decline of capital inflows.

QE is having a significant influence on the net capital inflows to emerging economies

The unconventional monetary policies, or so-called quantitative easing (QE), adopted by major central banks in the aftermath of the global financial crisis have had a significant influence on the net capital inflows to emerging economies. The QE programmes injected substantial liquidity into global financial markets and at the same time repressed long-term interest rates in developed countries. As a result, in a search for higher yields, a significant amount of capital flows was driven to markets of primary commodities and markets of equities and bonds in emerging economies in the period 2009-2012. However, in late 2012 and early 2013, as systemic risks associated with the sovereign debt crisis in the euro area abated and the prospects for economic recovery in the United States and Japan

---

4   See the G20 Labour and Employment and Finance Ministers' Communiqué, Moscow, 19 July 2013, available from http://www.g20.org/documents/#p3.

5   Data and definition of private capital inflows in this section are based on Institute of International Finance, "Capital flows to emerging market economies", IIF Research Note, 7 October 2013, while the forecasts for 2014 are revised based on Project LINK baseline forecasts. The data differ from those presented in chapter III, which cover all developing and transition economies and apply the "net net flows" concept, which is net inflows less net outflows. The use of "net inflows" would focus on the effects of volatility in foreign capital inflows, while the use of "net net flows" focuses on the effects of balance-of-payment.

improved, international capital flows started to move away from emerging markets back to developed markets, particularly developed equity markets. More recently, on the expectation that major central banks will taper their purchases of long-term assets and eventually sell their assets back to the markets, international investors have ratcheted up the repricing of assets and rebalancing of portfolios. This has led to the latest wave of declines in capital inflows to emerging economies. Given the prodigious size of the assets accumulated by major central banks through QE in the past few years, and the challenges for determining the timing and magnitude for unwinding these assets, more volatile movements of capital inflows to emerging economies are expected to occur in the next few years.

Among emerging economies, declines and volatility in capital inflows have been most pronounced in Asia. While growth in foreign direct investment (FDI) inflows to China seems to have resumed some strength recently, portfolio equity inflows to India and Korea and non-bank credit flows to Indonesia have registered significant falls. Latin America has also seen a notable retrenchment of inflows, mostly in portfolio equities. In contrast, Africa, Western Asia and emerging European countries continue to see increases in capital inflows. For example, in the past year Nigeria has registered significant increases in capital inflows to both its equity and bond markets. Egypt has, however, witnessed sharp declines in net private capital inflows due to continued political instability.

External financing costs for developing countries and transition economies have also risen in the second half of 2013, triggered by the anticipation of QE tapering. The spreads between yields on sovereign bonds issued by emerging economies and the benchmark yields on government bonds of major developed countries surged by more than 100 basis points in the two weeks immediately following the Fed's announcement in May 2013 of the possibility for reducing the size of its QE purchases (figure I.4). By taking into

External financing costs for developing countries are rising

Figure I.4
Daily yield spreads on emerging market bonds, January 2007 to 14 November 2013

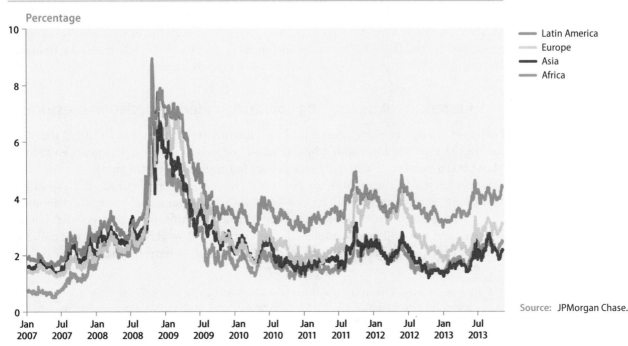

Percentage

Legend:
— Latin America
— Europe
— Asia
— Africa

Source: JPMorgan Chase.

account that the benchmark yields on government bonds in major developed countries also increased by about 100 basis points, the costs of external financing for emerging economies, in terms of the yields, actually increased 200 basis points on average. Among emerging economies, the spreads for Latin America are wider than others.

Outward capital flows from emerging economies have continued to increase. In addition to a continued increase in official foreign reserves, which are counted as part of outward capital flows and stood at about $7.5 trillion by mid-2013 for emerging and developing countries as a whole, private outward capital flows of emerging economies have increased in the past few years at a robust pace, reaching an estimated amount of about $1000 billion in 2013, almost to the same level as the net capital inflows to these countries. Among emerging economies, China has significantly increased its outward direct investment in recent years, supported by more encouraging government policies promoting its enterprises to "walk abroad". After registering a total of $88 billion in outward direct investment in 2012, available data have indicated another increase of about 20 per cent in 2013. Many economies in Latin America, such as Brazil, Chile, Colombia, Mexico and Peru, have also increased outward capital flows, mostly in the form of portfolio investments, reflecting the need by companies, banks and pension funds in Latin America to internationally diversify their assets.

ODA to developing countries has contracted in the past two years

Official development assistance (ODA) flows to developing countries contracted in the past two years, falling cumulatively 2 per cent in 2011 and 2012, down to $126.4 billion.[6] Of the 25 Development Assistance Committee (DAC) members, 16 decreased their ODA, mainly owing to fiscal austerity measures. Preliminary data show that bilateral aid from DAC donors to sub-Saharan Africa fell for the first time since 2007, with assistance totalling $26.2 billion in 2012, a decline of 7.9 per cent in real terms. Aid to landlocked developing countries (LLDCs) and small island developing States (SIDS) also fell. In 2012, the combined DAC donors' ODA was equivalent to 0.29 per cent of their combined gross national income (GNI), far from the United Nations target of 0.7 per cent. ODA flows in 2013 are estimated to remain at the same level as in 2012. Slight increases are expected for 2014-2015, as more DAC members see improvement in their economies and fiscal situations. A strengthening of political commitment in the international community spurred by the United Nations campaign for accelerating progress in the Millennium Development Goals (MDGs) is also expected to support increases.

Currencies of developing countries under depreciation pressures

Foreign-exchange markets experienced two distinctive episodes during 2013: the early part of the year was highlighted by a dramatic depreciation of the Japanese yen, and in May-June, a number of emerging and developing countries saw the sharp devaluation of their currencies. In the outlook for 2014-2015, major uncertainties and volatility in foreign-exchange markets will still be associated with the currencies of emerging economies.

Among major currencies, the yen devalued significantly vis-à-vis the United States dollar, from 80 yen per dollar by the end of 2012 to about 100 yen per dollar in March 2013, partly reflecting a set of drastically expansionary policies adopted by the

---

6   For more detailed information and analysis, see *MDG Gap Task Force Report 2013: The Global Partnership for Development—The Challenge We Face* (United Nations publication, Sales No. E.13.I.5), available from http://www.un.org/en/development/desa/policy/mdg_gap/mdg_gap2013/mdg_report_2013_en.pdf.

new Japanese Administration. The yen has since stabilized within a small range of about 98 yen per dollar. The euro-to-dollar exchange rate saw some fairly wide swings, between 1.28 and 1.34, but with no clear direction during the first half of 2013, and followed by a period of appreciation in the third quarter (reaching 1.38 before dropping to 1.34 during November). Changes in relative risk perceptions were an important driving force. For the last few years these have been evenly balanced between eruptions of the euro area debt crisis and United States fiscal impasses. As the year progressed, however, risks stemming from the European debt crisis subsided significantly, while those in the United States remained in play. In addition, the euro area current-account surplus began to widen notably, but stronger growth in the United States provided some counterbalance. Going forward, however, the shifting balance of monetary policies is expected to play an important role. The European Central Bank (ECB) cut its policy rates in November (the second time in 2013) leading to a sharp drop in the euro. In terms of unconventional policies, the United States is expected to taper its QE programme soon, while the ECB is still entertaining new forms of stimulus. The balance of expected policies in the three areas, coupled with the stronger growth outlook in the United States, leads to an expectation of the dollar appreciating moderately against both the yen and the euro.

Currencies in many developing countries and economies in transition have depreciated vis-à-vis the United States dollar and other major currencies in 2013. Currencies in a number of emerging economies depreciated by the greatest amount in May-June 2013, particularly in Brazil, India, Indonesia, South Africa and Turkey (figure I.6), at the same time that capital inflows to these economies declined. In contrast, the renminbi of China continued to appreciate gradually against the United States dollar and other major currencies. The difference between the trends in the exchange rates of China and other large emerging economies can be accounted for by a number of factors, including much larger foreign reserves, a less open capital account, higher domestic savings, and more concentration of FDI in the capital inflows to China (when compared with the other emerging

Currencies in many developing countries have depreciated

Figure I.5
Dollar exchange rates among major currencies, January 2007 to 14 November 2013

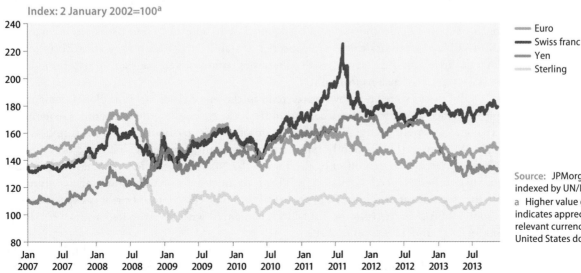

Source: JPMorgan Chase, indexed by UN/DESA.
a Higher value of index indicates appreciation of the relevant currency vis-à-vis the United States dollar.

Figure I.6
Dollar exchange rates of selected emerging economies, January 2007 to 14 November 2013

Index: 2 January 2002=100[a]

South African rand
Brazilian real
Indonesian rupiah
Indian rupee
Turkish lira

Source: JPMorgan Chase, indexed by UN/DESA.
a Higher value of index indicates appreciation of the relevant currency vis-à-vis the United States dollar.

economies). Given the remaining current-account surplus of China vis-à-vis the United States, the renminbi is expected to further appreciate slightly against the dollar in 2014-2015, unless China liberalizes its capital and financial accounts soon, which could trigger more capital outflows and renminbi depreciation. The currencies of other emerging economies are likely to remain under depreciation pressures.

Prices of primary commodities on a moderate downtrend

The downturn in commodity prices is expected to stabilize

The prices of most primary commodities have declined moderately during 2013 (figure I.7), mainly driven by generally weak global demand as global economic growth remained anaemic (see chapter II for more information). Different patterns continue to be evident across different commodity groups, as prices are also determined by various factors on the supply side. In the outlook, with global demand expected to pick up moderately in 2014-2015, commodity prices are expected to stabilize, although they are still subject to changes in supply-side factors, such as weather conditions (for agricultural commodities) and geopolitical tensions (for oil).

Oil prices were on a downward trend in the first half of 2013, as global demand for oil weakened along with the deceleration in world economic growth overall. Geopolitical tensions can entail a large risk premium on oil prices, particular when oil supply is also tight. Most recently, global oil supply has been declining modestly: increased oil supply in North America has been offset by declines in the North Sea, while high Saudi output only partly counterbalanced a collapse in Libyan production. In the outlook, by assuming no further significant eruptions in geopolitical tensions, the Brent oil price is expected to be about $108 per barrel (pb) for 2014-2015, compared with an estimated average of $108.1 pb for 2013 and $111.6 pb in 2012.

As production is expected to increase by a large margin in 2013-2014, food prices declined steadily during 2013, with prices for wheat, maize and rice declining by about

Figure I.7
Price indices of commodities, 2000-2015

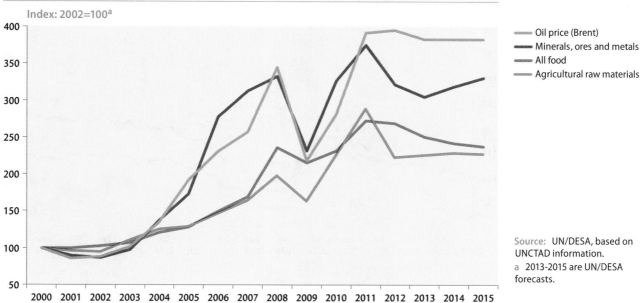

Index: 2002=100[a]

Oil price (Brent)
Minerals, ores and metals
All food
Agricultural raw materials

Source: UN/DESA, based on UNCTAD information.
a 2013-2015 are UN/DESA forecasts.

5-10 per cent. In the outlook, food prices are projected to moderate further in 2014-2015 based on the assumption of continued increases in the global production of these grains.

Prices of minerals, ores and metals strengthened in early 2013 but fell markedly in the latter part of the year, owing to weaker than anticipated global growth—the deceleration in the growth of emerging economies being particularly notable. For example, price indices for aluminium, copper, nickel, and zinc registered a steady decline during 2013, while the price of iron ore also declined significantly. In the outlook for 2014-2015, the prices of minerals, ores and metals are projected to stabilize and register modest gains as global demand improves.

International trade flows remain sluggish

International trade as the engine for global growth has shifted to a low gear over the past two years. After growing at a sluggish pace of less than 3 per cent in 2012, as measured by the volume of world exports, international trade flows are estimated to have grown by 2.3 per cent during 2013 (figure I.8). Notably, the ratio between the growth of world trade and the growth of global output is at a historical low. While protracted anaemic import demand from major developed countries can explain part of the cyclical downturn in trade activity, the lack of any progress in multilateral trade negotiations over the past decade may have reduced the momentum in creating new trade flows in the world economy. On the other hand, South-South trade is still demonstrating more dynamic patterns and becomes a major driver for the growth of international trade as a whole. The feedback effects of slow international trade growth have in turn dragged down the growth of global output. In the outlook, international trade is expected to pick up the momentum gradually, growing at 4.7 and 5.2 per cent in 2014 and 2015, respectively.

Trade as the engine for global growth has shifted to a low gear

Figure I.8
Index of world merchandise trade, January 2006-August 2013

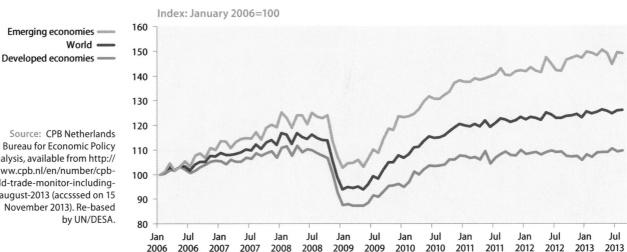

Emerging economies ━━
World ━━
Developed economies ━━

Index: January 2006=100

Source: CPB Netherlands Bureau for Economic Policy Analysis, available from http://www.cpb.nl/en/number/cpb-world-trade-monitor-including-august-2013 (accsssed on 15 November 2013). Re-based by UN/DESA.

Global imbalances narrowing to a benign level

Effort is needed to prevent imbalances from widening to excessive levels in the longer run

Global imbalances, namely, the current-account imbalances across major economies, continued to narrow to a benign level in 2013 (figure I.9). Such narrowing is not considered to be an imminent threat to the stability of the world economy, although efforts to strengthen international policy coordination should continue in order to prevent the imbalances from widening to excessive levels again in the longer run.

The United States remained the largest deficit economy, with an estimated external deficit of about $410 billion (2.4 per cent of GDP) in 2013, down from $450 billion in 2012, and substantially lower than its peak of $800 billion (6.0 per cent of GDP) registered in 2006. The external surpluses in China, the euro area, Japan and a group of fuel-exporting countries, which form the counterpart to the United States deficit, have narrowed accordingly, albeit to varying degrees. China, for instance, is estimated to register a surplus of just above 2 per cent of GDP in 2013, a sharp decline from a high of 10 per cent of GDP in 2007. Japan is expected to register a surplus of about 1 per cent of GDP in 2013, also a significant reduction from its peak level of 5 per cent of GDP reached in 2007. The current account for the euro area as a whole is in surplus of 2.5 per cent of GDP, with Germany's surplus remaining above 5 per cent of GDP. Large surpluses relative to GDP are still present in oil-exporting countries, reaching 20 per cent of GDP or more in some of the oil-exporting countries in Western Asia. These countries plan to share the wealth generated by the endowment of oil with future generations through a continued accumulation of surpluses in the foreseeable future.

Adjustment of the imbalances is both structural and cyclical

While some of the adjustment of the imbalances in major economies reflects certain improvements in the unbalanced domestic structure of these economies, a large part of the adjustment reflects a cyclical downturn—that is, a weakening in external demand from the deficit countries, rather than a strengthening of external demand from the surplus countries. In the United States, a corresponding narrowing of the saving-investment gap reflects a slight decline in the savings rate in 2013 and a large moderation in investment. In the outlook for 2014-2015, the current-account deficit in the United States is expected

Figure I.9
Global imbalances, 1997-2014

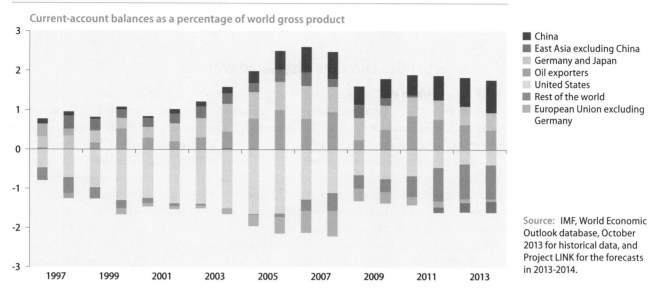

Current-account balances as a percentage of world gross product

Legend:
- China
- East Asia excluding China
- Germany and Japan
- Oil exporters
- United States
- Rest of the world
- European Union excluding Germany

Source: IMF, World Economic Outlook database, October 2013 for historical data, and Project LINK for the forecasts in 2013-2014.

to remain at the same level relative to GDP. In the surplus countries, the narrowing in the external surplus of China reflects a confluence of a more flexible exchange rate, and the policy measures to move the economy towards greater reliance on domestic demand. Global imbalances are not expected to widen by a significant margin in the next two years.

Uncertainties and risks

The baseline outlook presented above is subject to a number of uncertainties and risks, mostly on the downside. In *WESP 2013*, three major downside risks were identified, namely, a much more detrimental adjustment in the euro area, a "fiscal cliff" in the United States, and a hard landing in some large emerging economies. All three risks manifested themselves to some extent during 2013 and entailed certain costs for the global economy, although not to the full scale that was presented in the downside scenarios. In the outlook for 2014-2015, these risks remain relevant. While the systemic risks in the euro area abated, owing to a number of policy measures adopted over the past year, the real economy in the euro area, particularly in those member countries under debt distress, remains fragile. The United States averted a fiscal cliff in 2013, but fell into fiscal sequestration, and uncertainties remain high about the debt ceiling and the budget for 2014. The slowdown in a number of emerging economies in 2013 was "hard" enough, and many of these emerging economies remain vulnerable in the outlook.

In addition to these remaining risks, new risks are also emerging. One of them is the risk associated with the unwinding of the unconventional monetary policies by the central banks of major developed countries over the course of 2014-2015. As indicated by the mini–financial crisis of mid-2013, sparked by the Fed simply mentioning the possibility of tapering its purchases of assets (tapering should have far less impact than unwinding, as the former continues to add liquidity while the latter withdraws liquidity), this risk could cause substantial instability for the world economy. Moreover, beyond economic risks, geopolit-

Old risks remain and new risks are emerging

ical tensions in Western Asia and elsewhere in the world might spiral out of control. Such tension could lead to economic disruptions directly, or indirectly through rising oil prices. These and other risk factors, unfolding unexpectedly, could derail the world economy far away from the projections outlined in the baseline forecast.

Uncertainties and risks associated with QE

Great uncertainties and risks for global economic growth and the financial stability of the world in the coming years are inextricably associated with the unconventional monetary policies adopted in major developed countries, or, more precisely, with the process in which the central banks of these countries start to change their stances on these policies.

Since the eruption of the global financial crisis in 2008, central banks in major developed countries have implemented quantitative easing policies to purchase and hold increasingly large amounts of long-terms assets. These policy measures have played a critical role in stabilizing financial markets, injecting liquidity to the beleaguered banks and providing necessary support for economic recovery in general, although the significance of these positive effects is still in question. However, by moving a prodigious amount of financial assets from markets to their own balance sheets, these central banks have also created non-trivial market distortions that repress the risk premiums for certain classes of financial assets and generate moral hazard for commercial banks (allowing them to delay the clean-up of the balance sheets).

QE has led to increased volatility for developing countries

Certain side effects generated by QE have already manifested themselves in the past few years. For example, developing countries have repeatedly complained about the spillover effects of QE on their macroeconomic stability, seeing it lead to increases in volatility in capital inflows, in prices of primary commodities, and in their exchange rates (box I.3). The extra liquidity injected through QE turned out to be beyond the control of the central banks that issued it. From the first round of QE occurring in late 2008 to the current open-ended, ongoing QE, international capital flows have been moving erratically back and forth across developed equity markets, emerging markets and international commodity markets.

During the summer of 2013, the Fed signaled the possibility of tapering the size of its monthly purchases of long-term assets and triggered global financial turmoil. Both equity and bond markets worldwide experienced a sharp sell-off. While equity prices in developed countries recuperated, bond yields remain elevated relative to the level before May 2013. For instance, the yield on the 10-year United States Treasury bond soared by about 100 basis points, reaching the highest level since late 2011. By this measure, all the efforts by the Fed to lower long-term interest rates through the latest round of QE that began in late 2012 were completely undone by the market reaction in just a few weeks. The shocks to emerging markets were more pronounced, leading to substantial declines of capital inflows for the first time since 2009. Equity prices in emerging markets plummeted by about 20 per cent in two months and in the same period, the risk premia, as measured by the spreads of the bond yields, increased by 30 per cent on average. Declines of capital inflows were found to be more acute in such countries as Brazil and India because of the relatively high degree of liquidity in these markets, accompanied by sharp depreciations of the local currencies. Even in China, a seize-up of interbank lending in late June—although rooted mainly in the problems of its own banking system—was to some extent also related to the global financial turmoil.

Both policymakers and financial markets are aware that, in the future, when the central banks start to taper the pace of their asset purchases and eventually unwind the process

Box I.3
Spillover effects of unconventional monetary policies in major developed countries[a]

In the aftermath of the global financial crisis, the central banks of the major developed economies low-ered their policy interest rates to close to zero, while also aggressively pursuing unconventional mone-tary policy measures, including quantitative easing (QE)—an expansion of the monetary bases through purchasing and holding of long-term assets (figures I.3.1 and I.3.2).

As a result, developing countries and economies in transition have experienced waves of capi-tal flows over the past few years. These capital flows have directly impacted equity and bond prices in developing countries as well as exchange rates, while also indirectly affecting other variables in devel-oping countries, such as monetary growth, real GDP, exports and imports, and inflation. A number of recent studies have attempted to assess the size and importance of these spillover effects for developing

Figure I.3.1
Monetary policies for selected countries

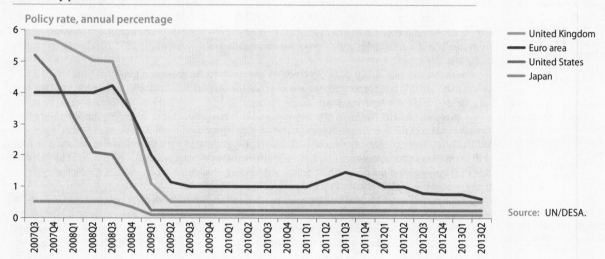

Policy rate, annual percentage

United Kingdom
Euro area
United States
Japan

Source: UN/DESA.

Figure I.3.2
Assets held in major central banks

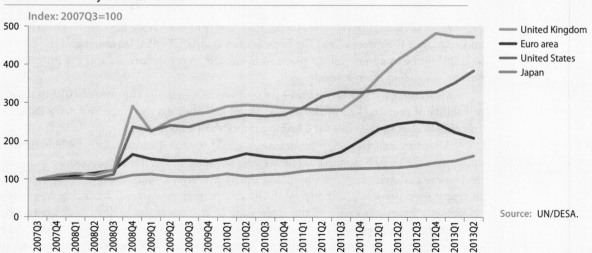

Index: 2007Q3=100

United Kingdom
Euro area
United States
Japan

Source: UN/DESA.

Box I.3
Spillover effects of unconventional monetary policies in major developed countries[a]
(*continued*)

economies.[b] While some controversies remain over the exact magnitude of the effects on the different variables, several important findings are summarized as follows.

First, the impact of QE on the developing economies has varied across countries, reflecting the scale of their exposure to developed countries (in terms of both trade and financial linkages), their individual cyclical positions, and the type and scale of responses to capital inflows by the national monetary authorities.

Second, QE seems to have exacerbated the procyclical aspects of capital flows to developing countries. The QE measures enacted in the midst of the global financial crisis—which successfully aimed at market repair and provision of liquidity to financial institutions—contributed to the increased moving of assets out of developing countries. The QE programmes in 2010-2011, by contrast, added significantly to the capital flows that were already moving to the rapidly recovering emerging economies.

Third, QE likely had a significant impact on financial market variables in developing countries, but the impact on the real economy has been much smaller. Overall, QE led to a decline in long-term bond yields, an increase in equity prices, and an appreciation of some, but not all, currencies. Among the largest developing economies, Brazil appears to have experienced the most significant spillover effects from the QE measures, including a significant appreciation of its currency in 2011-2012, which probably hampered the export sector.

Fourth, the availability of ample credit in low yields for an extended period of time led to an increase in household and corporate debt in some countries in East Asia (Indonesia, Malaysia and Thailand, for example) and Latin America (Brazil, among others).

In recent months, the focus of policymakers has shifted towards the upcoming tapering and eventual unwinding of the asset purchase programmes in developed economies, the United States in particular. The main financial stability risks of such an exit are associated with the following factors: potential shifts in market sentiment, which may lead to sharp increases in bond yields; financial market turbulence, due to massive global portfolio rebalancing; and funding challenges faced by banks, which may negatively impact the availability of credit to households and businesses.

The degree to which developing countries will be affected by the exit of QE policies could mirror—at least to some extent—the degree to which they were affected initially and will likely depend on similar factors, such as: trade and financial linkages with developed economies; the depth of their financial markets; the scale of their external imbalances; the size of the corporate and household debt levels; and the policy responses undertaken. However, as previous capital crises in developing countries have shown, reversals in capital flows can be much more abrupt and disruptive. Vulnerable countries should therefore take action to strengthen balance sheets, reduce external imbalances and improve macroprudential regulation.

[a] This box draws from Tatiana Fic's presentation at the UN/DESA Expert Group Meeting on the World Economy held on 21-23 October 2013 in New York, "The spillover effects of unconventional monetary policies in major developed countries on developing countries", available from http://www.un.org/en/development/desa/policy/proj_link/.

[b] In addition to the study by Fic (ibid.), this includes, for example, Qianying Chen and others, "International spillovers of central bank balance sheet policies", BIS papers, No. 66 (October, 2012), Basel, Swtizerland: Bank for International Settlements; and Marcel Fratzscher, Marco Lo Duca and Roland Straub, "On the international spillovers of US quantitative easing", ECB Working Paper Series, No. 1557 (June, 2013), Frankfurt, Germany: European Central Bank.

(by selling the assets back to markets), investors will inevitably have to reprice the assets and rebalance their portfolios. The hope is that, by then, banks, investors and the economy at large will be in a more robust position to endure such adjustments and the central banks will be able to engineer a smooth exit.

However, the market reaction—or over-reaction—in the summer of 2013 to the mere possibility of tapering QE in the United States has dimmed this hope and provided a vivid and timely alert to the risks for a bumpy rather than smooth exit.

A bumpy QE exit could lead to a surge in long-term interest rates

A bumpy exit from QE programmes could lead to a number of problematic developments: a surge in long-term interest rates, not only in developed economies but also in developing countries; a sell-off in global equity markets; a sharp decline of capital inflows to emerging economies; and a spike in the risk premia for external financing in emerging economies. Exactly because of the large scale of the assets the major central banks have accumulated in the past few years through QE, the magnitude of these shocks from the unwinding could be equally significant. For example, the QE programmes have led to a broad-based shift into fixed-income assets with longer durations; the increased duration has significantly increased the potential losses to the holders of those portfolios when interest rates rise. Moreover, as QE moved a large proportion of the long-term bonds out of the markets, it reduced market liquidity, which in turn could intensify the shocks and lead to an overshooting of long-term interest rates.

More importantly, those first-round shocks in international financial markets could transmit quickly to the domestic real economic sectors of both developed and developing countries. For example, in major developed countries, such as the United States, a marked increase in long-term interest rates would be detrimental not only to banks, in terms of funding challenges, but also to households and businesses, in terms of higher financial costs. This could stifle the fledgling recovery in private consumption and business investment. In fact, the 100-basis-point increase in benchmark long-term interest rates during the financial turmoil of May-June 2013 has already left a measurable imprint on the housing sector in the United States. As mortgage interest rates spiked, the recovery in the housing sector weakened notably.

Shocks in international financial markets could transmit quickly to the real economy

In emerging economies, higher benchmark interest rates, rising risk premia on external financing, and the decline in capital inflows would exacerbate the challenges they are already facing—that is, a slowdown in GDP growth and a further narrowing of policy space—especially for those economies with large twin deficits and elevated inflation (see more discussion below).

Vulnerability of emerging economies to external shocks

Many large developing countries, including Brazil, China, India and the Russian Federation, saw a significant deceleration in GDP growth in the past two years (box I.4), due to a combination of challenging external conditions and domestic impediments. In the baseline outlook discussed earlier, growth in these economies is expected to strengthen in some cases, such as Brazil and India, and to stabilize in others, such as China. Risks remain, however, for a hard landing for some of these economies.

The financial turbulence encountered by many emerging economies during 2013 has reminded the world of the Asian financial crisis of 1997-1998. Several aspects prompt comparison between the vulnerability facing emerging economies today and the situation in the run-up to the Asian financial crisis. A few indicators are selected from three Asian economies involved in the Asian financial crisis (Indonesia, the Republic of Korea and Thailand) to compare with five economies most affected by the current episode (Brazil, India, Indonesia, South Africa and Turkey).

Box I.4
Growth slowdown in the BRICS

In many large developing countries, including the BRICS (Brazil, the Russian Federation, India, China and South Africa), economic growth has weakened considerably over the past two years and is now well below the pre-crisis level. For 2013, weighted gross domestic product (GDP) growth in the BRICS is projected at 5.6 per cent, down from an annual average of about 8 per cent during the period 2000-2008.

An important question is how much of the recent slowdown in these emerging economies is cyclical and temporary, and how much is structural and longer-term. The former implies that growth in these economies could return to the same high growth paths they enjoyed prior to the global financial crisis, once the cyclical conditions (such as external demand from developed countries) improve. The latter, on the other hand, suggests that these economies would, in the longer-term, face a "new normal" growth path that is notably slower than before the crisis.

Box I.4
Growth slowdown in the BRICS *(continued)*

A standard growth decomposition exercise for the BRICS for the period 1996-2012 can reveal some interesting features about the growth deceleration in these countries.[a] By a production function approach, GDP growth can be decomposed into the contributions from three sources: growth in labour inputs, accumulation in capital, and increase in total factor productivity (TFP)—a catch-all category that measures the overall efficiency of the economy in transforming labour and capital into output. As illustrated in the figure below, most of the decline in GDP growth triggered by the eruption of the global financial crisis of 2008 can be attributed to a drop in the growth of TFP. However, the contributions from growth in labour (measured as total employment (quantity) adjusted for changes in the composition of labour) and capital have also been on a downward trend in recent years. One caveat about this exercise is that since TFP is estimated as the residual, a large part of its fluctuation in the aftermath of the financial crisis may reflect a cyclical movement caused by changes in aggregate demand, rather than a structural change in technological advance or other supply-side factors.

A number of recent studies, with various more sophisticated approaches, including structural modelling and time-series analysis techniques, have offered more information.[b] Estimates of potential output and output gaps (the gap between actual GDP growth and potential growth) in the BRICS suggest: First, prior to the crisis, from 2005-2008, actual GDP grew faster than potential output, resulting in a significant positive output gap at the onset of the crisis. The rising output gap was associated with a marked increase in inflation in all of these economies, except Brazil. The output gap was probably largest in the Russian Federation and South Africa. Second, potential GDP growth seems to have declined in the aftermath of the crisis in all five economies, with the decline most pronounced in China and India. And third, small negative output gaps are currently estimated for these economies, with the largest gap in India.[c]

The estimated decline in the potential growth, combined with relatively small negative output gaps, suggests that the pace of economic expansion in the BRICS will remain notably below the pre-crisis period. A moderate cyclical upturn is expected in the near term, particularly in India, but more lasting progress will depend on policies and reforms to remove supply-side bottlenecks to growth. In most economies, this will require increased efforts to stimulate capital accumulation, promote technological advances, strengthen human capital and improve the functioning of labour markets.

a See The Conference Board *Total Economy Database*™, January 2013, available from http://www.conference-board.org/data/economydatabase/.

b These analyses include work by the World Bank, including the Global Economic Prospects: Less volatile but slower growth (June, 2013), the IMF, as well as national authorities.

c Despite a significant negative output, inflationary pressures in India have remained elevated, largely owing to structural bottlenecks. This recently led India's central bank to raise interest rates even as current output growth is considered to be below potential.

Source: UN/DESA.

Figure I.4.1
Growth decomposition for the BRICS, 1996-2012

Total factor productivity ■
Labour (quantity and composition) ■
Capital (ICT and non-ICT) ■

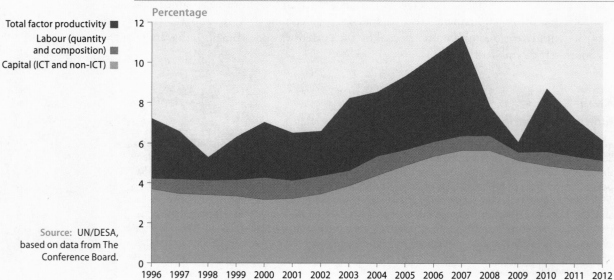

Source: UN/DESA, based on data from The Conference Board.

Volatility of capital inflows

As in the Asian financial crisis, the latest financial turmoil experienced by emerging economies has also been driven by procyclical movements in fickle international capital flows.

In the run-up to the Asian financial crisis, net private capital inflows to emerging economies increased by about 90 per cent from 1994 to 1996, followed by a sharp decline of 50 per cent. Currently, net private capital inflows to emerging economies increased by 85 per cent from the trough of 2008 to 2012, followed by an estimated decline of 12 per cent in 2013.

Current-account balances

In the three years before the Asian financial crisis, the three selected economies all experienced increases in their current-account deficits, with Thailand registering the greatest increase, from 5.4 per cent of GDP in 1994 to 8 per cent in 1996 (figure I.10). In comparison, all five sampled economies have been running current-account deficits in the past few years, with the largest deficit in Turkey, at 9.7 per cent of GDP in 2011. India's deficit was also sizeable at more than 5 per cent of GDP.

External debt

Measured by the ratio of foreign debt to GDP (figure I.11), among the three selected economies for the Asian financial crisis, Thailand had the highest external debt ratio of 50 per cent in 1996. In the current episode, India and Turkey have the highest external debt-to-GDP ratio of about 20 per cent.

In addition, currency and maturity mismatches in emerging markets' balance sheets (particularly of the private sector) played a central role in the Asian financial crisis, but are less pronounced this time. In South Africa, for instance, approximately two thirds of the total external debt is in domestic currency and only about 10 per cent of total external debt is short-term debt denominated in foreign currency. Similarly, India's short-term external debt accounts for only about 5 per cent of GDP.

Procyclical and fickle movements pervade international capital flows

Figure I.10
Current-account imbalances for selected countries

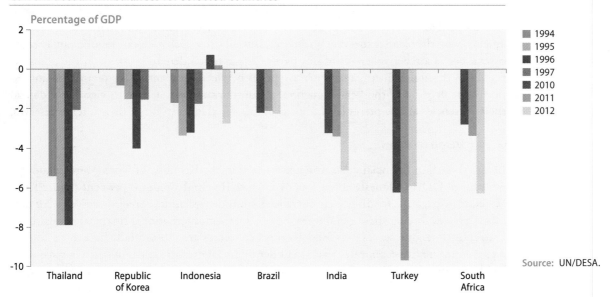

Source: UN/DESA.

Figure I.11
External debt for selected countries

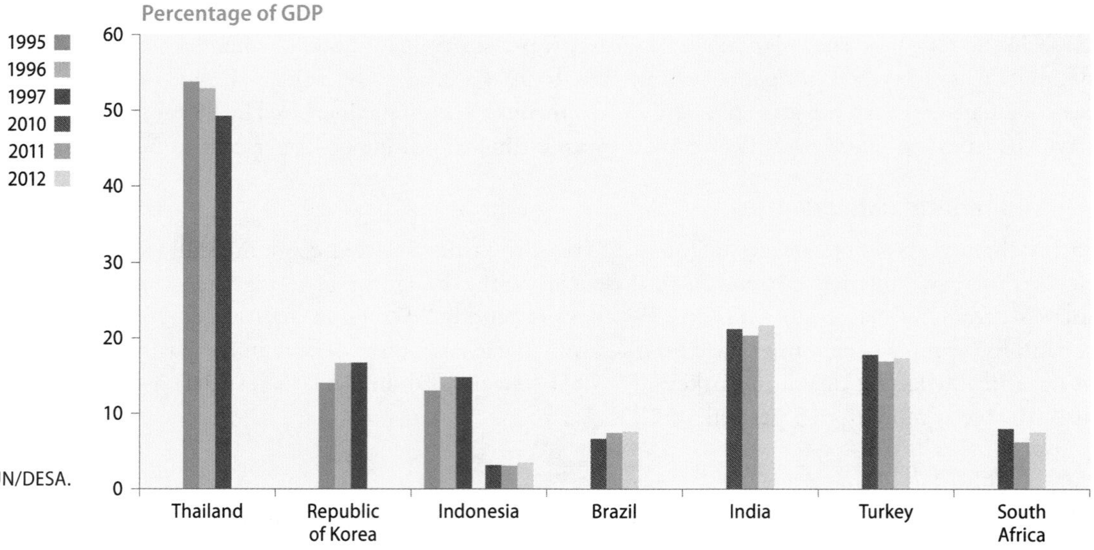

Percentage of GDP

1995
1996
1997
2010
2011
2012

Thailand Republic Indonesia Brazil India Turkey South
of Korea   Africa

Exchange-rate regimes

In the 1990s, most emerging economies adopted a fixed exchange-rate regime, pegging their currencies to the United States dollar, or other major currencies. The fixed exchange-rate regime caused at least two types of problems. First, in the run-up to the financial crisis, the fixed exchange-rate regimes tended to lead to overvaluation of the local currencies when these countries experienced higher inflation than that in the United States, and/or when they encountered adverse shocks to their exports. Second, when the crisis erupted, the fixed exchange-rate regime also obligated these countries to defend their currencies by selling their foreign reserves, only to watch those hard-earned reserves quickly drain away.

Most emerging economies have recently adopted more flexible exchange-rate regimes

In contrast, most emerging economies have recently adopted floating, or managed floating exchange-rate regimes. A sharp devaluation of the local currency in a short period is still harmful for emerging economies, in terms of the adverse effects on inflationary pressures and losses on the balance sheets of businesses. But a flexible exchange-rate regime can, to some extent, act as a relief valve—it offsets part of the external demand shocks on the domestic economy, through adjustments to relative prices between the external sector and the domestic sector. Because of the flexible regime, the authorities do not have to vigorously defend their currencies at any preset level, thus avoiding rapid exhaustion of their foreign reserves.

Foreign reserves

Before the Asian financial crisis, foreign reserves in the Republic of Korea were at about 5 per cent of GDP, Indonesia about 8 per cent and Thailand about 20 per cent (figure I.12). When they began defending their currencies from depreciation, foreign reserves were rapidly depleted, forcing these economies to seek aid from international financial institutions. Currently, foreign reserves in most emerging economies are substantially higher. For example, even in the five economies that are under financial pressure, each of them has accumulated foreign reserves above 10 per cent of GDP, not to mention a group of other emerging economies with much higher foreign reserves.

Figure I.12
Foreign reserves for selected countries

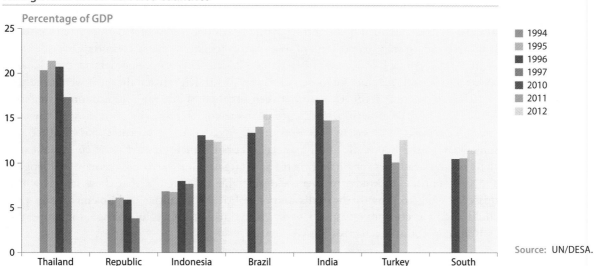

Source: UN/DESA.

Other aspects

Since the Asian financial crisis of the 1990s, as well as a few financial crises in other emerging economies in the late 1990s and the early 2000s, these economies have made a number of improvements. There is a greater transparency in the disclosure of financial information, including data on foreign reserves and non-performing loans; banking supervision and regulation has beeen strengthened so as to reduce mismatches in currencies and terms of debt; policy measures in managing capital inflows are more flexible; and better macroeconomic positions, in terms of more prudent fiscal and monetary policies and lower government debt-to-GDP ratios, have been achieved.

In the outlook, as major central banks (particularly the Fed) are expected to taper and eventually unwind their QE programmes, emerging economies are bound to face more external shocks, especially marked declines of capital inflows. Some of these economies, particularly those with large external imbalances, remain vulnerable. Nevertheless, economic fundamentals and the policy space in these economies are better than when the Asian financial crisis erupted.

Economic fundamentals in emerging economies are stronger now than when the Asian financial crisis erupted

Remaining risks in the euro area

The crisis in the euro area has cooled significantly but remains a significant risk factor for the world economy. The Outright Monetary Transactions (OMT) programme adopted by the ECB and other policy initiatives since late 2012 have significantly reduced sovereign risks and the risk of a euro area break-up. The OMT in particular has acted as a circuit breaker between the eruption of country-specific crises and sovereign bond markets. This explains why the political impasse in Italy and the Cypriot bank bailout during 2013 caused only limited disturbances. Despite this progress, considerable banking and fiscal risks remain.

A large number of banks still have weak balance sheets, particularly in the southern region, and could face insolvency. The Cypriot bailout in March 2013 actually raised risks in the banking sector by bailing in additional classes of creditors, thus increasing the pos-

A large number of European banks still have weak balance sheets

sibility of bank runs in the future. This has heightened the urgency to create a region-wide banking union. EU finance ministers have agreed on the first stage of a banking union, and the ECB will become the top bank supervisor in the euro area. However, in the continuing discussion over the form of the future banking union, the issue of bank resolution is far from resolved, so that the problem of weak banks remains a major concern. One side effect of the OMT policy has been that banks have added more sovereign debt to their balance sheets and would therefore be more vulnerable to sovereign instability if it were to return.

The dangerous feedback loop between fiscal consolidation and economic weakness remains a risk. The growth performance of the region is improving, but most of the crisis countries remain in recession. The pressure to enact austerity measures has been reduced somewhat, as the Economic and Financial Affairs Council granted some countries extensions on the deadlines for hitting their fiscal targets. But the targets remain challenging, and will continue to hinder recovery. Considerable risk remains that these targets will be missed, owing to growth shortfalls and/or political difficulties in implementation. This could lead to a return to crisis; and, as was seen during the Cypriot episode, the support for assistance to countries in crisis has weakened.

Uncertainties and risks from lingering budget issues in the United States

Over the course of 2013, the United States has experienced a series of small-scale fiscal crises caused by political divides over budget issues in Congress. At the beginning of the year, a full-scaled fiscal cliff was averted when an agreement was reached to permanently maintain a large part of the temporary tax cuts after they were due to expire. But Congress failed to agree on a long-term deficit reduction plan, triggering automatic, across-the-board spending cuts (sequestration) worth $1.2 trillion over the next nine years, with a cut of $85 billion for 2013. In early October, a failure in Congress to agree on the 2014 budget and to raise the debt ceiling led to a partial shutdown of the federal Government and heightened the risk of a default on the United States debt. At the last minute, an agreement was reached to fund the Government through 15 January 2014 and suspend the debt limit through 7 February 2014, merely postponing the issues.

There are two different types of economic costs associated with these uncertainties and risks. First, the recurrent uncertainties about the government budget, even if no large-scale crisis erupts, discourage business investment and hiring, thereby leading to lower growth and higher unemployment in the short run and damaging potential growth in the longer run.

If the debt ceiling were not raised, the consequences would be devastating

Second, should a crisis occur if the debt ceiling were not raised, for example, the consequences would be devastating not only for the United States, but also for the world economy. With the federal government budget deficit at more than 4 per cent of GDP, if no more net borrowing were allowed, the Government would be forced to take actions which would entail a combination of defaulting on the debt and cutting expenditures. Given that the United States has never defaulted, that the dollar is the major international reserve currency, and that half of the United States government debt is held by foreigners, including foreign central banks, it is difficult to make a plausible estimate for the costs of such a default. On the other hand, the impact of a cut in government spending can be estimated through model simulation (as the one simulating the fiscal cliff in *WESP 2013*, for example, which remains valid today.

Policy challenges

Macroeconomic policy stances in the world economy have become more diverse across countries, and some critical transitions are expected to occur in 2014-2015. While policies in most developed countries, except Japan, will continue to feature a combination of tightening fiscal policy and accommodative monetary policy, the degree of fiscal tightening will be less restrictive and the extent of monetary easing will taper off. The central banks of major developed countries have the primary responsibility for providing adequate and stable global liquidity, as they are the issuers of the international reserve currencies. Managing a smooth tapering of the QE will be the key challenge for the monetary authorities in major developed countries, as the risks associated with this transition will pose a threat not only for developed economies, but also for the rest of the world.

In developing countries and economies in transition, policymakers are facing a more challenging international economic environment, as well as more demanding domestic economic situations, that require tough tradeoffs amid a confluence of different policy needs. Moreover, some of the challenges facing developing countries and economies in transition may go beyond the reach of standard macroeconomic policies, requiring institutional and structural reforms. A number of developing countries, such as Brazil, China and India, have indeed embarked on various reforms, including reforms in social security, income distribution, the financial sector, taxation, energy, transportation, education and health care.

Managing a smooth tapering of the QE will be the key challenge

Fiscal policy

Most developed economies, with Japan as the exception, have continued fiscal tightening during 2013 by reducing government spending, raising taxes, and, in some cases, liquidating public assets. The average budget deficit of developed countries is estimated to have been reduced by 1.4 per cent of GDP to 4.5 per cent of GDP by 2013, compared with the peak of 8.9 per cent in 2009 at the height of the financial crisis. The average debt stands at 108.5 per cent of GDP. In the outlook, fiscal tightening will likely continue in most of these economies, but with a notably less acute stance.

In the United States, fiscal policy has tightened markedly in 2013, through increases in taxes and automatic spending cuts (sequestration). As a result, government spending in real terms is estimated to have declined by about 5 per cent in 2013 from the previous year. The outlook for fiscal policy in 2014-2015 is clouded by uncertainties emanating from political wrangling. Fiscal policy is expected to remain restrictive, but less severe than in 2013. In Western Europe, fiscal policy remains dominated by the need to reduce deficits under the euro zone rules and was reaffirmed by the ratification of the new fiscal compact this year. Progress has been made, but twelve out of seventeen euro area countries remain under the Excessive Deficit Procedure of the Stability and Growth Pact. The fiscal compact of the euro area entered into force in 2013, adding additional fiscal targets: the structural deficit should now be less than 0.5 per cent of GDP, and remedial action will now be required for countries with debt-to-GDP ratios above 60 per cent. Japan, despite facing the largest debt-to-GDP ratio in the world, has adopted expansionary fiscal policy during 2013, through a supplemental budget to increase government spending by about 2.2 per cent of nominal GDP. The Government decided to implement plans to raise the consumption tax rate from the current level of 5 per cent to 8 per cent in April 2014 and 10 per cent in October 2015. A new complementary package of about 5 trillion yen was introduced to compensate the negative impacts of the higher consumption tax.

A number of low-income
countries are experiencing
high budget deficits

Compared with developed economies, most developing countries and economies in transition have a better fiscal position in terms of budget deficits and public debt. However, their fiscal position has deteriorated measurably in 2013, with a number of low-income countries experiencing high budget deficits.

The fiscal deficit has deteriorated in much of Africa, as Governments across the continent are under continuous pressure to increase spending on public services, wages in the public sector and provision of subsidies on food and fuel. The deterioration is largely due to lagging revenues in oil-importing countries, while oil-exporting and mineral-rich countries have sizeable fiscal surpluses. In East Asia, fiscal policy has remained generally expansionary, as a number of countries adopted various stimulatory measures, including tax relief, expenditures in support of job creation, and infrastructure projects, to counter the slowdown in domestic demand. As a result, fiscal positions have worsened slightly in 2013. A similar stance is expected for 2014. Public finances in South Asia are under pressure, with Governments increasing already large deficits and regularly missing deficit reduction targets by a wide margin. Given the weak growth momentum in the region and the difficulties in raising tax revenues and curbing expenditure growth, fiscal deficits will remain large in the near term. In Western Asia, the active fiscal policy employed by oil exporters will remain, in contrast to more pronounced fiscal constraints of the non-oil exporters. In Latin America and the Caribbean, the fiscal position has deteriorated slightly in the past two years, mainly due to higher public expenditures in South America, but public revenues are also vulnerable to a softening of the prices of the primary commodities that the region exports.

In the CIS, the Russian Federation has maintained a prudent fiscal stance as budget revenue increased less than anticipated. While Ukraine is restrained by high fiscal deficit, a few oil and natural gas exporting countries, such as Azerbaijan, Kazakhstan and Turkmenistan, continued massive fiscal spending on public wages and public infrastructure.

Monetary policy

Major developed countries share a number of common features in their monetary policy. In addition to maintaining policy interest rates at zero or near zero, and adopting large-scale purchases of long-terms assets (see box I.3 in previous section), central banks in these countries have also increasingly turned to "forward guidance" as a policy tool, thus providing additional stimulus by anchoring expectations that interest rates will remain low for an extended period.

The Fed was the first central bank to adopt forward policy guidance; it stated publicly that it would keep the target range for the federal funds rate at exceptionally low levels as long as the unemployment rate remains above 6.5 per cent, or inflation between one and two years ahead is projected to be no more than a half percentage point above the two per cent longer-run target.

The Bank of England (BoE) has joined the Fed in framing its guidance as refraining from raising the bank rate from its 0.5 per cent level at least until the unemployment rate has fallen to a threshold of 7 per cent. The BoE also made it clear that the unemployment threshold is not expected to be breached until at least the second half of 2016. The Bank of Japan (BoJ) has announced that it will continue the Quantitative and Qualitative Monetary Easing until the CPI inflation rate reaches the target of 2 per cent. In comparison, the forward guidance recently instituted by the ECB is to confirm that their current policy setting will stay in place for an extended period of time without specifying a numerical target for exiting this setting.

Enhanced guidance by the central banks is seen as necessary for increasing policy transparency and reducing uncertainties, thereby limiting the risk of financial market volatility that diminishes policy effectiveness. In reality, however, confusion can still occur. For example, when the Fed announced in May 2013 the possibility of tapering the amount of its purchases of long-term assets by late 2013, financial markets reacted immediately by pushing up long-term interest rates significantly. When the Fed did not reduce its purchases in September 2013, markets seemed to be confused again. Managing public expectations, if possible, remains a big challenge for policymakers.

As delineated in box I.1 above, central banks in major developed countries are expected to maintain the policy interest rates at their current low levels at least until mid-2015, to be followed by a gradual increase in the rates. The Fed is expected to taper QE in 2014.

Among central banks in developing countries and economies transition there is no apparent common trend in monetary policy, as some of them are tightening while others are easing. In the outlook, the monetary authorities in these countries are expected to adopt appropriate monetary policy stances in accordance with the challenges they face, including the responses to spillovers from the changes in QE of major developed countries, fluctuations in exchange rates, volatility in capital inflows, and the movements in inflation, unemployment and growth. More details about monetary policy in these countries can be found in chapter IV.

Enhanced guidance by the central banks is necessary

Policy challenges in managing the risks associated with the unwinding of QE

The tapering and unwinding of the unconventional monetary policies in major developed economies in the next few years pose significant risks for global growth and the stability of the world economy. It is a challenge for policymakers in these countries to harness a smooth process for this transition. Central banks should develop a clear communication strategy to articulate the timing and the targets of the policy action, and avoid repeating the episodes resulting from the actions of the Fed in May-June and September of 2013. At the macroeconomic levels, the timing and the pace of the unwinding are crucial: a premature and rapid unwinding may risk choking off the economic recovery, but a delayed unwinding could risk creating financial bubbles. At the technical level, contingency plans are also needed to deal with the overreaction of financial markets and prevent contagion. Efforts are needed to enhance supervision, regulation and surveillance of financial markets, in order to be able to identify and mitigate risks and vulnerabilities associated with the liquidity of some assets, market structure, and other problems in advance.

For developing countries and emerging economies, the challenge is to shield themselves from the spillover effects of the unwinding of QE in major developed countries, which will be transmitted through international finance and trade. As shown by the financial market turmoil in the summer of 2013, the spillover shocks to these countries can be consequential and costly, particularly to those emerging economies that are highly exposed to international capital markets and have large external imbalances financed by short-term external capital flows. Before the next episode of shocks arrives, these economies need to address external and internal imbalances and build policy space. Supervision and regulation should also be strengthened to prevent a build-up of mismatches in foreign currency funding on bank balance sheets. Prudential oversight should be tightened, particularly for shadow banking activity.

A challenge for developing countries will be to shield themselves from the spillover effects of the QE exit

Many emerging economies today have gained policy flexibility from adopting a more flexible exchange-rate regime, compared with the Asian financial crisis of the 1990s. However, central banks in these economies may still have to defend their currencies from sharp depreciation in case of a significant decline in capital inflows. How to do it effectively remains a challenge.

During the most recent financial turmoil of mid-2013, some countries, such as Brazil, India and Indonesia, raised interest rates in an attempt to curb currency depreciation. Alternatively, the central bank of Turkey has adopted a different policy scheme by creating an interest-rate corridor without increasing the policy interest rate. Individual countries can and should adopt measures that are most suitable to their institutional settings and policy targets.

International policy coordination

Stronger recovery should be the primary focus of the globally coordinated policy

The multiple and complex challenges in the world economy call for strengthening of international policy coordination. While the primary focus of globally-concerted and coherent policy actions should be a stronger recovery—particularly the recovery of jobs—increasing attention should also be given to mitigating the spillover effects emanating from the large-scale, unconventional monetary policies adopted by major developed countries regarding developing countries and economies in transition.

Maintaining an open multilateral dialogue on the economic policy intentions of all countries, particularly the major economies, is a crucial element in international policy coordination to promote policy coherence and concerted action. Such dialogue has so far been frequently held in the context of the Group of 20 (G20), but it should also be promoted to more broadly representative international forums, particularly the United Nations.

Most recently, at the G20 Summit held in St. Petersburg on September 5 and 6, 2013, members reaffirmed the framework for strong, sustainable and balanced growth. The G20 has committed to undertaking further policy adjustments towards rebalancing global demand between surplus and deficit countries. The surplus countries will achieve stronger domestic demand while the deficit countries will increase savings, and countries are encouraged to make their exchange rates more flexible. The Summit also called for urgent action to increase the momentum of the global recovery and generate higher growth and better jobs. The effectiveness of the G20 policy coordination, however, will still need to be enforced by compliance at the individual country level.

Advancing the reforms of the international financial system

International policy cooperation and coordination are needed to advance the reforms of the international financial system on several fronts. Progress in financial regulatory reform has been slow, encountering growing resistance from the financial industry. Some progress has been made in amending the global financial safety standards for the banking sector. A dozen countries have issued final regulations to implement Basel III and more countries have committed to do so during 2013. Progress has also been made in implementing over-the-counter derivatives reforms. On the other hand, the question of ending the "too big to fail" approach is still pending, and recommendations from the Financial Stability Board for the oversight and regulation of the shadow banking sector have yet to be issued. More forceful efforts are needed to address the issues of international tax avoidance and evasion, particularly through tax havens.

The current phase of reforming both the International Monetary Fund (IMF) and the World Bank needs to be completed to make their governance structures more representative, responsive and accountable. While there has been progress in ratifying the 2010

IMF quota and governance reforms, the process has not been finalized. The new review of the IMF quota formula should be resolved quickly to enhance the voice and participation of developing economies.

International policy cooperation should ensure that sufficient resources are made available to developing countries—especially the least developed countries—and countries that possess limited fiscal space and face large financing needs for sustainable development and poverty reduction. The decline in ODA flows over the past two years should be reversed. As the target date for the MDGs is approaching, international donors should redouble their efforts to deliver on existing commitments. These resources are greatly needed in order for developing countries to accelerate progress towards the achievement of the MDGs by the end of 2015, and to build a solid foundation for long-run sustainable development beyond 2015.

Sufficient resources must be ensured for the least developed countries

Chapter II
International trade

With demand in many developed countries still low, and growth faltering in developing countries, 2013 has seen a further slowdown in trade. There is some improvement expected in the forecast period, with demand rising in developed economies and activity recovering in developing countries. Trade balances are expected to remain virtually the same between now and then. Trade in services has fared somewhat better than goods, particularly exports from developing countries. There has been some progress on multilateral trade, with a limited agreement reached on 7 December 2013 at the World Trade Organization (WTO) Ninth Ministerial Conference, held in Bali. Significant developments are also possible in the area of large regional trade agreements (RTAs), which have the potential to cover a majority of world trade if they are approved. For the moment trade is being driven by larger macroeconomic trends as opposed to changes in policy; this may shift in the medium term.

Growth of international trade flows weakened even further in 2013, after anaemic growth in 2012. Sluggish global output growth has weighed on international merchandise trade flows, with feeble import demand in major developed economies and moderate demand in a number of large developing countries. World export volumes are set to increase only 2.3 per cent for 2013, lower than the pace of 3.1 per cent in 2012 and well below trend growth prior to the global financial crisis (figure II.1).

Slow growth continued in world merchandise trade in 2013, but some improvement is expected

Some improvement is expected in world trade flows in the outlook for 2014-2015, as global output is projected to strengthen gradually. Slightly improved demand in Europe (from a recession, admittedly), a continuation of the recovery in the United States of America, and an expected rebound in the trade dynamism of Asia are anticipated to drive growth of world exports to 4.6 per cent in 2014 and 5.1 per cent in 2015—more in line with the historical pattern of the ratio of trade growth to global output growth.

The geographic pattern of world trade flows continues to shift. The share of exports is almost equal for developed and developing countries, although imports of developed countries are still leading developing countries. South-South trade has continued to grow, rising from about one fifth of world trade to about one fourth in the past decade. Growth of South-South trade has accounted for a majority of the growth of world trade. North-North trade has grown at a slower clip and now accounts for about the same proportion of world trade as South-South trade (figure II.2). Much of the growth in South-South trade has been driven by trade in fuels—owing to both higher prices and increased demand in developing countries—and by communications equipment, which has shifted production from developed to developing countries.[1] Trade flows between developing and developed countries still account for a significant portion of world trade. Despite some increase, shares of least developed countries (LDCs) in world trade remain low at less than 1 per cent.

South-South trade is now nearly equal to North-North trade as a proportion of world trade

---

[1]   See UNCTAD, "Key trends in international merchandise trade", UNCTAD/DITC/TAB/2013/1 (Geneva) for more details.

Figure II.1
World trade growth, 2002-2015

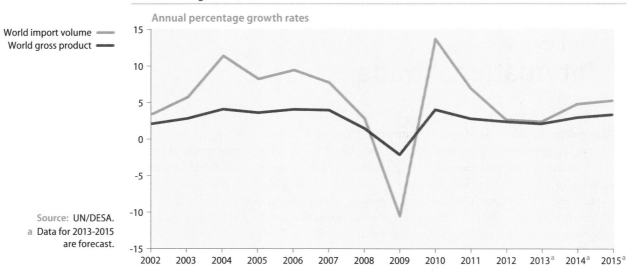

Annual percentage growth rates

World import volume ——
World gross product ——

Source: UN/DESA.
a Data for 2013-2015
are forecast.

Figure II.2
North-South distributions of world trade, 1995-2012

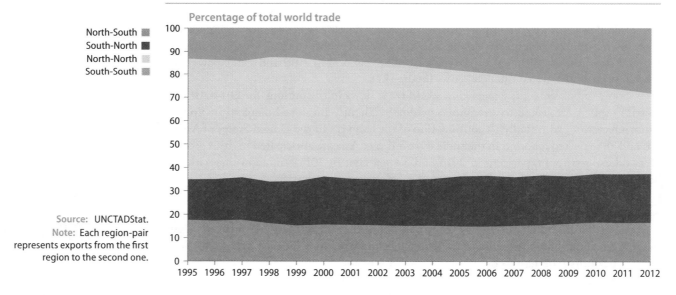

Percentage of total world trade

North-South ▨
South-North ■
North-North ▨
South-South ▨

Source: UNCTADStat.
Note: Each region-pair
represents exports from the first
region to the second one.

Among developing countries, intraregional trade makes up a significantly large proportion of overall trade only in East Asia, particularly owing to trade in intermediate products; yet, intraregional trade accounts for a much smaller proportion of trade growth in Latin America and the Commonwealth of Independent States (CIS), as trade in these two regions is based more on primary products and agriculture. The degree of regional integration varies by countries and regions, with some East Asian countries, such as Lao People's Democratic Republic, Mongolia and Myanmar, registering upwards of 80 per cent of their trade as intraregional. Larger economies, such as those in Latin America, have considerably lower shares of intraregional trade. Overall, in value terms, a majority of trade continues to occur within and between Europe, North America and East Asia.[2] Evidence of this is apparent when examining the global liner shipping network, in which these regions play a central role (box II.1).

In developed countries, growth of imports was down to almost zero at 0.5 per cent for 2013, pulled down by a significant deceleration in developed Asia and Oceania. Import growth improved slightly in Europe in 2013, but that was only from -0.2 per cent to 0.0 per cent. In contrast, import volume for developing countries increased by 4.6 per cent in both 2012 and 2013 (figure II.3). An upward shift is expected in trade for major developed countries in the outlook for 2014-2015.

Among developed countries, for 2014-2015, relatively strong import growth is expected in Japan—to 5 per cent, which is higher than its average growth rate of the past 15 years. Import growth in Canada and the United States is also expected to grow at a pace of about 5 per cent. Growth in imports in Europe will only improve modestly from the zero growth registered in 2013 (figure II.4).

Developed-country trade growth is expected to improve in the outlook period

Figure II.3
Import trends of developed and developing countries, 2000-2015

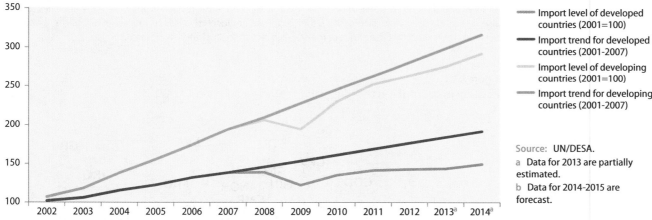

Import level of developed countries (2001=100)
Import trend for developed countries (2001-2007)
Import level of developing countries (2001=100)
Import trend for developing countries (2001-2007)

Source: UN/DESA.
a Data for 2013 are partially estimated.
b Data for 2014-2015 are forecast.

Figure II.4
Import volume growth across groups of countries, 2011-2013

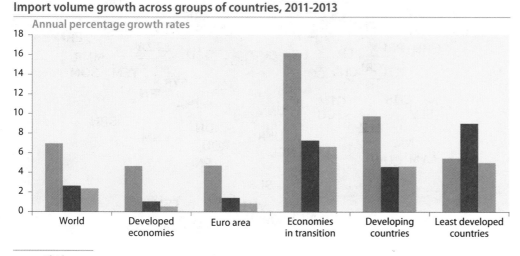

Annual percentage growth rates

2011
2012
2013[a]

Source: UN/DESA.
Note: Import includes goods and services.
a Data for 2013 are partially estimated.

2   Ibid.

Box II.1
Maritime trade: the role of the global liner shipping network

The importance of containerization for global trade has only recently started to be understood. A new study[a] covering the introduction of containerization until 1990 concluded that containerization had a stronger impact on driving globalization than trade liberalization. A study by ESCAP and the World Bank[b] found that liner shipping connectivity was a more significant determinant of trade costs than the indicators for logistics performance, air connectivity, costs of starting a business, and lower tariffs combined.

In order to analyse the structure of the global container shipping network, the United Nations Conference on Trade and Development (UNCTAD) has developed the Liner Shipping Connectivity Matrix database, which includes both country-level data as well as information on container shipping services between pairs of countries. The country-level Liner Shipping Connectivity Index is generated from the following five components that capture the deployment of container ships by liner shipping companies to a country's ports of call: 1) the number of ships; 2) their total container carrying capacity; 3) the number of companies providing services with their own operated ships; 4) the number of services provided; and 5) the size (in twenty foot equivalent units (TEU)) of the largest ship deployed.

Based on this database, it is possible to visually capture the structure of the global network of container shipping services (figure II.1.1). The best connected countries, such as China, Germany, the Republic of Korea and the United States of America, are at the centre of the global shipping network and they are also well connected with each other. Other countries are located closer to the periphery of the global network, represented at the edges of the star-like structure illustrated in Figure II.1.1.

Figure II.1.1
Position of countries in the global liner shipping network

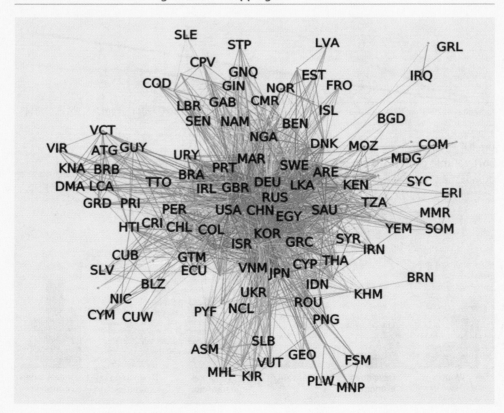

Source: UNCTAD, based on data provided by Lloyd's List Intelligence.
Note: The three-letter code is the country code defined by the International Organization for Standardization.

With the database, it is also possible to examine important trends in container ship deployment, namely, that ships have become significantly larger over time and these ships are being deployed by fewer companies (Figure II.1.2).

Figure II.1.2
Trends in container ship fleet deployment, mid-2004–mid-2013

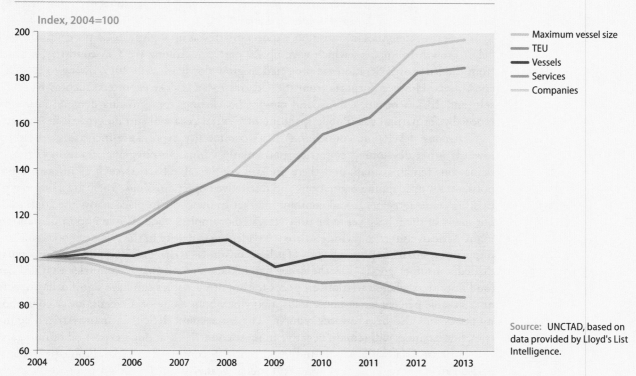

Index, 2004=100

Legend:
- Maximum vessel size
- TEU
- Vessels
- Services
- Companies

Source: UNCTAD, based on data provided by Lloyd's List Intelligence.

Regarding vessel sizes, since 2004, the average container-carrying capacity of the largest ship in the 159 countries covered by the UNCTAD database has almost doubled, from 2,812 TEU ten years ago to 5,540 TEU in 2013. The trend towards larger ships can be expected to continue. The current containership orderbook is dominated by ships that are far bigger than today's average.[c]

As regards the number of companies per country, the average has decreased by 27 per cent during the last ten years, from 22 in 2004 to just 16 in 2013. This trend has important implications for the level of competition, especially for smaller trading nations, many of which are located at the periphery of the network (figure II.1.2). While an average of 16 service providers may still be sufficient to ensure a functioning competitive market with many choices for shippers for the average country, on given individual routes, especially those serving smaller developing countries, the decline in competition has led to oligopolistic markets. For example, in 2004, there were 22 countries served by three or fewer carriers, while in 2013, 31 countries were facing this situation.

From the shippers' perspective, larger ships and more total TEU carrying capacity could be positive developments. It should lead to lower freight costs, both by ensuring sufficient available carrying capacity for the growing trade in containerized goods, and by the doubling of ship sizes to allow them to achieve economies of scale. However, lower operational unit costs achieved by shipping lines, thanks to newer, larger and more fuel-efficient ships, may not necessarily be passed on to the shippers (that is, the importers and exporters). The very process of concentration of cargo in larger ships may also lead to the same capacity being offered by fewer providers, thereby decreasing competition. In some oligopolistic markets shippers may in fact be confronted with higher freight rates and less choice of services.[d]

a Daniel Bernhofen, Zouheir El-Sahli and Richard Kneller (2013), "Estimating the effects of the container revolution on world trade" CESifo Working Paper, No. 4136 (February 2013).

b Jean-François Arvis and others, "Trade costs and development: a new data set ", World Bank Economic Premise, No. 104 (January 2013).

c Clarksons, *Container Intelligence Quarterly*, (Clarkson Research Services Ltd: London).

d UNCTAD, *The Review of Maritime Transport 2013* (United Nations publications, Sales No. E.13.II.D.9).

Source: UNCTAD.

The same patterns of trade deficits and surpluses continued among most developed countries, with the United States in deficit and the euro area in surplus—the latter mainly driven by surpluses in Germany. The exception was Japan's shift from surplus to deficit.

Exports from the new European Union (EU) members in Eastern Europe picked up over the course of 2013 and should strengthen further in 2014 and 2015, in line with the recovery in external demand. Despite the strong import content of exports, imports to those countries will expand at a lower pace, as investment has yet to recover and austerity measures continue to dampen domestic demand.

For the economies in transition, export growth was up slightly to 1.4 per cent, still well below growth in imports, which were up 7.9 per cent. Among the CIS countries, exports from the Russian Federation are projected to grow slowly in 2014-2015, owing to capacity constraints. However, exports from the Central Asian energy exporters, such as Kazakhstan and Turkmenistan, will expand rapidly, benefitting from growing demand in China especially for natural gas. Public spending in Central Asia will sustain growth in imports.

Among developing countries, Africa's commodity exports are increasingly heading towards other developing countries, particularly China. Intraregional trade in Africa is rising, but remains small, and there are still considerable barriers such as infrastructure bottlenecks, overlapping regulations and restrictive border crossings. There are a number of existing trade agreements and common market frameworks in place across the continent, but many of them have yet to be fully activated or implemented. While import demand in many African countries is rising, there is a widening disparity in the types of goods that are imported; a small but growing class of urban consumers is driving demand for more sophisticated consumer goods. On the other hand, there are still many countries that are net food importers where variations in prices for imported staples can have significant impacts on a sizeable percentage of households, many of whom are poor. Overall, lower commodity prices will also help towards reducing current-account deficits in many African countries, but balances will remain negative in most countries that don't export oil or minerals.

In East Asia, while export and import growth continued to expand robustly in comparison to other regions, they were still much weaker than the period prior to the crisis (figure II.5). Both export and import growth are expected to improve slightly over the forecast period, with exports rising from 4.9 per cent in 2013 to 6.1 per cent in 2014 and 6.2 per cent in 2015. Within the region, China will continue to be the powerhouse, but it has begun to increase its share of both regional and world imports in efforts to strengthen domestic demand (Box II.2). There have also been some shifts in the trade patterns between East Asia and Japan, mainly owing to exchange rate changes.

In Western Asia trends vary across subregions. In Gulf Cooperation Council (GCC) countries, trade surpluses shrank as oil revenues declined, while demand grew at a rapid pace, driven by solid domestic demand. The conditions in the Syrian Arab Republic have increasingly impacted their neighbouring countries, particularly Jordan. Import growth jumped in Turkey, driven in particular by rising oil imports. There was a drastic drop in export growth for Turkey between 2012 and 2013, from over 16 per cent to about 3 per cent. The combination of these two trends pushed the trade deficit up by 17 per cent for the first nine months of 2013, compared to the same period in 2012. Some recovery is expected in the outlook period as demand from Europe recovers.

In Latin America, slowing growth in emerging economies such as China caused a notable decline in export growth in Brazil. More generally, decreased commodity demand—also to some extent a function of slowing growth in China—further contributed to a reduction in exports from Latin America. Domestic demand continued to be strong in many countries in

Figure II.5
Import volume growth across regions, 2001-2013

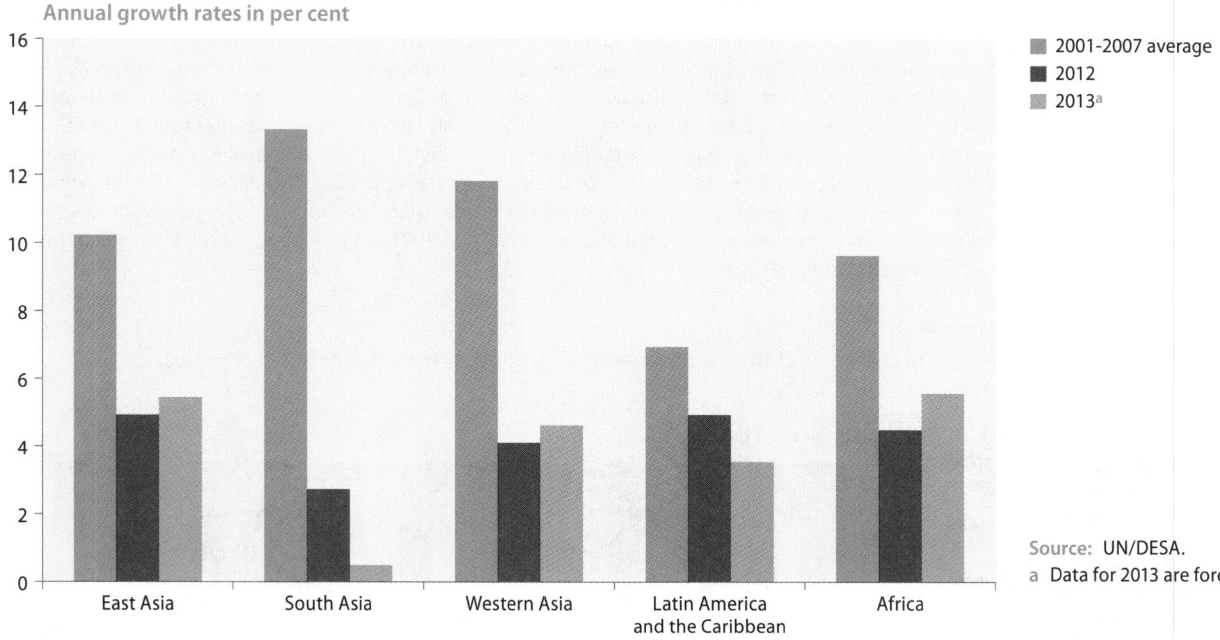

Annual growth rates in per cent

Legend:
- 2001-2007 average
- 2012
- 2013[a]

Source: UN/DESA.
a Data for 2013 are forecast.

Box II.2
The impact of China's structural changes on its major trading partners

A structural shift in the composition of China's gross domestic product (GDP), away from investment and net exports and towards efforts to promote household consumption might affect the size and composition of its import basket.

Between 2000 and 2008, China's rapid growth was led by an increase in investment as a share of GDP from 36 per cent to 42 per cent and an increase in the share of net exports from about 2 per cent to over 8 per cent. Increases were driven mainly by rising exports, whose share in GDP went from 23 per cent to 38 per cent.[a] Over the same period, the share of household consumption fell from 46 per cent to 36 per cent.

After the global crisis, the Chinese Government's stimulus package further increased the share of investment in GDP to almost 50 per cent to support strategic emerging industries, urbanization, the construction of social housing, and the development of infrastructure and higher technology products. The share of household consumption has changed little, however, while the share of net exports declined to 3.5 per cent, mainly as a result of a sharp deceleration in the growth of exports.

Given the large size of China's economy, significant shifts in the composition of its trade basket may affect global commodity prices and the terms of trade for other countries, particularly for resource-based economies such as those in Africa. Therefore, the changes in China's trade basket resulting from structural changes in the Chinese economy may have significant impacts on its trading partners.

Different GDP components have different import intensity. An increase in the share of private consumption in China's GDP is unlikely to bring sizable benefits to countries exporting consumer goods, because much of the consumption increase will come in the form of increased demand for services, such as health care and other social services with low import intensity. On the other hand, changes in the shares of investment and exports in its GDP would lead to more substantial effects on China's imports.

Box II.2
The impact of China's structural changes on its major trading partners (*continued*)

Empirical evidence on the composition of China's imports (figure II.2.1) indicates that the recent increase in the share of investment in gross domestic product (GDP) was accompanied by an increase in the share of minerals and metals—especially iron ore and copper—in China's total imports from about 9 per cent in 2005-2007 to about 13 per cent in 2009-2012. This increase was mostly due to strongly rising infrastructure investment during the latter period. By contrast, the share of machinery in total imports declined from about 16 per cent in 2005-2007 to about 12 per cent in 2012. This decrease reflects the decline in net exports as a share of GDP, while the decline in the shares of imports of parts and components for electrical and electronic goods, from 24 per cent in 2005-2007 to 14 per cent in 2012, is a result of the decline in processing trade.

Figure II.2.1
The composition of China's merchandise imports, selected product categories, 2000-2012

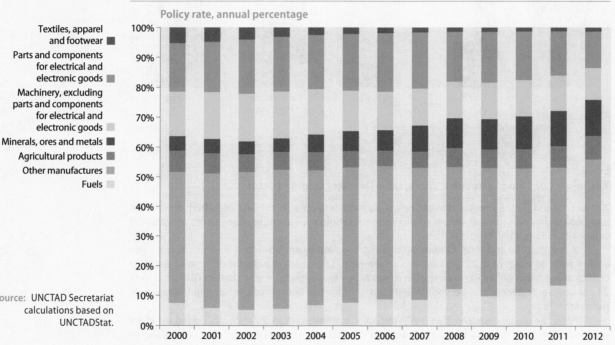

Textiles, apparel and footwear ■
Parts and components for electrical and electronic goods ■
Machinery, excluding parts and components for electrical and electronic goods ■
Minerals, ores and metals ■
Agricultural products ■
Other manufactures ■
Fuels ■

Policy rate, annual percentage

Source: UNCTAD Secretariat calculations based on UNCTADStat.

In the outlook, a structural shift in the composition of China's GDP away from investment and net exports towards a greater importance of household consumption would lead to changes in China's imports. The groups of countries most heavily exposed would include: Australia and Brazil, which account for about two thirds of China's iron ore imports; Chile, which accounts for about one third of China's copper imports; Germany, Japan and the Republic of Korea, which account for almost half of China's machinery imports; and Japan, Malaysia, the Republic of Korea and Taiwan Province of China, which account for over two thirds of China's imports of parts and components for electrical and electronic goods. However, the impact would likely be spread over a number of years, and would not be sudden and sharp. Moreover, given that China's rapid pace of urbanization is set to continue, and a shift in the composition of its GDP towards greater importance of household consumption will require enhanced transportation and distribution networks, China's infrastructure investment is likely to remain high in the medium term. This would mean that those countries exporting minerals and metals, in particular, are unlikely to experience a significant, if any, adverse effect.

a Given its fairly stable level of about 13-16 per cent during the period 2000-2011, the share of government consumption in GDP will not be considered here.
Source: UNCTAD.

the region, which helped to support overall growth and also added to import growth, but led to rising trade deficits. Most of those imports, however, were coming from outside of Latin America, as exports within the region were generally lower. The prospects for 2014-2015 will benefit from expected increases in external demand from developed countries, particularly the United States, but the demand from emerging economies in other regions, including China and India, will remain moderate compared with the period prior to the global financial crisis.

Commodity markets

Since January 2013, commodity prices have generally eased, although trends of commodity groups vary (figure II.6). The United Nations Conference on Trade and Development (UNCTAD) Non-oil Nominal Commodity Price Index[3] fell 9.44 per cent between January and September 2013. However, the index remained generally high relative to its long-term trend.[4]

Food and agricultural commodities

Since January 2013, prices in food markets have been easing, thanks to good harvests, which have also allowed a continuation of the ongoing replenishment of stocks (figure II.7).

The food price index registered a steady decline, reaching 245.1 points in September 2013 after its peak of 286 points in August 2012. Between January and September 2013, prices for wheat and maize declined by 9 per cent and 26 per cent, respectively. Expectations of continued growth in wheat and maize production will likely prompt further drops in cereal prices in 2014. The price of rice has been trending downward since 2012, despite short-term fluctuations. During the first nine months of 2013, the Thailand rice price index recorded

Food prices decline on good harvests

Figure II.6
Price indices of non-oil commodities, all food and minerals, ores and metals, January 2009-September 2013

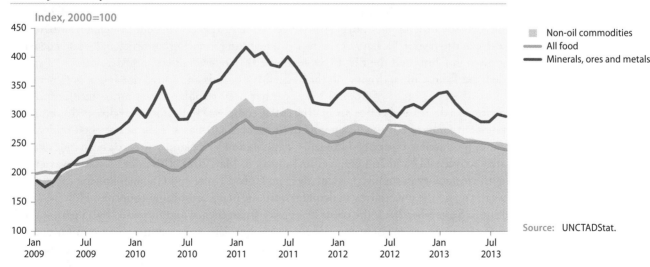

Source: UNCTADStat.

---

3   The UNCTAD Non-oil Nominal Commodity Price Index covers these subgroups of commodities: food, tropical beverages, vegetable oilseeds and oils, agricultural raw materials, and minerals, ores and metals.

4   In September 2013, the Index was 250.3 points, 32 points higher than its 10-year average of 218 points (between October 2003 and September 2013).

Figure II.7
Price indices of selected food and agricultural commodity groups, January 2009-September 2013

All food
Agricultural raw materials
Food
Tropical beverages
Vegetable oilseeds and oils

Source: UNCTADStat.

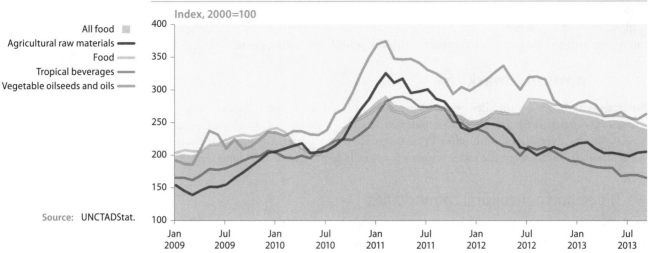

an 18 per cent decline, underpinned by comfortable levels of stocks and the ongoing release of rice from the Thai Government's public stock. The sugar price fell by 11 per cent from January 2013 to reach 16.84 cents per pound in July 2013 as a result of a production surplus and the retreat of speculative funds from the sugar futures market. However, owing to falling crop output in Brazil and a rise in demand, especially from China and Indonesia, sugar prices rebounded in August, reaching 17.4 cents per pound in September 2013. Looking forward, trends in sugar prices will depend on the level of global stocks and the demand from the main consuming countries.

The UNCTAD Vegetable Oilseeds and Oils Price Index trended downwards over the first eight months of 2013, despite some short-term fluctuations, mainly as a result of improvements in soybean supplies. Soybean prices recorded a 13 per cent decline from January to August 2013, due to favourable harvests in the main soybean producing countries and weaker demand growth in China and the EU. In September 2013, soybean prices surged as a result of strong demand from China, driving up the Vegetable Oilseeds and Oils Price Index by 3 per cent.

The price index of tropical beverages has been trending downwards since early 2013, owing to a decrease in coffee prices. The coffee composite indicator index dropped from 207.6 points in January 2013 to 178 points in September 2013 as a result of the good outlook for coffee production, especially in Brazil, Colombia and Viet Nam. The cocoa bean index fluctuated between 242 and 264 points from January to May, 2013. This price volatility was a result of the instability in supply, particularly from Côte d'Ivoire and Ghana following dry and hot weather, and the uncertainty in demand from the main consuming countries. However, from June to September 2013, the cocoa bean price strengthened and increased by 15 per cent over this period, owing to rising demand from the chocolate manufacturing sector in Europe and North America. Expected improvements in the economic outlook of the major consuming areas, albeit slow, are likely to keep the cocoa market firm through 2014.

The UNCTAD Agricultural Raw Materials Price Index strengthened in early 2013, driven by higher prices of rubber, tropical logs and cotton. The index fell from 219.5 points to 198.4 points between February and July 2013, owing to a 24 per cent decline in rubber prices during the same period. However, as China's manufacturing pace picks up, the demand for rubber from the automobile manufacturing sector has been boosted. As a result, the Raw Materials Price Index increased by nearly 3.5 per cent from July to September 2013. The cotton index has been fluctuating within a band from 144 to 160 points. Furthermore, the cotton market is sensitive to China's policy with respect to its reserves, given the country's large state cotton reserves. Prices for agricultural raw materials are expected to be mostly flat over the forecast period.

Minerals, ores and metals

Minerals, ores and metals prices are sensitive to worldwide supply, the macroeconomic context, and manufacturing demand from major consuming countries including China, the United States and the EU. After a brief recovery in the first two months of 2013, base metal prices softened in the remaining first half of the year (figure II.8). This can be attributed to a combination of factors, including uncertainty over the economic outlook of the euro area, a slowdown in China's economy, the indecisive pace of recovery in the United States, a supply surplus in the context of relatively high stock levels, and the strengthening of the dollar.

Metals prices declined as world growth remained tepid

Prices of several industrial commodities dropped below their end-2012 levels, partly owing to the deceleration of growth in major economies (China especially) in the first half of 2013. In July 2013, the UNCTAD Minerals, Ores and Metals Price Index was down 15 per cent relative to the 340 points recorded in February 2013. Price indices for aluminium, nickel, and zinc registered a steady decline from January 2013 to July 2013. Over the same period, price indices for copper and lead, while recording some short-term fluctuations, showed an overall downward trend. The iron ore index declined by 23.67 per cent from January to June

Figure II.8
Price indices of selected minerals, ores and metals, January 2009-September 2013

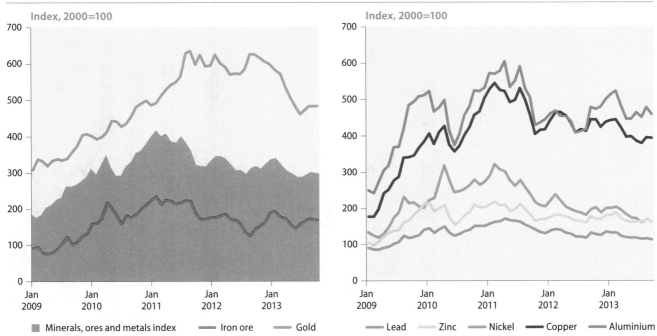

Source: UNCTAD, UNCTADStat.

2013, largely owing to shrinking demand for steel by China's construction and manufacturing industries—a consequence of the ongoing structural change in China's economy (box II.2).

However, owing to positive expectations for global industrial activity and China's economic revival beginning in mid-2013, several metals prices rebounded in August 2013, then retreated the following month based on strong supply in global metals markets. For example, the iron ore index regained 19.33 per cent of its June 2013 value, reaching 171.6 points in August and falling to 168 points in September. Although global industrial prospects are expected to put upward pressure on metals prices in the short run, the strong supply induced by increased investments in the extractive sector (due to the recent price boom) will probably soften the metals markets. Moreover, trends in these markets in the coming years will greatly depend on ore grades, environmental issues and energy costs.

A group of other metals not included in the index discussed above has also become increasingly important (box II.3).

Oil prices

Oil prices were on a downward trend in the first half of 2013 (after a spike in January and February caused by geopolitical tensions with Iran), as global demand for oil weakened along with the deceleration in world economic growth overall. Moderation in the growth of emerging economies was particularly notable, as they have been the major source for the incremental increases in global oil demand in recent years. However, oil prices surged in July and August as geopolitical tensions in the Syrian Arab Republic escalated. The Brent oil price increased by about $18 per barrel (pb) within two months to above $117 pb. Later,

Figure II.9
**Brent spot price in relation to significant geopolitical and economic events,
January-November 2013**

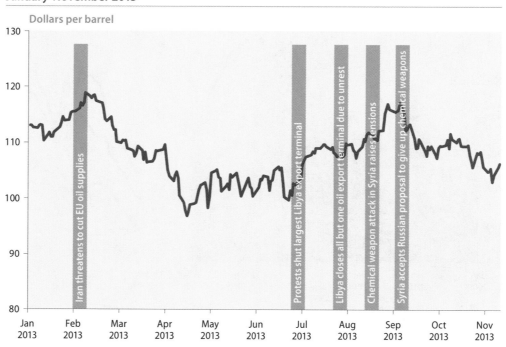

Source: UN/DESA, based on data from United States Energy Information Administration.

Box II.3

The strategic importance of rare earth metals

Rare earth metals (REMs) or rare earth elements (REEs) are a group of 17 elements,[a] which are vital inputs in high-tech device manufacturing, military and defence applications, as well as clean energy technologies. For example, they are essential to battery and magnet technologies, laser technology, radar systems, cellular telephone manufacturing, energy-efficient lighting, fibre optics, and flat screens for television and computers. REMs are indeed considered to be critical raw materials.[b] REMs are not as rare as their name suggests; they are classified as "rare" because their deposits are not concentrated in commercially viable quantities. Hence, it is difficult to mine them cost effectively.

The strategic importance of REMs stems from two main factors: they have very few substitutes, and they are associated with high supply risk as their reserves and production are highly concentrated in a handful of countries. REMs global reserves and production are mainly concentrated in China and, to a limited extent, the United States of America. Although information on REMs reserves, production and use varies, the January 2013 United States Geological Survey estimates suggest that in 2012, China and United States accounted for about 50 per cent and 12 per cent of global reserves, respectively.[c] Australia, Brazil, India, Malaysia, and the Russian Federation also have some reserves. China accounts for over 80 per cent of total production and is also a major user and exporter of REMs.

Recently, global demand for REMs has increased significantly, reaching an estimated 136,000 tons per year between 2010 and 2012. From 53,000 tons in 1990, world REMs production increased about twofold to reach 90,000 tons in 2000. Thereafter, production continued its upward trend to finally reach 110,000 tons in 2012. Excess demand partly explains the recent price increases.

REMs prices—which are not quoted on international markets—were relatively stable until 2010. Between 2010 and 2012, prices increased markedly as a result of a global supply deficiency that was induced by increasing demand in high technology industries as well as China's export quotas—set partly to preserve domestic stock and increase domestic processing, and partly to start addressing severe environmental damages associated with past REMs mining and processing.[d] As a result, depending on which element is considered, prices increased by 1.2-14.0 times between the first half of 2010 and the first half of 2011 before declining in the second half of 2011 and 2012. Indications are that the prices have recovered in 2013, but remain below their peak level of mid-2011.

In order to reduce world dependence on Chinese exports, several Governments have initiated a series of new legislations and actions. For example, the United States National Strategic and Critical Minerals Policy Act of 2011 was adopted to address the potential supply vulnerability and to support domestic production and supply chain development of REMs. The European Union adopted its Raw Materials Initiative in 2008 to maintain fair and undistorted access to raw materials including REMs. Moreover, many countries have launched new projects to increase production. They include the new Mountain Pass project in the United States with its 19,050 tons of REMs production capacity; the Mount Weld mine project in Australia, launched in 2012 with its production capacity estimated at 20,000 tons per year; and the Zandkopsdrift Rare Earths project in South Africa, currently at an advanced phase of feasibility, with a potential reserve of 950 kilotons of REMs.

By 2015, global demand for REMs is expected to range from 180,000 tons to 210,000 tons per year. China will continue to play a major role in the global REMs market, but its dominance is expected to decline. The increasing demand for REMs from high tech industries will keep the demand firm. On the other hand, despite the opening of new projects, concerns about the negative environmental impact of mining REMs, and the high cost of cleaning up polluted old mines (as currently experienced by China) will heavily weigh on REMs supply, keeping the prices relatively high.

a REMs or REEs consist of the following elements: scandium (Sc), yttrium (Y) and the 15 so-called lanthanoids (Ln) including lanthanum (La), cerium (Ce), praseodymium (Pr), neodymium (Nd), promethium (Pm), samarium (Sm), europium (Eu), gadolinium (Gd), terbium (Tb), dysprosium (Dy), holmium (Ho), erbium (Er), thulium (Th), y tterbium (Yb) and lutetium (Lu).

b In 2010, the European Commission analysed a selection of 41 minerals and metals and listed four teen critical mineral raw materials, including REMs based on their low substitutability, high supply risk and high economic importance. See http://ec.europa.eu/enterprise/policies/raw-materials/critical/index_en.htm.

c U.S. Department of the Interior, U.S. Geological Survey, "Mineral Commodity Summaries, January 2013", available from http://minerals.usgs.gov/minerals/pubs/mcs/2013/mcs2013.pdf.

d However, many countries interpreted these measures as unfair trade practice prompting Japan, the European Union and the United States to file complaints against China to the WTO in 2012. A WTO ruling has judged these measures as incompatible with WTO rules; it is likely that China will appeal the decision. See Lucy Hornby and Shawn Donnan, "WTO rules against China on rare earths export quotas", *Financial Times*, 29 October 2013.

Source: UNCTAD.

when progress was made in the Syrian Arab Republic's agreement to surrender its chemical weapons, the Brent oil price retreated to $108 pb in September.

Geopolitical tensions can entail a large risk premium for oil prices, particularly when oil supply is also tight. Most recently, global oil supply has been declining modestly: increased oil supply in North America has been offset by declines in the North Sea, while high Saudi output only partly counterbalanced the recent collapse in Libyan production.

Oil prices fluctuated with geopolitical tensions

Oil exporters have continued to register trades surpluses, but lower than in 2012, partly because of an increase in domestic oil production in the United States (box II.4) and the general decreases in the demand for oil. In the outlook, global demand for oil is expected to grow above 1 per cent for 2014, moderately stronger than 2013. By assuming no further significant eruptions in geopolitical tensions, the Brent oil price is expected to be about $108 pb for 2014-2015, compared with an estimated average of $108.1 pb for 2013 and $111.6 pb in 2012.

Box II.4
Effects of increased oil production in the United States of America on exporters of similar grade

A significant contributor to the decrease in the trade deficit of the United States of America over the past few years has been the rise in domestic oil production that has resulted in a substantial decrease in oil imports. Countries like Algeria and Nigeria, that export the same light sweet crude that the United States has begun to produce in relatively massive quantities, have been significantly affected (figure II.4.1). There had been some shifts in Algerian and Nigerian exports towards Asia, which still has considerable demand for this oil variant, but the situation has still put measurable downward pressure on those countries' trade surpluses.

While the United States is not the largest market for Algeria's oil, it still absorbs almost 13 per cent of Algerian exports, the large majority of which are crude oil and petroleum related products. The scope of the decline can be seen in figure II.4.1, with imports down from an average of 500,000 barrels per day (bpd) in 2010 to closer to 100,000 bpd in 2013. A similar decline can be observed in Nigeria, from an average of about 1 million bpd to about 300,000 in 2013. This trend has also affected other producers such as Angola and Libya, albeit to a lesser degree. Overall, imports of the United States from OPEC, which includes producers of both light sweet crude and heavier sour varieties, was down from an average of almost 5 million bpd in 2010 to 3.75 million bpd in the first eight months of 2013.

In addition, generally flat oil prices—with some significant fluctuations—have continued to put pressure on the budgets of some of these countries. Algeria relies on revenue from oil and petroleum products, which make up 90 per cent of the country's exports, to cover significant portions of the Government's budget. Recent increases in spending have also pushed up estimates for the price per barrel necessary to balance the budget well above current prices. As it appears that U.S. production is set to continue expanding, these countries will have to diversify both their oil trading partners and their overall export baskets.

Source: UN/DESA.

Figure II.4.1
United States imports of Algerian crude oil and petroleum products, January 2010-August 2013

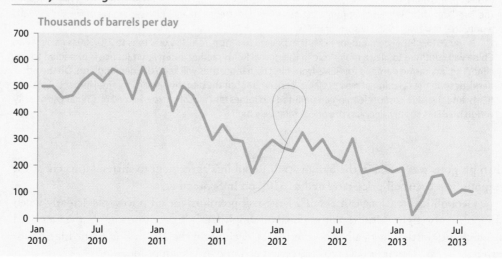

Source: United States Energy Information Administration.

Terms of trade and trade shocks

The outlook for global merchandise trade is unlikely to fulfill expectations of a net-exported recovery for a number of countries. Trade volume demand is only estimated to grow moderately across the world; on a country-by-country basis, small declines will mostly offset small rises. Overall, this will result in relatively flat patterns in the terms of trade and thus in limited changes to import and export bills.

Using historical and forecast changes in trade volume and prices, the Global Vulnerability Monitor[5] provides a decomposition analysis to quantify the size of trade shocks relative to gross domestic product (GDP) that world regions experience in the event of changes in volume or terms of trade. As shown in figure II.10, these shocks were significant for most countries during the periods of the boom years, the eruption of the

Figure II.10
Trade shocks of major country groups and major regions

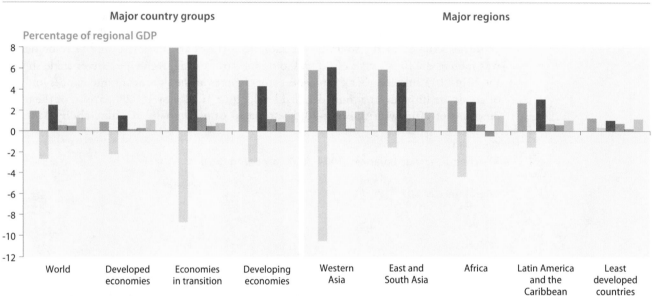

| Years | Major country groups | | | | Major regions | | | | |
	World	Developed economies	Economies in transition	Developing economies	Western Asia	East and South Asia	Africa	Latin America and the Caribbean	Least developed countries
2004-2007	1.9	0.9	7.9	4.8	5.8	5.9	2.9	2.7	1.2
2009	-2.7	-2.2	-8.8	-3.0	-10.5	-1.6	-4.4	-1.5	0.3
2010-2011	2.5	1.5	7.3	4.3	6.1	4.7	2.8	3.1	1.0
2012	0.5	0.1	1.3	1.1	2.0	1.2	0.6	0.7	0.7
2013	0.5	0.2	0.4	0.8	0.2	1.2	-0.5	0.6	0.2
2014-2015	1.2	1.0	0.7	1.6	1.9	1.8	1.5	1.0	1.1

Source: UN/DESA, World Economic Vulnerability Monitor.

---

5   See UN/DESA, World Economic Vulnerability Monitor, available from http://www.un.org/en/development/desa/policy/publications/wevm.shtml.

crisis and the immediate aftermath. Particularly for net exporters (and correspondingly importers) of primar y commodities and energ y, huge shocks mostly reflect wide swings in their terms of trade. However, in the most recent period (2012-2013) and the short-term outlook (2014-2015), trade shocks are mostly fading away, remaining very small in the forecast period.

At the aggregated level of figure II.10, and for most countries individually, large positive shocks in the two years following the crisis compensated for the high negative shocks of 2009. In addition, as trade shocks in 2012-2013 were only marginal, the balances of merchandise trade for most countries in 2013 will be of a similar size and magnitude as those prior to 2009. This is illustrated in figure II.11, a scatter-plot constructed at the country-level, showing the balances of goods in 2013 against those of the pre-crisis period. With most observation points lying close to the diagonal 45-degree line, the figure confirms that in spite of the traumatic shocks around the global financial crisis, countries with deficits (of merchandise trade) in the years before the crisis were experiencing similar deficits by the end of 2013, and conversely for countries in surplus.[6]

Figure II.11 calls attention to the fact that there are a number of countries which, up to 2013, were facing chronic deficits in the balance of goods. Indeed, for many of the countries situated in the south-west quadrant of the chart, the merchandise trade deficit was more than 10 per cent of GDP. Going forward, the aggregate picture of trade shocks for 2014-2015 suggests that the prospects for changes in the significant imbalances in trade of goods are limited. At a more detailed level, figure II.12 shows a comparison of the trade positions of 2013 with those of 2015, estimated using the Global Vulnerability Monitor

Figure II.11
Merchandise trade balances, 2004-2007 compared to 2013

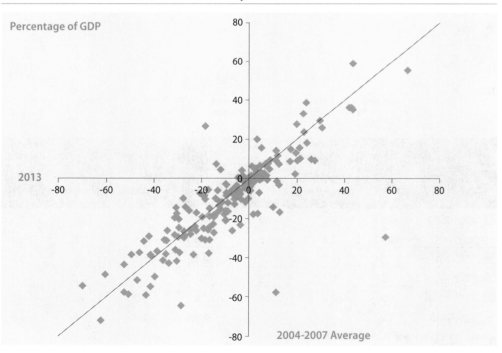

Source: UN/DESA, World Economic Vulnerabilit y Monitor.

---

6   There are a few exceptions to this such as Ghana, which went from a merchandise trade deficit to a surplus, mainly owing to the start of oil exports between the two periods.

Figure II.12
Merchandise trade balances, 2013 and 2015

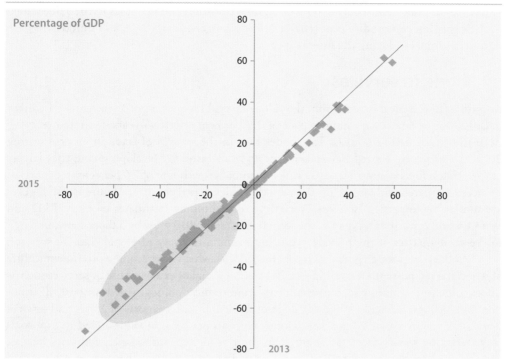

Source: UN/DESA, World
Economic Vulnerability Monitor.

tool. The countries highlighted within the red circle are those that were in deficit in 2013 and are not expected to see notable change in the outlook, as they are mostly situated in the diagonal line.

This situation is of particular importance for a majority of LDCs. Many are low-performing primary commodity exporters and often net importers of energy and food, facing a configuration of price changes in the outlook which is either flat or only minimally positive in net terms. Further analysis of a number of countries for which more detailed information is available corroborates this predicament, as presented in figure II.13. Deficits

Large LDC trade deficits are likely to persist throughout the forecast period

Figure II.13
Merchandise trade balance deficits as a percentage of GDP for selected LDCs

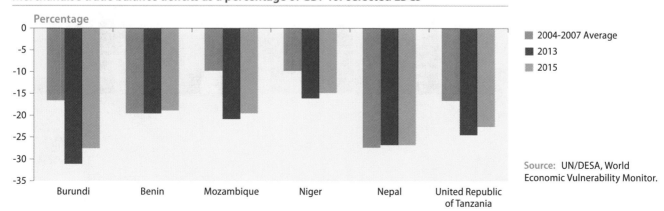

Source: UN/DESA, World
Economic Vulnerability Monitor.

in merchandise trade have been and will likely continue to be large, and all the more so if growth prospects involve a greater demand for imported manufactures. In these instances in particular, policy efforts need to focus on diversification and increases in the value added to their existing commodity exports; but this is a longer-term process and unlikely to have significant impacts during the forecast period.

Trade in services

Services exports expand at a modest pace, driven by developing country exports

According to the latest information, the value of world services exports reached $4.4 trillion in 2012, but expanded at a modest pace of 2.2 per cent after two years of a rapid recovery from the global financial crisis. The moderation in the growth of trade in services during 2012 was primarily caused by weaker exports from Europe. Developing countries largely outpaced developed countries, registering an annual growth rate of 7.6 per cent in exports of services, compared with a pace of -0.3 per cent in developed countries (figure II.14). Figures are similar for imports of services. According to preliminary estimates by UNCTAD and WTO, world exports of services in the second quarter of 2013 grew by 5.0 per cent compared to the same quarter of the previous year, indicating a recovery of global trade in services.

Production through global value chains (GVCs), which has become a prominent feature of world merchandise trade over the last two decades, makes extensive use of services such as information and communication technology, communication, logistics, transport, distribution and business services. While the share of services in gross exports of goods and services worldwide is only about 20 per cent, almost half (46 per cent) of value-added in exports is contributed by service-sector activities. This share is higher in developed countries (50 per cent) than in developing countries (38 per cent). This fact confirms that greater value-added tends to be captured by developed countries, in which many transnational corporations are headquartered, to a large extent through services activities. Two thirds of global foreign direct investment (FDI) stock indeed concentrates on services (figure II.15). In the aftermath of the global financial crisis, the manufacturing sector in major developed countries lost ground to the services sector in terms of attracting FDI projects, especially greenfield projects.

Figure II.14
Growth of services exports by development status

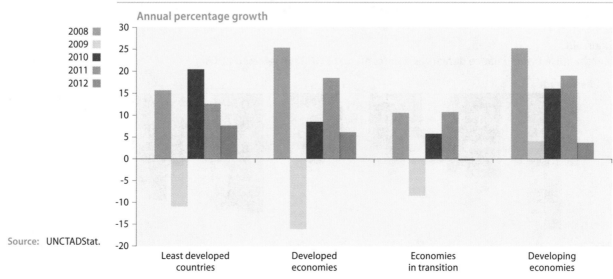

Source: UNCTADStat.

Figure II.15
Share of services in trade, employment, GDP and FDI in 2011

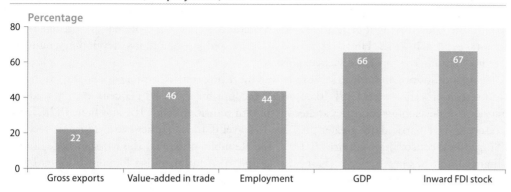

Source: UNCTAD, *World Investment Report 2013* (United Nations publication, Sales No. E.13.II.D.5); UNCTADStat; and ILO, *Global Employment Trends 2013* (Geneva).

Developing countries have steadily increased their participation in trade in services over the last decade, particularly in the past five years.[7] Their share in world services exports climbed to 31 per cent in 2012, owing largely to a rapid expansion of exporters in Asia services, with a similar pattern observed for imports where developing countries' share in world services imports was almost 32 per cent in 2008 and jumped to more than 37 per cent in 2012 (figure II.16). The shares for the economies in transition and the LDCs have changed only marginally since 2008.

Trade flows in services have been concentrated in a small number of countries, with the top 10 exporters accounting for 51 per cent of world exports. This reflects their high shares in trade in travel and transport services, which represent more than fifty percent of total services. It also reflects the predominance of a few countries—especially that of the United Kingdom of Great Britain and Northern Ireland and the United States—in trade in financial and insurance services sectors. A breakdown of services exports according to

Trade flows tend to be concentrated, particularly among developing countries and economies in transition

Figure II.16
Share in world services trade by development status, 2000 and 2008-2012

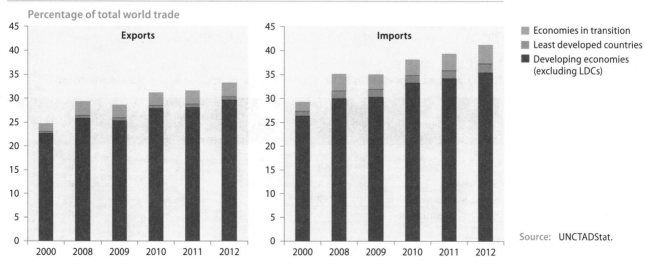

Economies in transition

Least developed countries

Developing economies (excluding LDCs)

Source: UNCTADStat.

---

7   For a discussion of the effects of trade in services on poverty and employment, see UNCTAD, "The impact of trade on employment and poverty reduction", TD/B/C.I/29, 8 April 2013.

regions indicates that only developing economies in Asia have significantly expanded their services exports over the last decade; the share of Latin American economies has fallen, while the share of Africa has not changed. Exports of services originating from France, Germany, Japan, the United Kingdom and the United States together still represent almost one third of total exports in 2012. However, China has surpassed Japan, and five developing countries are now among the top 13 services exporters.

Concentration in trade in services is even more pronounced among developing countries and transition economies. Only 10 countries account for about 70 per cent of total trade in services for developing countries and economies in transition (table II.1 and table II.2). These countries have particularly greater presence in travel (China, Turkey) and transport services (Singapore), construction services (China, the Republic of Korea, the Russian Federation), financial and business services (Hong Kong Special Administrative Region of China) and computer and information services (India). The share in world travel services of Macao Special Administrative Region of China has doubled over the last five-year period to reach about 4 per cent in 2012. The increases of imports of services in most developing countries and the economies in transition have outpaced that of exports, leading to deterioration in their trade balances in services (figure II.17). However, the deficits in their services balances have been

Table II.1

Top 10 services exporters in 2012: developing countries and economies in transition

	Share in world exports			
	Rank in 2008[a]	Share in 2008[a, b]	Rank in 2012[a]	Share in 2012[a, b]
China	1	3.8	1	4.4
India	2	2.7	2	3.2
Hong Kong SAR[c]	4	2.4	3	2.8
Singapore	3	2.5	4	2.6
Korea, Republic of	5	2.3	5	2.5
Russian Federation	6	1.3	6	1.4
Thailand	9	0.8	7	1.1
Taiwan Province of China	7	0.9	8	1.1
Macao SAR[c]	14	0.5	9	1.0
Turkey	8	0.9	10	1.0

Source: UNCTADStat.
a Among developing economies and economies in transition.
b In percentage points.
c Special Administrative Region of China.

Table II.2

Top 10 services importers in 2012: developing countries and economies in transition

	Share in world imports			
	Rank in 2008[a]	Share in 2008[a, b]	Rank in 2012[a]	Share in 2012[a, b]
China	1	4.3	1	6.8
India	3	2.4	2	3.1
Singapore	4	2.4	3	2.9
Korea, Republic of	2	2.6	4	2.6
Russian Federation	5	2.0	5	2.6
Brazil	7	1.3	6	2.0
Saudi Arabia	6	2.0	7	1.8
United Arab Emirates	10	1.2	8	1.5
Hong Kong SAR[c]	8	1.3	9	1.4
Thailand	9	1.2	10	1.3

Source: UNCTADStat.
a Among developing economies and economies in transition.
b In percentage points.
c Special Administrative Region of China.

more than compensated by surpluses in their goods balances. The LDCs, however, have seen deficits in their trade balances in both goods and services. Travel and transport services remain the core sectors of exports in services for developing countries, especially high- and middle-income developing countries. Almost 60 per cent of exports in services are either travel services or transport services. Outsourcing associated with the global dynamic growth of computer and information and travel services associated with tourism (box II.5) have continued to drive services exports of developing countries (figure II.18). Construction services seem to have accelerated the speed of recovery lately. The financial services and the royalties and fee payment sectors are the only sectors showing a negative growth rate in 2012. Communications services associated with merchandise trade, despite positive records in terms of growth over the last two years, is the only sector that has still not recovered its pre-2008 level of exports.

Figure II.17
Trade balances by development status

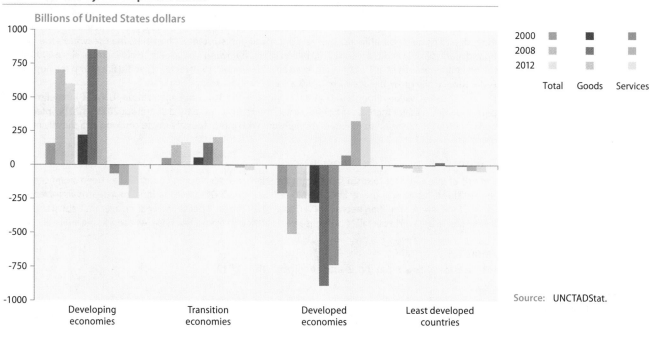

Source: UNCTADStat.

Figure II.18
Developing country exports of services by category, 2008-2012

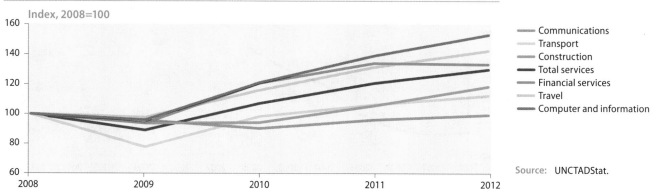

Source: UNCTADStat.

Box II.5
International tourism

International tourist arrivals (overnight visitors) exceeded the 1 billion mark for the first time ever in 2012 with 1035 million tourists crossing borders, up from 995 million in 2011. Over half of global travel was for leisure and 14 per cent for business, with the rest being for health, religious or other purposes, including visiting friends or family. Demand for international tourism remained strong throughout the first eight months of 2013, with arrivals growing by 5 per cent compared to the same period last year, boosted by arrivals in Europe (5 per cent) and Asia and the Pacific (6 per cent). An estimated 747 million overnight visitors crossed borders through August 2013 worldwide, about 38 million more than in the same period of 2012. In view of these results, the January 2013 projection of 3 per cent to 4 per cent growth for the full year could well be surpassed, despite the weak world economy.

In tourism receipts, preliminary data through August also point to good results for 2013, with approximately three quarters of countries reporting an increase in tourism earnings and over a quarter with double-digit growth. After growing 4 per cent in real terms in 2012, tourism receipts hit a record $1075 billion. In addition, international passenger transport generated $213 billion in export earnings last year, bringing total tourism exports (tourism receipts plus passenger transport) to $1300 billion in 2012.

As for outbound markets, emerging economies continue to show rapid growth in tourism expenditure, due to rising disposable incomes and improved infrastructure. China became the world's top outbound market in 2012 with a record $102 billion spent, following a nearly eightfold increase since 2000. In the first eight months of 2013, China reported another double-digit increase, as did Brazil and the Russian Federation, while growth was slower in advanced economy source markets.

The latest survey among the United Nations World Tourism Organization (UNWTO) Panel of Experts revealed a major increase in confidence in the tourism industry throughout 2013. In 2014, international tourism is expected to maintain momentum with international arrivals growing at a slightly more moderate pace of about 4 per cent.

Tourism as a source of development

Growth of international tourism in emerging market and developing countries has been significant in the last three decades. In the 49 least developed countries (LDCs), international tourist arrivals increased from 1.4 million to 21 million between 1980 and 2012 (almost 9 per cent a year on average), substantially faster than in the world overall (4 per cent a year), although from a low base. As a result, the share of LDCs

Figure II.5.1
International tourist arrivals and receipts, 2000-2012

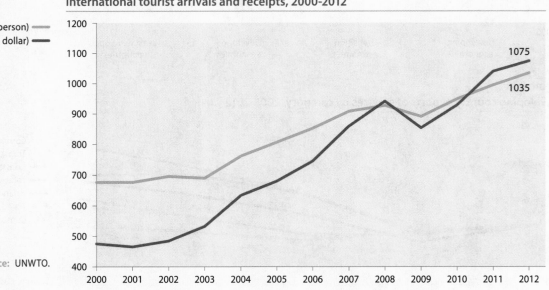

Arrivals (million person)
Receipts (billion dollar)

Source: UNWTO.

in global tourist arrivals has quadrupled from 0.5 per cent to over 2 per cent in this period. This growth is also reflected in international tourism receipts, which rose 25 times in LDCs—from $0.5 billion in 1980 to over $12 billion in 2012. Earnings growth was also much faster in LDCs than globally. In current dollar terms, the average growth rate of tourism receipts in LDCs was 11 per cent per year between 1980 and 2012, as compared to 8 per cent worldwide, 9 per cent in emerging markets and developing countries overall, and 7 per cent in developed economies.

In the full group of emerging economies, international tourists spent $386 billion in 2012, over five times the level of official development assistance received by those countries.

Tourism offers LDCs an opportunity to compete in the global economy, as it accounts for 6 per cent of overall exports (10 per cent among non-fuel exporters) and 52 per cent of services exports. Tourism has been identified by most LDCs and small island developing States (SIDS) as a powerful engine for poverty reduction and development. This is reflected in the sector's role in the three countries that have so far graduated from the LDC category: Botswana, Cabo Verde and Maldives. In Cabo Verde and Maldives particularly, tourism accounts for a large percentage of exports: 56 per cent and 80 per cent respectively, while in Botswana it is approximately 11 per cent.

The five pillars for assessing sustainable tourism

While tourism can be a significant force for poverty alleviation in developing countries through the creation of jobs and businesses, sustainability is an inseparable condition of tourism development and requires careful planning and management. The *Sustainable Tourism for Development Guidebook* identifies five pillars in the assessment of the sustainability of tourism development, which constitutes a methodology for identifying and implementing strategies, policies and measures.

1. Tourism should be given due recognition in Governments' development plans and incorporated into development studies and frameworks to ensure that the sector is correctly positioned as a force for sustainable development.
2. In order to effectively assess competitiveness, countries must put systems in place to effectively measure and monitor the sector. Many developing countries will require assistance in establishing a reliable system of national tourism statistics.
3. Tourism also requires a sufficient supply of suitably skilled labour, which will necessitate coordination between government, private enterprise and employee representatives to ensure the sector can fulfill its full employment-creation potential.
4. As a labour-intensive and diverse sector, tourism presents special opportunities for benefiting poor and disadvantaged people. This requires commitment from government and the private sector, applying relevant policies and tools.
5. Finally, the tourism sector can be an effective partner in supporting the preservation of nature and local cultural heritage because it depends on these to attract visitors. Sustainable consumption of natural resources such as water and energy can be part of a broader strategy of protecting the country's natural capital.

Source: UNWTO.

Between 2000 and 2012, developing countries increased their market share in 7 out of 10 subsectors reported. The share of developing countries is the highest in construction and travel services at 40 per cent, followed by transport and other business services. Developing countries saw a substantial increase in their share in computer and information services, together with construction, during this period.

Trade policy developments

The successful outcome of the Ninth WTO Ministerial Conference in December 2013 in Bali[8] somewhat renewed faith in the multilateral trading system. There remains much unfinished multilateral business under the Doha Round, while regional and national

The WTO Bali Package contains agreements on agriculture, development and trade facilitation

---

8   WTO, Bali Ministerial Declaration, WT/MIN(13)/DEC/W/1/Rev.1, 7 December 2013.

trade liberalization continues unabated—although the picture is mixed.[9] Overall, the international trading system is becoming more uncertain and fragmented, and less able to provide a coherent, development-oriented framework that enables international trade to optimally boost economic growth and development—all of which leads to renewed questioning of the benefits arising from trade. These challenges have affected progress in reaching Millennium Development Goal Target 8.A (to develop an open, rule-based, predictable, non-discriminatory trade and financial system) and poses a serious risk for global economic welfare.

The multilateral trading system: the Bali "mini" Package and variable geometry of trade agreements

The more than twelve-year Doha Round negotiations have finally led to some limited outcomes agreed within the Bali "mini" Package, representing an early harvest from the much broader Doha Round. The Doha Round[10] will continue, and a work programme to address the remaining issues will be established during 2014. The programme will build upon the Bali outcome (particularly with regard to agriculture, development and LDC issues, and prioritizing issues where legally binding outcomes were not achieved), as well as all other Doha issues central to concluding the Round.

Salient elements of the agriculture component of the Bali Package include: a peace clause for existing food stockholding programmes for traditional staple crops (subject to certain conditions) that will continue until a permanent solution is found, with the aim of finding that solution within four years; rules for tariff-rate quota administration when the quota is persistently under-filled, with some countries (including the United States) reserving the right not to apply the system after six years; political commitments to continue reducing export subsidies, and measures that have an equivalent effect; continuing negotiations and enhanced transparency and monitoring on cotton; and clarification that land reform and rural livelihood security programmes are considered to be non-trade-distorting general services.

On development, there are provisions for: extending duty-free quota-free (DFQF) treatment to those LDC exports going to countries that have not provided DFQF for at least 97 per cent of products, in order to increase the number of products covered; guidelines on preferential rules of origin for LDCs; discussions on operationalizing the LDC services waiver; and a monitoring mechanism for implementation of special and differential treatment for developing countries.

On the Agreement on Trade Facilitation, which is perhaps the most important element in the Bali Package in terms of rule-making, there are, inter alia, provisions on: publication and availability of information; consultation; advance rulings; appeal procedures; impartiality, non-discrimination and transparency; fees and charges; clearance of goods; border agency cooperation; formalities; freedom of transit; customs cooperation; and timing flexibilities and capacity-building assistance for developing-country and

---

9   For more details, see UNCTAD, "Key statistics and trends in trade policy", UNCTAD/DITC/TAB/2013/2 (Geneva), available from http://unctad.org/en/pages/PublicationWebflyer.aspx?publicationid=685.

10   For a review of developments in the international trading system from a development perspective, see United Nations, Report of the Secretary-General on international trade and development (A/68/205).

LDC members to implement obligations. The non-discrimination principle of Article V of the General Agreement on Tariffs and Trade 1994 on freedom of transit is reaffirmed.

Clearly, this "Doha-lite" outcome attempts far less than the original ambitious Doha Round agenda, and achieves little in securing development-oriented outcomes. The likely trade and development gains from its implementation are unclear, despite over-optimistic predictions about the welfare gains from the trade facilitation agreement amounting to up to $1 trillion. In any event, the Bali outcome will take time to implement and thus will not affect world economic prospects in 2014, and probably not in 2015. Yet the Bali Package does provide reassurance that trade multilateralism can still deliver in terms of agreed negotiating results. However, what further WTO negotiations could produce in the short and medium term remains an open question.

Another positive outcome of Bali was the approval of the WTO accession of Yemen, the thirty-fifth LDC member, bringing WTO membership to 160 (Lao Democratic People's Republic and Montenegro also acceded in 2013). Twenty-three more countries are currently negotiating membership. While this demonstrates the continuing attractiveness of WTO, the former Director-General of WTO has offered a cautionary message against creating a divide between R A Ms (recently acceding members)—who have higher commitments on average—and ROMs (rest of the members).[11]

Meanwhile, prospects for WTO sectoral discussions outside the Doha Round appear uncertain. Negotiations on expanding the product coverage of the 1997 Information Technology Agreement (ITA) are currently suspended over China's request for exclusion of a number of information technology (IT) products from trade liberalization, and no timeline for resumption has been set.[12] However, progress was registered in September 2013 when the Russian Federation became the seventy-eighth member of the ITA.

> There has been limited progress on some sectoral negotiations such as the ITA and TISA

Discussions continue among some 23 WTO members (the majority of which are Organization for Economic Cooperation and Development (OECD) countries) on a plurilateral Trade in Services Agreement (TISA) to cover about 70 per cent of global services trade. China is seeking to join these negotiations, but the United States is requesting that certain preconditions be met first.[13] The TISA proponents' aim is that the outcome of the negotiations will be brought into the multilateral system, although the modalities for such a development remain unclear.

At the Bali Conference, participants in the negotiations on expansion of the plurilateral Agreement on Government Procurement affirmed their objective of bringing its 2012 revision extending market access commitments into force by March 2014.

Regional trade agreements: major initiatives, uncertain outcomes and implications

The pace and scale of negotiations on regional trade agreements (RTAs) further accelerated in 2013. As of 31 July 2013, some 575 notifications of RTAs (counting goods and services and accessions separately) had been received by the WTO, and, of these, 379

---

11   Pascal Lamy, "Looking back, moving forward", VOX, 29 July 2013, available from http://www.voxeu.org/article/looking-back-moving-forward.

12   See Inside U.S. Trade's World Trade Online of 22 November 2013. While negotiated plurilaterally, the zero tariffs, duties and charges on IT products covered under the ITA are extended to all WTO members on a most favoured nation basis.

13   Ibid.

were in force.[14] Current RTA negotiations often involve multiple parties and/or parties accounting for major shares of world trade; they aim at high-standard integration through WTO-plus or WTO-extra provisions on behind-the-border regulatory measures, such as technical regulations, standards, conformity assessment systems, sanitary and phytosanitary regulations, services, investment, intellectual property, State aid and State-owned enterprise (SOEs), public procurement, competition policy, environment, or labour market regulations.[15]

Two new large RTAs—the TTIP and the TPP—are currently being negotiated

Major RTA developments in 2013 have included the launch of negotiations on a Trans-Atlantic Trade and Investment Partnership (TTIP) between the United States and the EU, the joining of the negotiations on the Trans-Pacific Partnership Agreement (TPP) by Japan,[16] the start of negotiations on an EU-Japan free trade agreement, and agreements (pending final approval or ratification) on RTAs between the EU and Canada, China and Switzerland, and Australia and the Republic of Korea .

It is reported that a leaked version of the TPP chapter on intellectual property revealed major divergences and has raised controversy within the United States.[17] Plans for finalizing the TPP negotiations by December 2013 did not materialize. On 10 December 2013, TPP participants decided to extend these negotiations to 2014.

In the TTIP, the EU has placed relatively more emphasis on mutual recognition in specific sectors, and the United States on horizontal rules regarding issues such as transparency.[18] However, it is agreed there will be a post-negotiations long-term regulatory mechanism to work on breaking down new regulatory barriers.[19] The ultimate outcome of both these "mega-regional" negotiations may hinge upon whether fast-track negotiating authority to conclude trade agreements is extended by the United States Congress to the Administration.

The EU is negotiating RTAs with a large number of other countries or regional groupings[20] and has recently concluded association agreements with Georgia and the Republic of Moldova; Armenia and Ukraine, however, have cancelled similar negotiations on EU association agreements, with Armenia intending to accede to the Eurasian Customs Union forming among Belarus, Kazakhstan, the Russian Federation and, eventually, Armenia and some Central Asian countries (Kyrgyzstan and Tajikistan).

South-South regional integration arrangements and interregional organizations are increasing

In parallel, many developing countries are exploring South-South regional integration schemes to promote scale economies, diversification and resilience. Building upon existing initiatives, such as the tripartite initiative among SADC, COMESA and ESA, the African Union decided in 2012 to fast-track the operationalization of the Continental Free

---

14   See World Trade Organization's regional trade agreements section of the website, available from http://www.wto.org/english/tratop_e/region_e/region_e.htm.

15   "WTO-Plus" provisions relate to areas already subject to some commitments in WTO agreements, and provide for additional obligations. "WTO-extra" provisions relate to areas outside current WTO coverage.

16   Countries participating in these negotiations include Australia, Brunei Darussalam, Canada, Chile, Japan, Malaysia, Mexico, New Zealand, Peru, Singapore, the United States and Viet Nam. Some other Asian countries have expressed interest in joining.

17   See Inside U.S. Trade's World Trade Online of 14 and 22 November 2013.

18   See Inside U.S. Trade's World Trade Online of 27 September 2013.

19   See Inside U.S. Trade's World Trade Online of 22 November 2013.

20   Including Armenia, Georgia, India, the Republic of Moldova, Singapore, Thailand, 6 Central American countries, 4 Mediterranean countries, most African, Caribbean and Pacific Group of States (ACP) countries, the Andean Community, the Gulf Cooperation Council and Mercado Común del Sur (MERCOSUR).

Trade Area by the indicative date of 2017, and, to this end, implement an Action Plan for Boosting Intra-African Trade.[21] At the interregional level, the successful conclusion of the Sao Paulo Round negotiations under the Global System of Trade Preferences in 2010 has provided a major additional opportunity for further strengthening the expansion of South-South trade on an interregional scale.

Major motivations for attempts to form RTAs have been to spur progress in the Doha Round negotiations and to promote deeper commitments in new areas that will eventually be incorporated at the multilateral level. RTAs may sometimes be driven by the desire for predictable and less restrictive trade and investment rules that support the establishment and evolution of GVCs, which mainly exist in developed countries and in Asia.[22] The conclusion of RTAs has also politically triggered other RTAs, as countries have sought to avoid isolation.

Regarding "mega-RTAs", such as TPP and TTIP, it has been suggested that they aim at constituting alternatives to multilateral liberalization and updating of trading rules, while enabling parties to avoid marginalization from non-participation in rival trade pacts;[23] they can also enhance coherence and promote improved WTO trade rules, most favoured nation (MFN) liberalization, and deeper regional integration worldwide.[24]

Mega-RTAs are intended as "Doha by other means"

However, doubts have been expressed over the reach and effectiveness of TPP and TTIP negotiations. There are questions as to whether the two would fit with each other and with other RTA negotiations, particularly the Regional Comprehensive Economic Partnership Agreement (RCEP) between ASEAN and Australia, China, India, Japan, New Zealand and the Republic of Korea; and if they would promote global trade liberalization and multilateral convergence, given they may involve discriminatory market-distorting trade-offs (concessions and preferential market access), avoid addressing agricultural subsidies and other global challenges, and lock in regulatory divergences.[25] Differences between rules applicable inside and outside mega-RTAs could indeed pose major problems for the constantly changing operations of GVCs (box II.6).[26]

Many participating developing countries see regional trade agreements (RTAs) as a way to lock in access to their major markets. However, it has been suggested that: (a) the proliferation of RTAs has reduced transparency and uniformity in the global trading system and increased transaction and administration costs, particularly for developing-country customs authorities and firms less able to deal with multiple and complex rules of

---

21 "Decision on boosting intra-African trade and fast tracking the Continental Free Trade Area" (Assembly/AU/Dec.394(XVIII)), adopted by the Assembly of the African Union on its 18th Ordinary Session in Addis Ababa, Ethiopia from 23-30 January 2012.

22 See OECD, *Interconnected Economies: Benefiting from Global Value Chains* (Paris, 2013); and Richard Baldwin, "Global supply chains: why they emerged, why they matter, and where they are going", in *Global Value Chains in a Changing World*, Deborah K. Elms and Patrick Low, eds. (Fung Global Institute, Nanyang Technological University and World Trade Organization, 2013).

23 See David Pilling and Shawn Donnan, "Trans-Pacific Partnership: Ocean's Twelve", *Financial Times*, 22 September 2013; and Shawn Donnan, "Pascal Lamy questions US-led regional talks", *Financial Times*, 18 July 2013.

24 See Lucian Cernat, "TPP, TTIP and multilateralism: stepping stones or oceans apart? VOX, 8 November 2013.

25 See David Pilling and Shawn Donnan, "Trans-Pacific Partnership", op. cit.; and Shawn Donnan, "Pascal Lamy questions US-led regional talks", op. cit.

26 Michitaka Nakatomi, "Global value chain governance in the era of mega FTAs and a proposal of an international supply-chain agreement", VOX, 15 August 2013.

origin; (b) while RTAs enable developing countries to import international regulatory systems that are pre-tested and represent best practices, potentially limiting costs, the fact that they are often negotiated under substantive power asymmetries could lead to developing countries being pressured to adopt common rules inappropriate for their level of development, and utilization of standards by advanced economies to close markets to poor countries.[27] It has further been argued that, while the establishment of systems of "hub-and-spoke" bilateral agreements by Japan, the United States and the EU would mitigate conflicts, "spoke countries" having RTAs with more than one of these parties would face particular problems.[28]

Regarding developing countries not party to major RTAs, their adherence to the harmonized standards of these RTAs could reduce their trading costs with both RTA parties and non-parties adopting these standards.[29] However, developing-country non-parties with limited capacity may run risks of marginalization and damage to their competitiveness, particularly if they do not substantially participate in world trade or are unable to conform to higher standards. Moreover, although some RTA provisions are extended to non-members because they are embedded in broader regulatory frameworks, discrimination might arise from mutual recognition agreements recognizing only standards of RTA parties as equivalent, mandating more advance transparency notifications, or providing for services provider recognition.[30]

Box II.6
Global value chains: policy implications for developing countries

Greater participation and capture of value addition by developing countries in global value chains (GVCs) could offer a promising path to enhanced growth and development. However, benefits of GVCs do not accrue automatically, and appropriate policies are needed to harness the potential economic and social upgrading opportunities.

The international fragmentation of production, while not a new phenomenon, has in the past two decades reached an unprecedented magnitude and scale. Driven by progressive trade liberalization and technological advances (especially in transport and telecommunication), GVCs have become a dominant feature of many industries, involving both developed and a growing number of developing countries. Since the 1980s, firms have turned to offshoring and outsourcing of production processes to locations with quality and low cost inputs and skills. In the past years, the nature of GVCs has been shaped by a shift in production and market demand from North to South, especially emerging economies. Multinational enterprises now coordinate as much as 80 per cent of global trade through GVCs.[a] Following the 2008 2009 global economic crisis and other unforeseen events such as the 2011 Japanese tsunami and nuclear disaster, as well as the Thai floods, GVCs have resorted to forming geographical hubs and reorganizing, as lead firms seek to deal with smaller numbers of larger, more efficient and strategically located suppliers.[b] Delocalization of production to other developing-country regions, although increasing, is still limited. An

a UNCTAD, *World Investment Report 2013— Global Value Chains: Investment and Trade for Development* (United Nations publication, Sales No. E.13.II.D.5).

---

27   See *Trade and Development Report 2007: Regional cooperation for development* (United Nations publication, Sales No. E.07.II.D.11); and WTO, *World Trade Report 2011—The WTO and preferential trade agreements: from co-existence to coherence* (Geneva).

28   Richard Baldwin, "Global supply chains: why they emerged, why they matter, and where they are going", op. cit.

29   See Lucian Cernat, op. cit.

30   See Pravin Krishna, Edward D. Mansfield and James H. Mathis, "World Trade Report 2011. The WTO and Preferential Trade Agreements: From Co-Existence to Coherence by World Trade Organization Geneva: World Trade Organization, 2011", *World Trade Review*, vol. 11, Issue 2 (May), pp. 327-339.

arguably more insightful picture of patterns of global production and trade is painted by new metrics of value-added trade, which distinguish between use of domestic and foreign inputs to fuel export-oriented growth. The high share of trade in intermediates, which comprises about 40 per cent of total world trade, is also indicative of the fragmentation of production in the context of global/regional supply chains. However, this is a phenomenon largely confined to developed countries and to the East Asian region.

In theory, greater participation and value capture in value chains could be important avenues for developing countries to benefit from enhanced trade and investment, competitiveness, economic growth and employment. GVCs can facilitate access to global markets without developing entire export industries, but instead focusing on fewer specific tasks or components within industry value chains. GVCs can also help build productive capacity—including through transfer of technology, finance, knowledge and skills—thus opening up opportunities for longer-term industrial upgrading. Evidence shows that faster growing developing economies also have the fastest growing GVC participation.[c]

Not all countries have joined global production networks to the same extent, with most countries in Africa and Latin America accounting for a limited share of world GVC income and trade. Moreover, even developing countries that manage to join global supply chains can still remain locked into relatively low valued-added activities (typically resource-based and/or purely manufacturing-related) and a narrow technology base.[d] Connecting to GVCs can also carry other risks, including: greater exposure to the transmission of crises and shocks through trade; unequal sharing of gains; exposure to predatory behaviour of powerful global players (which could be linked, for example, to unstable and hazardous employment, land grabbing, or depletion of natural resources); as well as environmental degradation and climate change acceleration, exacerbated by the fact that internationally traded goods generate on average 50 per cent more carbon emissions than locally traded goods.[e]

Smaller and/or resource poor developing countries, including least developed countries, which may also have high costs of production, are often unable to compete in GVCs, even by specializing in niche segments of the chain. In such cases, regional, national and local value chains may potentially present a viable alternative, by promoting integration and industrial development, and presenting an opportunity to diversify production and export structures and capture higher value in the chain. More localized value chains could also enhance food security, environmental sustainability (linked to lower CO_2 emissions from transport[f]), and other development goals. A successful example includes South African supermarkets and clothing manufacturers that have expanded via regional value chains involving neighbouring and other sub-Saharan African countries.[g]

Overall, the potential development benefits of GVCs are not automatic; hence, carefully designed and proactive policies are necessary for promoting increased participation as well as upgrading to higher value-added and technologically sophisticated activities in GVCs. While GVC-led development strategies need to be country and sector specific, with no one-size-fits-all approach, a number of broad policy prescriptions can nonetheless be identified.

GVCs strengthen the economic case for limiting traditional and non-tariff barriers in trade, as the cost of protection may be magnified when intermediate and final goods are traded across borders numerous times. However, this case is challenged by the need to devise a more sustainable development path compatible with environmental sustainability and climate stabilization; the cost of protection must be weighed against the environmental cost of incentives that encourage transporting goods across borders and oceans many times. In addition, gainful participation of low-income countries in GVCs necessitates a global trading system that permits sufficient flexibility and space to implement trade policies that support industrial, agricultural and services development, and at the same time ensures unrestricted global market access for exports.

Importantly, GVC policies need to be embedded in broader national development strategies that focus on a rapid pace of capital formation, economic diversification and technological upgrading. Appropriately tailored complementary policies—including investing in infrastructure and skills, improving public and corporate governance, and facilitating adjustment through well-designed labour market, social and environmental policies and standards—are therefore central to engaging and upgrading in value chains and reaping associated development benefits. Finally, international cooperation can also contribute greatly to fostering a supportive and coherent multilateral trade and investment climate, and to building productive capacities—including through initiatives such as Aid for Trade—to help developing countries realize the development gains of GVCs in today's highly interconnected world.

b Olivier Cattaneo and others, "Joining, upgrading and being competitive in global value chains: a strategic framework", World Bank Policy Research Working Paper, No. 6406 (April, 2013); and, Gary Gereffi, "Global value chains in a post-Washington consensus world", *Review of International Political Economy*, DOI: 10.1080/09692290.2012.756414.

c OECD, WTO and UNCTAD, "Implications of global value chains for trade, investment, development and jobs", Prepared for the G-20 Leaders Summit at Saint Petersburg in September 2013.

d UNCTAD, "Integrating developing countries' SMEs into global value chains", UNCTAD/DIAE /ED/200 9/5; and, Rashmi Banga, "Measuring value in global value chains", UNCTAD Regional Value Chains Background Paper, No. RVC8 (Geneva).

e See *World Economic Situation and Prospects 2013* (United Nations publications, Sales No. E.13. II.C.2), Box. II.1, pp. 39-41; and, Anca D. Cristea and others, " Trade and the greenhouse gas emissions from international freight transport", NBER Working Paper, No. 17117 (Cambridge, Massachusetts: National Bureau of Economic Research).

f See Anca D. Cristea and others, Ibid.; and WTO, *World Trade Report 2013: Factors shaping the future of world trade* (Geneva). This will be true in general, although there are some particular regional or sectoral shifts where there could be potentially greater emissions such as a switch from ocean going transport to truck-based overland transport.

g Gary Gereffi, "Global value chains in a post-Washington consensus world", op. cit.

Source: UNCTAD.

The G20 Leaders' Declaration at the St. Petersburg Summit, held on 6 September 2013, commits to ensuring that RTAs support the multilateral trading system (MTS).[31] The Annex on Advancing Transparency in Regional Trade Agreements expresses G20 member commitment to ensuring full compliance with transparency obligations for RTAs under the WTO and proposes further transparency obligations, including further steps to ensure consistency of RTAs with WTO principles and rules. The Annex further reaffirms that RTAs should remain complementary to—not substitute for—the MTS, and urges WTO members to advance their discussions of the systemic implications of the increasing number of RTAs on the MTS.

Unilateral trade liberalization: a mixed picture

Global tariff liberalization continues, although more slowly than before the crisis

The last decade has seen the process of global tariff liberalization continue largely unabated. Developed countries further reduced tariffs or maintained them at very low levels since 2002, while the vast majority of developing countries reduced their tariffs, in some cases quite substantially. Tariff liberalization occurred to a greater extent during the pre-crisis period (2002-2007), with the average level of developing-country tariffs falling by almost 5 per cent. Since 2008, tariff liberalization has continued, but at a slower pace. In 2012, with the exception of some countries (mainly in sub-Saharan Africa), the average tariffs applied by developing countries on imported goods has generally been lower than 10 per cent. Overall, the average tariff on world trade in 2012 was about 2 per cent.

Many countries have reduced MFN tariffs, while the proliferation of preferential trade agreements has contributed to further reducing applied tariffs. By 2012, almost 40 per cent of international trade was fully liberalized under MFN terms, with an additional 35 per cent free because of preferential tariff regimes.[32]

More recently, some backsliding has occurred. A review of G20 trade policies, since a standstill on new protectionist measures was announced at the first economic crisis-era G20 summit (November 2008), found that the number of trade-related protectionist measures increased by 23 per cent between 2009 and 2012, and 90 per cent of crisis-era G20 protectionism still needed to be unwound.[33] A comparison of the G20 nations' performance with the ten next largest trading countries in terms of different measures of protectionism[34] since the announcement of the standstill found that the performance of the G20 was markedly better only with regards to "murky", non-transparent protectionism.

---

31 See G20 Leaders' Declaration at the St. Petersburg Summit from 5-6 September 2013, available from http://en.g20russia.ru/events_summit/20130905/780962092.html.

32 See, UNCTAD, "Key statistics and trends in trade policy", op. cit.

33 Simon J. Evenett, "What restraint? Five years of G20 pledges on trade", 14th Global Trade Alert Report (London: Centre for Economic Policy Research), available from http://www.globaltradealert.org/sites/default/files/GTA14_0.pdf. The review drew upon nearly 3,800 reports of trade-related measures taken since the pledge was made, and compared the annual totals up to 19 August 2010 (273) and 19 August 2013 (335).

34 Those are: shares of all measures since November 2008 that are harmful; shares of all measures since last G20 summit that are harmful; share of harmful measures still to be unwound; shares of tariff linesaffected by all implemented harmful measures; shares of tariff lines affected by remaining harmful measures; and share of harmful measures that are "murky" (non tariff measures).

Conclusions and ways forward

Tariff liberalization has proceeded at all levels: multilaterally, regionally, bilaterally and unilaterally. WTO disciplines still remain at the core of global trade governance and their credibility has been boosted by the Bali "mini" Package. However, the uncertainty and fragmentation of the international trading system, the meagreness of progress regarding more effective development-oriented multilateral trade rules and disciplines, and the scale of outstanding issues may accelerate a shift in multilateral focus from trade liberalization to monitoring compliance with established trade rules, together with a variable geometry approach to WTO member commitments. Such trends may be further accelerated by the potential impact of RTAs involving multiple parties and/or major trading countries (mega-RTAs) upon developing parties and non-parties, and upon the wider trading system and international trade. Meanwhile, the record of achievements in terms of unilateral trade liberalization may be stained by the common trend of resorting to "low intensity protectionism" in national trading regimes, despite pledges made to the contrary.

Accordingly, to promote systemic coherence and development-oriented trade liberalization, transparency, analysis and discussions need to be furthered regarding: (1) outstanding multilateral issues left over from Bali, particularly with regard to agriculture and development issues; (2) types of provisions in selected policy areas commonly found within RTAs, particularly "WTO-plus" and "WTO-extra" provisions in RTAs of major trading countries; (3) effects of RTAs upon developing country parties and outsiders, particularly in areas having spillover effects (such as agriculture and non-tariff measures, industrial policies, GVCs, the environment, or sectoral employment composition); (4) RTA best practices in terms of asymmetric provisions favouring developing countries; (5) how best to exploit the potential of South-South RTAs to expand markets for poorer and smaller countries and facilitate broader cooperation, consistent with national developmental objectives; and (6) interrelationships among RTAs and between RTAs and WTO provisions.

While tariff liberalization has continued, the overall picture is fragmented and uncertain

Chapter III
International finance for development

The global financial crisis demonstrated the substantial risks that the international financial system can pose to the real economy and global development. Yet, despite efforts by the international community to implement reforms (particularly in the area of financial regulations), significant risks in the financial system remain, more than five years after the crisis. Risks include vulnerabilities in the banking and shadow banking systems, as well as in short-term volatile capital flows, global imbalances, weakening fiscal positions and sovereign debt overhangs.

At the same time, discussions on the post-2015 development agenda have highlighted the enormous needs for financing the social, economic and environmental dimensions of sustainable development. Long-term financing will be essential for raising the resources required for a transition to a green economy and for promoting sustainable development. Yet, to date, the international financial system has failed to adequately allocate resources for long-term sustainable development needs. There has been insufficient investment in a number of critical areas: infrastructure; health, education and sanitation services for the world's poor, small- and medium-sized enterprises (SMEs); financial services for all; and the green technologies necessary to address climate change in both developed and developing countries.[1]

Nonetheless, estimated financing needs still represent a relatively small portion of global savings. Annual global savings are estimated to be about $17 trillion as of 2012, with global financial assets at about $218 trillion as of 2011.[2] Furthermore, despite turbulent markets and deleveraging across the developed world, global financial assets have grown at least 10 per cent since the end of 2007.[3] Although reallocating the pool of global financial assets would be challenging, reinvesting a small percentage in sustainable development could have an enormous impact. The challenge lies in promoting a global financial system that incentivizes such a reallocation in a sustainable manner, while also building stable domestic capital markets for long-term investment in developing countries.

Significant vulnerabilities remain in the global financial system...

...a system that failed to adequately allocate savings to investment in sustainable development

---

1   UN/DESA, "Financing for sustainable development: review of global investment requirement estimates", Report of the UNTT Working Group on Sustainable Development Financing, chap. 1 (New York, 2013); Peer Stein, Tony Goland and Robert Schiff, "Two trillion and counting: assessing the credit gap for micro, small, and medium-size enterprises in the developing world" (World Bank International Finance Corporation and McKinsey & Company, October 2010).

2   International Monetary Fund (IMF), *World Economic Outlook 2012* (Washington, D.C.); TheCityUK, *Fund Management Report 2012* (London, November 2012).

3   McKinsey & Company, "The Hunt for Elusive Growth: Asset Management in 2012: Will the goose keep laying golden eggs?", McKinsey's annual perspective on the global asset management industry (June 2012).

Trade-offs exist between
reducing risks in the
international financial
system and enhancing
access to credit for achieving
sustainable development

Ultimately, stability, sustainability and inclusiveness are mutually reinforcing: stable and inclusive markets encourage greater investment, while long-term investment can play a stabilizing, countercyclical role in financial markets and the real economy.[4] Nonetheless, there are also trade-offs between lowering risk and enhancing access to the credit necessary for achieving sustainable development.

Global imbalances and international reserves accumulation

Global imbalances have
narrowed but remain an
issue in the long run

As discussed in Chapter 1, global imbalances on the current accounts of major countries narrowed in 2013, continuing a general trend since the financial crisis, with only a temporary reversal in 2010. In the medium term, global imbalances are projected to decrease modestly, helped by lower surpluses among energy exporters.[5] To an extent, the reduction in global imbalances reflects a cyclical downturn and weak external demand in deficit countries. In addition, it reflects some structural improvements in several major economies. For example, the narrowing in the external surplus of China reflects in part a more flexible exchange rate. Global imbalances are not expected to widen by a significant margin in the coming two years. Nonetheless, much of the structural issues underlying global imbalances remain, which continue to pose a risk to long-term economic stability.

Global imbalances have been interlinked with the increase in global foreign-exchange reserves in the last decade, which increased more than fivefold from $2.1 trillion to $11.7 trillion between 2000 and 2012. Although reserves fell across regions following the crisis, reserves have stabilized since 2010, but this is mainly owing to a large increase in reserve accumulation in Western Asia. For example, over the past year, reserves increased slightly across developing countries and economies in transition, although the situation varied significantly across regions (figure III.1). Western Asia sharply increased its level of international reserves to gross domestic product (GDP), from 33 per cent in 2011 to 40 per cent in 2013. By contrast, reserves to GDP fell in Indonesia and Ukraine, mirroring the decline in capital inflows. Emerging and developing countries held an estimated $ 7.5 trillion in the second quarter in 2013, accounting for 67 per cent of the total.[6] Accumulated reserve holdings are particularly significant in East and South Asia, where they amount to almost 38 per cent of GDP, largely because of China, compared to 31 per cent for developing and emerging market countries overall (figure III.1).

Countries have been
accumulating large
international reserves for a
variety of reasons...

The accumulation of international reserves is influenced by a range of motivations.[7] In the aftermath of the emerging market crises of the 1990s, reserve accumulation came to be seen by a number of emerging economies as protection—or "self-insurance"—against risks associated with volatile private capital flows. Reserve accumulation can also be a by-product of interventions of central banks on foreign-exchange markets, especially during episodes of surges in capital inflows. As such, reserve accumulation has been highly correlated with global liquidity and changes in international investor sentiment. Finally, reserves can be a

---

4   UN/DESA, "Challenges in raising private sector resources for financing sustainable development", Report of the UNTT Working Group on Sustainable Development Financing, chap. 3 (New York, 2013).

5   IMF, *World Economic Outlook 2013: Transitions and Tensions* (Washington, D.C., October 2013).

6   UN/DESA calculations based on IMF COFER database, second quarter 2013.

7   United Nations, *World Economic Situation and Prospects 2013* (United Nations publication, Sales No. E.13.II.C.2).

by-product of export-led growth strategies that maintain an undervalued currency through direct interventions in the currency market. Overall, empirical studies suggest that no single explanation for reserves accumulation can account for the behavior of all countries at all times. Precautionary demand and self-insurance motives provided prominent roles for the increase in international reserves following the East Asian crisis, although mercantilism in the form of an undervalued real exchange rate also appears to have contributed in some cases.[8]

Figure III.1
Foreign-exchange reserves, 1992-2013[a]

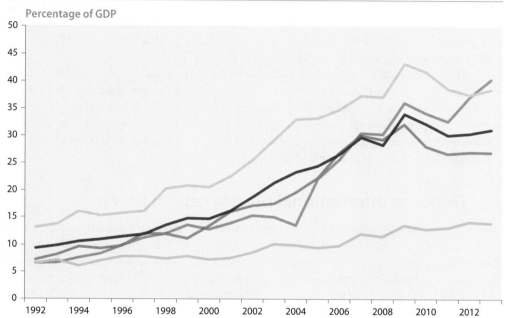

Percentage of GDP

Legend:
- Africa
- East and South Asia
- Latin America and the Caribbean
- Western Asia
- Economies in transition and developing countries

Source: UN/DESA, based on IMF, International Financial Statistics and World Economic Outlook database.
a Data for 2013 are forecast.

Nonetheless, there are costs associated with the buildup of reserves. Most international reserves are held in United States treasuries, which are considered safe, but are low-yielding. Foreign-exchange reserves thus represent a form of "constrained saving" since national savings allocated to reserves withhold funds that could be invested elsewhere, possibly with greater social benefit. Second, accumulation of foreign-exchange reserves tends to increase the domestic money supply (since the central bank buys foreign currency and sells local currency).[9] In addition, that a large share of international reserves is invested in assets abroad implies a net transfer of resources from poorer countries to wealthier ones. Overall, net transfers from developing economies and economies in transition were $622 billion in 2013, down from $740 billion 2012. Net transfers of resources are negative for most developing and emerging economies, with the exception of least developed countries (LDCs), which continue to receive net positive transfers (figure III.2). In addition, Latin American

...but there are costs to accumulation, including diverting resources from sustainable development

---

8 Atish R. Ghosh, Jonathan D. Ostry, Charalambos G. Tsangarides, "Shifting motives: explaining the build-up in official reserves in emerging markets since the 1980s", IMF Working Paper, No. WP/12/34 (Washington, D.C., January 2012).

9 On occasion, to minimize expansion in the money supply, authorities may choose to sterilize the monetary effect of foreign-reserve accumulation through off-setting intervention that involves selling government bonds to the general public (thereby reducing the amount of money in circulation).

economies recorded positive transfers of $23 billion in 2013, for the first time since 2001, due primarily to a fall in reserve accumulation in Brazil, in response to falling portfolio inflows. Finally, precautionary reserve accumulation, while sensible at the national level, adds to global imbalances and a less stable financial architecture at the global level.

Several proposals have been put forth to address global imbalances. A sustained reduction in global imbalances is an important objective of the Group of Twenty (G20), although there are challenges in arriving at politically agreed upon solutions, given the divergent interests of deficit and surplus countries. The Commission of Experts of the President of the United Nations General Assembly recommended that the international reserve system make greater use of International Monetary Fund (IMF) Special Drawing Rights as a way to reduce systemic risks associated with global imbalances, and as a low-cost alternative to accumulation of international reserves. However, this idea has not gained sufficient political support in policy discussions.[10]

To reduce developing countries' self-insurance, it is necessary to address the risks associated with the global financial system

The lack of political agreement underscores the importance of reducing risks embedded in the international financial system in order to lessen the perceived need for self-insurance, and to free up reserves for productive investment. Such risk reduction can be achieved, in part, through better management of the risks associated with volatility of cross-border private capital flows, excessive leveraging in the financial system, too-big-to-fail institutions, shadow banking and sovereign debt distress.

Trends in international private capital flows

A significant proportion of private capital flows remains short-term oriented and volatile

Attracting stable and long-term private investment into development-enhancing sectors, human resources, and critical infrastructure sectors—including transport, energy, and communications and information technology—is of increasing importance for developing countries to accomplish sustainable development objectives. Yet, today, a significant share of private capital flows to developing countries remains short-term oriented, which is inappropriate for long-term investment needs.

Financial investors, particularly institutional investors, have been considered a potentially significant source of financing for sustainable development. Institutional investors, for example, are estimated to hold between $75 trillion and $85 trillion in assets. However, many of them fit the profile for long-term investors. For example, pension funds distribute about 40 per cent of their assets within 10 years, and 60 per cent within 20 years, so that, to match liabilities, they could hold 60 per cent of their assets in relatively long duration instruments. Similarly, life insurers need to distribute about 60 per cent of their assets to beneficiaries within 10 years, and 40 per cent of their assets within 20 years. Moreover, many sovereign wealth funds are meant to preserve and transfer wealth to future generations, with few short-term liabilities. However, despite their long-term liabilities, most institutional investors have traditionally held relatively liquid portfolios. As a result, investment by institutional investors in many sectors necessary for long-term sustainable development remains limited in both developed and developing countries. For example, direct investment in infrastructure globally, represents less than 1 per cent of pension fund assets, with lower allocations to infrastructure in developing countries and low-carbon infrastructure. At the same time, many developing countries lack a domestic long-term institutional investor base for long-term investment.

---

10   United Nations, Report of the Secretary-General on international financial system and development, (A/68/221).

Figure III.2
Net transfer of resources to developing economies and economies in transition, 2001-2013[a]

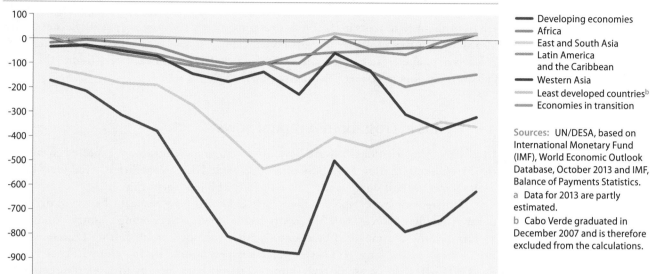

Developing economies
Africa
East and South Asia
Latin America
and the Caribbean
Western Asia
Least developed countries[b]
Economies in transition

Sources: UN/DESA, based on International Monetary Fund (IMF), World Economic Outlook Database, October 2013 and IMF, Balance of Payments Statistics.
a Data for 2013 are partly estimated.
b Cabo Verde graduated in December 2007 and is therefore excluded from the calculations.

There is also evidence that since the crisis, institutional investors shifted their asset allocations toward more liquid assets and shorter-term investments.[11] In particular, during the financial crisis, institutional investors experienced difficulties in refinancing liabilities, which led them to reduce their exposure to long-term investments in favor of more liquid assets.[12] This, in combination with other factors—such as a move towards mark-to-market accounting (requiring long-term illiquid portfolios to be evaluated relative to a public market benchmark for some investors), stricter capital requirements, and the structure of staff evaluation/compensation schemes and internal decision-making/governance—is argued to have restricted the proportion of assets employed by these institutional investors for long-term investing.

There has recently been a renewed focus on corporate responsibility and sustainable finance. Yet, despite some significant achievements and major breakthroughs, sustainable finance practices are still far from the mainstream. In 2009, for example, 7 per cent—or $6.8 trillion of investments in the $121 trillion global capital markets—was subject to environmental, social and governance (ESG) considerations.[13] Sustainable finance implies a shift in the financial sector to make sustainable development, including the three pillars of economic, social and environmental stewardship, a central concern for the global financial sector. While the financial industries have traditionally focused on creating economic value, their short-term investment horizon has meant that they have often overlooked the long-term value of sustainable ESG practices, and may have not given adequate attention to the long-term risks associated with neglecting them.

---

11 Ibid.

12 World Economic Forum (WEF), "The future of long-term investing", WEF report in collaboration with Oliver Wyman (New York, 2011).

13 United Nations Environment Programme, *Towards a Green Economy: Pathways to Sustainable Development and Poverty Eradication* (Nairobi, 2011).

The short-term outlook of most investors has manifested in both developed-country capital markets, as well as in the volatility of international capital flows to developing countries. In the United States of America, for example, the average holding period for stocks fell from about eight years in the 1960s to approximately six months in 2010. Recent studies also show that the sensitivity of cross-border capital flows—especially portfolio flows—to risk aversion, interest rate differentials and other global factors has increased since the financial crisis, leading to greater volatility of flows.

Trends in cross-border capital flows

In 2013, net international private flows to developing countries are expected to increase to $284 billion, up from $137 billion in 2012 (table III.1). Nonetheless, total cross-border capital flows are still significantly below the $439 billion reached in 2010.

Different types of capital inflows have exhibited heterogeneous behavior, driven by diverse underlying forces. In 2013, net portfolio flows to developing countries underwent a sharp decline accompanied by extremely high volatility, amid shifting expectations on the tapering of the large-scale asset purchases programme by the United States Federal Reserve (Fed). There was some revival in cross-border bank lending to developing countries, although this continues to be subdued, with banks in the euro area still facing deleveraging pressures. On the other hand, foreign direct investment (FDI) has remained relatively strong and stable (table III.1).

Foreign direct investment

FDI inflows to developing and transition economies have been growing strongly

While net FDI flows to developing countries fell somewhat from 2012 to 2013, this was mostly owing to an increase in outward FDI, rather than a fall in inflows. Overall, the contribution of developing and transition economies to FDI outflows has grown from 17 per cent in 2007 to about 31 per cent in 2012. In terms of inflows, FDI flows to developing and transition economies rose by 18 per cent in the first half of 2013, absorbing about 60 per cent of global capital inflows—a record share.[14] This increase was driven by acquisitions in Latin America and the Caribbean and record inflows into the Russian Federation. Although flows to developing Asia fell slightly, the region continues to absorb more than half of the FDI directed to developing economies as a group, and one quarter of global FDI flows (figure III.3).

After a slight decline in 2012, FDI flows to Latin America and the Caribbean jumped by 35 per cent in the first half of 2013, to $165 billion. Belgian brewer Anheuser-Busch Inbev's $18 billion acquisition of a 44 per cent share of Grupo Modelo explains most of the increase in FDI for Mexico and Central America. However, FDI to Chile, South America's second largest recipient in 2012, fell by almost 50 per cent. FDI flows to Brazil remained stable at $30 billion in the first half of 2013, while those to Colombia increased by 6 per cent, driven by investment in the mining and manufacturing sectors.

In developing Asia, the recovery of FDI inflows was weak. In the first half of 2013, total inflows to the region amounted to $192 billion, slightly lower than for the same period in 2012. Inflows to China resumed growth after a slight drop in late 2012, thanks to increasing FDI in services, such as real estate and distribution trade. At the same time, FDI fell to a

---

14   UNCTAD, Global Investment Trend Monitor, No. 13, 31 October 2013.

Figure III.3
**Growth rate and amount of FDI inflows to groups of economies, first half of 2012
to first half of 2013**

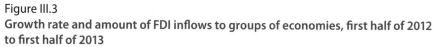

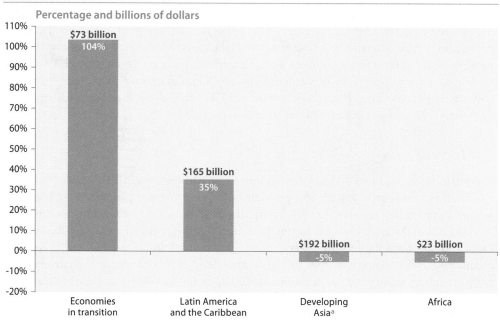

Source: UNCTAD.
Note: Dollar figures are the inflow amounts for the first half of 2013.
a Includes East Asia, South Asia and Western Asia.

number of the region's major recipients, such as Hong Kong Special Administrative Region of China, Singapore and Thailand. In Western Asia, FDI flows dropped by 19 per cent in the first half of 2013 compared to the first half of 2012; this continued the downward trend that began in 2009 due to the regional political instability and a near absence of large deals in Turkey, a major destination for FDI in this subregion. FDI to transition economies in South-Eastern Europe, the Commonwealth of Independent States (CIS) and Georgia more than doubled in the first half of 2013 compared with the same period in 2012, reaching $73 billion, primarily owing to FDI inflows to the Russian Federation involving British Petroleum (United Kingdom) and Rosneft (Russian Federation). At the same time, FDI to Africa decreased slightly over the period. While flows to North Africa and Southern Africa recorded positive growth rates, flows to other regions fell, although several countries (e.g., Ghana and Nigeria) are expecting to see a rise in industrial and manufacturing investment, particularly in the automotive industry, which would help diversify investments away from the oil and mining sectors.

Overall, FDI can play an important role in development, particularly when it contributes to promoting employment, new sectors, linkages, technology transfer and capabilities accumulation. However, the evidence on the impact of FDI on the domestic economy remains mixed.[15] In countries that experienced positive spillovers, there is evidence that government policies played an important role in facilitating the spillovers. For example, explicit policies—such as local content requirements, training requirements and mandated joint research and development programmes—helped to promote positive

---

15   Xiaolan Fu, Carlo Pietrobelli and Luc Soete, "The role of foreign technology and indigenous innovation in emerging economies: technological change and catching up", Inter-American Development Bank Technical Notes, No. IDB-TN-166 (Washington, D.C., September 2010).

spillovers in countries such as China, Costa Rica and Singapore.[16] This underscores the importance of the public sector role in ensuring that private flows, such as FDI, contribute to public goals.

At a global level, and in terms of flows to developing countries, the composition of FDI (between equity, reinvested capital and other capital representing intracompany loans) has remained relatively stable during the past eight years. However, for transition economies, the share of intracompany loans has increased, which may suggest that FDI may also be becoming more volatile in this region.[17] In addition, databases that exclude intracompany transfers show a much smaller increase in FDI—only about 7 per cent for emerging economies versus 18 per cent for net FDI inflows overall.[18]

Portfolio flows

Portfolio flows remain extremely volatile

Net portfolio capital flows to developing countries turned negative in 2013 (table III.1). The decline in net flows represented a 50 per cent fall in portfolio inflows, along with a slight increase in portfolio outflows. The 2013 drop in capital flows has been most pronounced in East and South Asia, particularly in portfolio equity inflows to India and the Republic of Korea and non-bank credit flows to Indonesia. Portfolio outflows have resulted in declines in equity markets, albeit to varying degrees, and sharp depreciations in the currencies of many emerging economies, such as Brazil, India, Indonesia, Mexico, South Africa and Turkey, as discussed in chapter I.

Quantitative easing (QE) in the developed economies in 2009 and 2010 led to a surge in portfolio flows into developing economies, which tapered in 2011. The third round of easing led to another surge in flows in 2012. In mid-2013, however, expectations of an end of the QE in the United States led to a sell-off of financial assets in emerging economies. This pattern of expansion and retrenchment in portfolio flows in recent years underscores the volatility in international capital flows, as well as the spillover effects of advanced-economy policies on developing countries.[19] In addition, the current economic weakness of some large emerging economies—Brazil, India, Indonesia, the Russian Federation and South Africa, for example—has also contributed to capital outflows.

While the recent expectations of an end to QE proved to be premature, the likely normalization of monetary conditions in developed countries over the coming years may lead to a continued retrenchment in portfolio flows to developing countries. The most vulnerable countries are those with large current-account deficits who recently received large short-term inflows, such as Brazil, India, Indonesia, South Africa and Turkey.

---

16   United Nations, *World Economic and Social Survey 2011: The Great Green Technological Transformation* (United Nations publication, Sales No. E.11.II.C.1); Rajneesh Narula and Sanjaya Lall, eds., *Understanding FDI-Assisted Economic Development* (London and New York: Routledge, 2006); Sunil Mani, *Government, Innovation and Technology Policy: An International Comparative Analysis* (Cheltenham, United Kingdom: Edward Elgar, 2002).

17   Database from UNCTAD on FDI components.

18   Institute of International Finance (IIF) database.

19   Shaghil Ahmed and Andrei Zlate, "Capital flows to emerging market economies: a brave new world?", International Finance Discussion Papers, Board of Governors of the Federal Reserve System (June, 2013); IMF, *Global Financial Stability Report: Old Risks, New Challenges* (Washington, D.C., April 2013).

Table III.1

Net financial flows to developing countries and economies in transition, 2000-2014 (*Billions of United States dollars*)

	Average annual flow		2010	2011	2012	2013	2014
	2000-2003	2004-2009					
Developing countries							
Net private capital flows	67.5	206.1	439.1	360.8	137.1	284.7	206.1
Net direct investment	146.4	264.9	343.8	479.6	427.0	378.1	375.1
Net portfolio investment[c]	-44.7	-59.1	11.2	-19.5	84.3	-21.1	-58.4
Other net investment[d]	-34.1	0.4	84.1	-99.2	-374.2	-72.2	-110.5
Net official flows	-31.1	-61.3	45.6	-31.4	-38.0	-108.9	-79.1
Total net flows	36.5	144.8	484.7	329.4	99.0	175.9	127.1
Change in reserves[e]	-148.3	-660.0	-875.5	-732.5	-445.5	-614.0	-544.8
Africa							
Net private capital flows	6.6	20.3	-7.7	-6.2	7.6	35.2	41.8
Net direct investment	17.6	36.3	34.7	44.0	42.0	51.7	53.5
Net portfolio investment[c]	-4.0	-6.8	-0.4	-16.3	-10.2	-12.4	-2.7
Other net investment[d]	-7.0	-9.3	-42.0	-33.9	-24.2	-4.0	-9.0
Net official flows	-1.1	2.1	31.4	21.6	27.9	25.2	35.9
Total net flows	5.5	22.4	23.8	15.4	35.5	60.4	77.7
Change in reserves[e]	-12.2	-54.7	-25.8	-30.1	-29.0	-18.0	-26.5
East and South Asia							
Net private capital flows	27.5	110.1	327.7	251.5	9.4	133.9	52.7
Net direct investment	63.5	122.4	193.5	276.1	228.0	171.3	163.8
Net portfolio investment[c]	-33.6	-42.1	9.2	15.0	26.5	-65.4	-79.4
Other net investment[d]	-2.5	29.8	125.0	-39.5	-245.1	28.0	-31.8
Net official flows	-9.6	-11.2	9.0	-25.2	-13.1	-21.0	-17.0
Total net flows	17.9	98.9	336.7	226.3	-3.8	112.9	35.7
Change in reserves[e]	-142.0	-492.9	-690.7	-514.8	-213.5	-465.3	-419.9
Western Asia							
Net private capital flows	-0.3	45.5	51.3	-47.2	-3.4	19.6	14.2
Net direct investment	7.9	41.2	38.0	28.4	29.7	24.5	30.4
Net portfolio investment[c]	0.3	2.4	4.6	-30.2	45.3	37.3	25.6
Other net investment[d]	-8.5	1.9	8.7	-45.4	-78.4	-42.2	-41.8
Net official flows	-26.0	-53.7	-37.4	-57.5	-108.6	-156.9	-135.6
Total net flows	-26.2	-8.1	13.8	-104.7	-112.0	-137.3	-121.4
Change in reserves[e]	-4.7	-89.5	-93.0	-101.6	-172.5	-131.4	-105.2
Latin America and the Caribbean							
Net private capital flows	33.8	30.3	67.8	162.6	123.5	96.1	97.4
Net direct investment	57.3	64.9	77.6	131.1	127.3	130.7	127.3
Net portfolio investment[c]	-7.5	-12.6	-2.2	11.9	22.7	19.4	-2.0
Other net investment[d]	-16.1	-22.1	-7.5	19.7	-26.5	-54.0	-27.9
Net official flows	5.6	1.4	42.6	29.7	55.8	43.8	37.6
Total net flows	39.3	31.7	110.4	192.3	179.4	139.9	135.1
Change in reserves[e]	10.7	-22.9	-66.0	-86.0	-30.5	0.7	6.7

Table III.1

Net financial flows to developing countries and economies in transition, 2000-2014 (*Billions of United States dollars*) (*continued*)

	Average annual flow		2010	2011	2012	2013	2014
	2000-2003	2004-2009					
Economies in Transition							
Net private capital flows	2.5	19.7	-20.1	-52.3	-28.0	-52.2	-16.1
Net direct investment	4.3	27.6	11.7	17.2	18.5	21.2	25.9
Net portfolio investment[c]	1.5	-1.0	8.7	-25.9	-3.3	-3.8	0.1
Other net investment[d]	-3.3	-6.9	-40.6	-43.6	-43.1	-69.6	-42.1
Net official flows	-5.7	-3.1	11.4	-10.0	4.7	-3.8	-5.9
Total net flows	-3.2	16.6	-8.7	-62.2	-23.4	-56.1	-21.9
Change in reserves[e]	-21.6	-69.3	-50.1	-22.1	-31.5	13.4	-11.5

Source: IMF World Economic Outlook database, October 2013.

Note: The composition of developing countries above is based on the country classification located in the statistical annex, which differs from the classification used in the IMF World Economic Outlook.

a Partly estimated.

b Forecasts.

c Including portfolio debt and equity investment.

d Including short- and long-term bank lending, and possibly including some official flows due to data limitations.

e Negative values denote increases in reserves.

Cross-border bank lending

Cross-border bank lending to developing countries remains subdued and volatile

Short-term commercial bank flows to many developing countries have been the most volatile form of capital inflows, experiencing more surge and reversal cycles than any other types of flows. Lending to large countries with open capital accounts, such as Brazil and South Africa, has been particularly volatile.[20] Net commercial bank flows to developing countries remain subdued as a number of international banks—particularly in Europe—have continued to face significant deleveraging pressures. The reduction in cross-border lending activity has been most severe in emerging economies that were more dependent on banks from the euro area (emerging European economies, for example).

Despite the aggregate situation, there were some positive developments in early 2013, as cross-border loans to some emerging economies increased noticeably in the first quarter—mainly to larger economies in Asia-Pacific and Latin America, but also to emerging economies in Europe[21] (with large economies, such as Brazil, China, and the Russian Federation accounting for 85 per cent of the increase). In addition, loans to emerging economies by banks from the euro area, notably by France and the Netherlands, rose for the first time since 2011. Still, it is not clear whether these emerging recovery signs will persist, especially considering the slowdown in many emerging economies.

One key concern is that long-term financing from banks has been constrained during the past few years.[22] In particular, long-term financing from banks to developing countries

---

20   Susan Lund and others, "Financial globalization: retreat or reset?", Global capital markets 2013 report of McKinsey Global Institute (March, 2013).

21   Bank for International Settlements (BIS), "International banking and financial market developments", BIS Quarterly Review (September, 2013).

22   United Nations, Report of the Secretary-General on international financial system and development, op. cit.

in the Asia-Pacific region has increased at a slower pace than short-term financing, causing the proportion of long-term financing to the region to decrease (figure III.4). In addition, total international claims of European banks, including all cross-border and local claims in foreign currency with a maturity of over two years, have decreased.[23]

Historically, commercial banks have played an important role in financing long-term projects in developing countries. This is especially the case for infrastructure investment in countries where corporate bond markets are relatively undeveloped and unable to raise the required levels of long-term finance. In 2012, however, deal volumes were at a historical low and global project financing fell by 6 per cent from the previous year.

Figure III.4
Shares of long-term financing for developing regions,[a] first quarter 2006-second quarter 2013

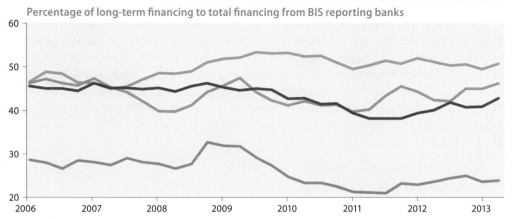

Percentage of long-term financing to total financing from BIS reporting banks

Africa and Middle East
Asia and Pacific
Europe
Latin America and the Caribbean

Source: UN/DESA, based on data from the Bank for International Settlements (BIS).
a Regions are based on the BIS classification.

Nonetheless, on average, commercial bank loan maturities average 4.2 years in developed economies and 2.8 years in emerging economies, which is shorter than other forms of borrowing, such as through bond markets. In particular, given the increasing share of short-term deposits, banks are not in a position to provide longer-term financing. This is further reinforced in regulatory systems for banks, such as Basel III, which make long-term financing more expensive in terms of capital requirements, as discussed below.

Remittances

As emphasized by the Monterrey Consensus and the Doha Declaration, remittances have become a significant source of cross-border financing. However, remittances are of a different nature than the capital flows discussed above. Remittances are private flows related to personal transactions from migrants to friends and families that are recorded in the income balance of the current account. Remittances flow directly to households, thereby having an effective role in reducing poverty and financing imports, but with limited direct effect on investments at the microeconomic level.[24] However, the effects of remittances on aggregate

---

23 "Long-term investment financing for growth and development: umbrella paper". Prepared by World Bank staff based on input from the staffs of the OECD, IMF, UNCTAD, UN/DESA, World Bank Group, and the Financial Stability Board. Presented at the meeting of the G20 Ministers of Finance and Central Bank Governors, February 2013, Moscow.

24 Dilip Ratha, "Leveraging remittances for development", Migration Policy Institute Policy Brief (Washington, D.C.: World Bank, June 2007).

investment in the economy are determined by macroeconomic investment behavior, not by how remittances are used by the individual households that receive them.

In the last decade, remittances to developing countries have become increasingly relevant as a form of cross-border finance. Remittances are larger than private debt and portfolio equity flows, and are more than twice the level of official development assistance (ODA) for developing countries. In some countries, such as Haiti, the Kyrgyz Republic, Lesotho, Nepal and Tajikistan, officially recorded remittances represent more than 25 per cent of GDP. Moreover, some estimates suggest that the inclusion of informal transfer channels would increase total remittances flows by almost 50 per cent.[25] Remittances have been more stable than capital flows; they can be a countercyclical source of balance-of-payment financing, thus playing a macroeconomic stabilizing role as their level is more dependent on the economic situation in the host country than in the recipient country.[26]

Remittance flows continue to increase, but the costs of sending remittances must be reduced

In 2013, remittance flows to developing countries are expected to increase by 6.3 per cent to $414 billion, continuing the upward trend observed in the last decade that was only temporarily reversed during the financial crisis.[27] Remittances to developing countries are expected to increase further in the coming years, surpassing $500 billion in 2016. One of the key challenges is to reduce the costs of sending remittances. While remittances costs are falling in high-volume corridors, the global average cost has remained relatively stable in recent years at just under 9 per cent. Furthermore, in some small-volume corridors, such as in Africa and the Pacific Islands, remittances costs remain exorbitant.

Management of volatile capital flows and other policy measures

Short-term volatile capital flows complicate macroeconomic management, and have been a major concern for many emerging economies. Surges in capital inflows generally expand credit in an unsustainable manner, while the sudden stops and withdrawals caused by heightened global risk aversion can contribute to spreading financial crises and to a decline in long-term investments.[28] This has led to a renewed interest in capital-account management, including capital controls.

As discussed above, during the past decade, some emerging economies have accumulated large levels of international reserves, which have placed those countries in a better position than in the past to respond to sudden outflows. Nevertheless, excessive reserve accumulation has costs. Greater attention is therefore being given to other tools to manage volatile capital flows. Traditional approaches to managing cross-border capital flows focused on macroeconomic policies. However, fiscal and monetary policies may not be enough to stabilize large volatile financial flows and may have undesired side effects. In this context, macroprudential policies as well as more direct controls have gained recognition among experts and policymakers as important tools to complement traditional policy approaches.

25 Dilip Ratha and Xu Zhimei, *Migration and Remittances Factbook 2008* (Washington, D.C.: World Bank, 2008).

26 Jeffrey A. Frankel, "Are bilateral remittances counter cyclical?", NBER Working Paper, No. 15419 (Cambridge, Massachusetts: National Bureau of Economic Research, October 2009).

27 World Bank, "Migration and remittance flows: recent trends and outlook, 2013-2016", Migration and Development Brief, No. 21 (Washington, D.C., 2 October, 2013).

28 Joseph E. Stiglitz and others, *Stability with Growth: Macroeconomics, Liberalization and Development*, (Oxford, United Kingdom: Oxford University Press, 2006).

For example, in 2012, the IMF changed its earlier position of opposing the use of capital-account management techniques in all cases, to acknowledging that there are circumstances where such measures may be useful—particularly when the room for macroeconomic policy adjustment is limited, when necessary policy steps or macroeconomic adjustments require time, and when surging capital inflows raise risks of financial system instability.[29]

Over the past few years a range of countries, including Brazil, Indonesia, Malaysia, Peru, Philippines, the Republic of Korea, Taiwan Province of China and Thailand, have implemented different direct and indirect capital-account regulations. The majority of the new initiatives were aimed at limiting the build-up of systemic risks, such as currency mismatches and credit bubbles, using macroprudential tools through the banking system[30] (for example, balance-sheet restrictions that limit the foreign-exchange mismatches of banks). The evidence on the effectiveness of macroprudential measures in managing cross-border inflows remains mixed: while they appear to have lengthened the maturity composition of capital inflows in some countries—particularly those where a large degree of financial intermediation occurs through the banking system, such as Croatia and Peru—the effect on total capital flows was limited.[31] In some cases, it has been important to address mismatches in the corporate sector as well.

Effectiveness of macroprudential measures in managing cross-border inflows is mixed

Some countries, such as Brazil, India and Indonesia, have implemented direct controls on capital inflows. These direct controls can be price based, in the form of levies or taxes on capital inflows, or quantity based, in the form of direct limits. For example, Brazil increased its tax on fixed-income foreign investment in 2010 to raise the cost of speculation (although the tax has since been cut), while Indonesia imposed a six-month holding period for Bank of Indonesia certificates to limit short-term hot money inflows. More recently, during the latter half of 2013, the Reserve Bank of India implemented measures to discourage capital outflows by banning private firms from spending more than their book value on direct investment abroad, unless given specific approval from the central bank. In addition, the Reserve Bank of India outlined a plan to provide concessional swaps for banks' foreign-currency deposits.[32]

Empirical evidence suggests that price-based capital controls have also been effective in changing the composition of inflows away from short-term debt.[33] For example, between 1991 and 1998, price-based controls on inflows in Chile appeared to have been effective in altering the composition of inflows, with short-term debt declining as a proportion of total liabilities while the stock of FDI increased from about 34 per cent to about 53 per cent. The impact on the volume of flows is, however, more ambiguous, with regulations appearing to have been more successful in some cases than in others. The varying results of similar mechanisms across countries and times suggest that there is no one-size-fits-all solution.

Capital-account regulations need to be adapted to country-specific circumstances

---

29   IMF, "The liberalization and management of capital flows: an institutional view" (Washington, D.C., 14 November 2012).

30   United Nations, Report of the Secretary-General on international financial system and development, op. cit.

31   Jonathan D. Ostry and others, "Managing capital inflows: what tools to use?", IMF Staff Discussion Note, No. SDN/11/06 (Washington, D.C., 5 April 2011); Mahmood Pradhan and others, "Policy responses to capital flows in emerging markets", IMF Staff Discussion Note, No. SDN/11/10 (Washington, D.C., 21 April 2011).

32   The Reserve Bank of India, "RBI to open a swap window to attract FCNR(B) dollar funds", Press release No. 2013-2014/494, 4 September 2013; and "RBI announces measures to rationalise foreign exchange outflows by resident Indians", Press release No. 2013-2014/323, 14 August 2013.

33   United Nations, *World Economic Situation and Prospects 2012* (United Nations publication, Sales No. E.12.II.C.2).

The design of regulations thus needs to take into account the specific circumstances of individual countries, including the economic situation, existing institutions and regulatory framework, and the structure and persistence of inflows.[34]

One reason often cited for why controls might not be effective is the risk of evasion.[35] In particular, capital-account regulations may be particularly difficult to implement in countries where there is a large derivatives market, since speculators can often circumvent the restrictions through this market. For this reason, some countries, such as Brazil and the Republic of Korea, implemented restrictions directly into the derivatives market, albeit at relatively low initial rates.[36] However, both countries also adjusted these and other controls countercyclically in response to changes in investor sentiment. For example, the Republic of Korea tightened limits on domestic and foreign banks' exposure to foreign-exchange derivatives towards the end of 2012 in an attempt to stem volatility in the rapidly appreciating won.[37] On the other hand, by mid-2013, Brazil reversed some of the capital controls implemented in previous years, when the real was under strong appreciation pressures. In particular, the central bank eliminated reserve requirements on short-dollar positions held by local banks, and the Government removed taxes on currency derivatives and foreign purchases of bonds.[38] Although some observers, such as the IMF in its institutional view on capital controls, have called for such mechanisms to be temporary, the flexibility of this approach argues for permanent regimes, which can be adjusted countercyclically.

The short-term, volatile character of private capital flows is also influenced by the compensation incentives for financial managers

In addition to managing capital flows to reduce volatility, policymakers should consider policies to incentivize longer-term and more stable investment. Many fund managers are compensated on the basis of annual performance, in packages that reward risk-taking on the upside but don't penalize losses on the downside. This incentivizes excessive short-term risk-taking, and makes it unlikely that the private sector will invest sufficiently in long-term sustainable development on its own. Indeed, according to the Financial Stability Board (FSB) surveys of market participants, more than 80 per cent of respondents believe that compensation packages contributed to the accumulation of risks that led to the crisis, with general agreement that without changes in such incentives, other reforms are likely to be less effective.[39]

Changes could include both top-down public and bottom-up private sector responses, at the international and national level. Public pension funds, sovereign wealth funds,[40] and endowments represent enormous pools of capital that ultimately report to the pension-

---

34   United Nations, Report of the Secretary-General on international financial system and development, op. cit.

35   Shari Spiegel, "How to evade capital controls, and why they can still be effective", in *Regulating Global Capital Flows for Long-Run Development*, Pardee Center Task Force Report (Boston, Massachusetts: Boston University, March 2012).

36   In the case of Brazil, in particular, these were initial measures to assess the reactions of financial markets as well as difficulties with implementation. However, evaluating their effectiveness is a difficult task given the low initial rate and the many factors that drive investors' behavior.

37   Simon Mundy and Song Jung-a, "South Korea tightens derivatives limits", *Financial Times*, 27 November 2012.

38   David Biller and Maria Luiza Rabello, "Brazil scraps tax on currency derivatives to stem real drop", *Bloomberg News*, 12 June 2013.

39   Financial Stability Board, "FSB principles for sound compensation practices: implementation standards", (Basel, 25 September 2009).

40   Some sovereign wealth funds are mandated to focus on financial stabilization. These types of funds are not providers of long-term finance. However, a larger set of sovereign wealth funds are investing

ers or to citizens who could put pressure on the industry to alter compensation structures. It remains an open question, however, whether the market on its own can develop changes to better align intermediaries with the goals of their long-term providers of capital. This implies a role for government through improved regulations.

Overall, capital market volatility needs to be better managed in both developed and developing countries. Developing countries have an imperative to develop local capital markets to provide long-term investment in productive sectors, but to do so in ways that minimize volatility. This includes managing volatility associated with inflows from international investors, while at the same time promoting the development of domestic investor bases that incorporate incentives for long-term investment in a stable manner. Developed countries have a responsibility to improve international coordination and better regulate international capital and financial markets to reduce global volatility, with a focus on longer-term stable investment.

Strengthening international financial regulation

The 2008 financial crisis prompted Governments and the intergovernmental community to undertake a number of important reforms in financial sector regulation. To date, these reforms have focused on ensuring the safety and soundness of the financial system, primarily by adhering to the banking sector regulations in Basel III, supplemented by a series of recommendations from the FSB.

The ultimate goal of the financial system is to facilitate the flow of funds from savers to borrowers[41] and to effectively allocate funds throughout the economy. Safety and soundness (of both individual institutions and the financial system more broadly) is crucial for this effort. However, the financial system also needs to address the broader goal of access to credit if it is to effectively contribute to sustainable development. Reducing risks while promoting access to credit presents a complex challenge for policymakers since there can be trade-offs between the two. For example, in the extreme, a completely safe financial system would only lend to AAA or other highly rated borrowers, such as sovereigns, but that clearly would not be an effective allocation of resources for long-term growth. The regulatory and policy framework thus needs to strike a balance between stability, particularly in reducing systemic risks, and access, especially for long-term investments, in order to ensure that the financial system works in the interest of sustainable global development.

Financial regulation should strike a balance between reducing risks and promoting access to finance

Reforms to the banking system

The main regulatory instrument, Basel III, is designed to increase the capacity of banks to withstand future shocks. Reforms include higher minimum capital requirements[42] and an improved quality of capital. In particular, core capital, which includes common equity, was

---

national wealth for future generations. A majority of their investments are in long-term finance, either through equities, real estate, private equity, or direct stakes in infrastructure or other projects.

41 A second function is to facilitate payments.

42 The original Basel III rule from 2010 was supposed to require banks to hold 4.5 per cent of common equity (up from 2 per cent in Basel II) and 6 per cent of Tier I capital (up from 4 per cent in Basel II) of risk-weighted assets. Basel III introduced additional capital buffers: (i) a mandatory capital conservation buffer of 2.5 per cent and (ii) a discretionary counter-cyclical buffer, which would allow national regulators to require up to another 2.5 per cent of capital during periods of high credit growth.

strengthened to exclude some hybrid instruments, such as subordinated debt, that were included in core capital as part of Basel II. Moreover, a new leverage ratio[43] and larger liquidity buffers[44] have been added. The new rules[45] require banks to have sufficient high-quality liquid assets to withstand a thirty-day stressed funding scenario specified by supervisors. One of the important innovations is to include off-balance-sheet obligations of the banks.

Basel III also introduces a countercyclical capital buffer, although it is unclear whether this will achieve its purpose

Along with the traditional microprudential approaches, which focus on reducing risks of individual banks, Basel III also attempts to strengthen the macroprudential policy framework through a countercyclical capital buffer that is introduced when authorities consider credit growth to be creating an unacceptable build-up of systemic risk. Thus, during periods of strong growth, capital requirements can be raised up to 2.5 per cent, whereas during slowdowns the buffer can be reduced to zero. The purpose is to mitigate the pressures on banks to reduce lending during an economic slowdown—a time when access to finance is particularly needed for economic growth (and vice versa during periods of economic booms). However, it is unclear whether this countercyclical capital buffer will be strong enough to achieve its intended purpose.

During the global financial crisis, large financial institutions in particular were found to have spread systemic risks. Such global systemically important financial institutions (G-SIFIs) carry an implicit government guarantee, which has lowered their borrowing costs while shifting the risk of covering the cost of a potential bailout to taxpayers. The IMF has estimated that the implicit subsidy to big banks in terms of lower borrowing costs to be about 0.8 percentage points.[46] In response, the FSB has suggested that G-SIFIs should have a loss-absorbing capacity beyond the general standards of Basel III, that G-SIFIs develop recovery and resolution plans (also known as living wills), and that countries prioritize this in national regulatory frameworks. The FSB also called for the adoption of cross-border cooperation agreements, pointing out that national jurisdictions need to put in place the powers and arrangements for cross-border cooperation, and that separate jurisdictions must be able to share firm-specific information.

Progress in implementing reforms of the banking system

While efforts to formulate the regulatory framework have been carried out mainly in international forums, such as the FSB and the Bank for International Settlements, their implementation takes place at the national level. To date however, implementation has been slow,

---

43   Basel III introduced a minimum leverage ratio, which is calculated by dividing Tier 1 capital by the bank's average total consolidated assets; banks are expected to maintain a leverage ratio in excess of 3 per cent under Basel III. In July 2013, the Fed announced that, in the United States, the minimum Basel III leverage ratio would be 6 per cent for 8 systemically important financial institution (SIFI) banks and 5 per cent for their bank holding companies.

44   Basel III introduced two required liquidity ratios: the Liquidity Coverage Ratio was supposed to require a bank to hold sufficient high-quality liquid assets to cover its total net cash outflows over 30 days; the Net Stable Funding Ratio was to require the available amount of stable funding to exceed the required amount of stable funding over a one-year period of extended stress.

45   Stephany Griffith-Jones, Shari Spiegel and Matthias Thiemann, "Recent developments in regulation in light of the global financial crisis: implications for developing countries", Background note prepared for the Conference on "Managing the Capital Account and Regulating the Financial Sector" in Rio de Janeiro on the 23-24 August 2011.

46   Christine Lagarde, "The global financial sector: transforming the landscape", speech delivered at the Frankfurt Finance Summit on 19 March 2013.

owing to a variety of factors, including political obstacles, limited national capacities and challenges in adapting global principles to the diversity of national-level specificities—especially in the light of the reluctance of national authorities to adopt regulatory standards that could place their financial industry at an internationally competitive disadvantage.

The implementation of Basel III was originally planned for 1 January 2013, but delays have caused this deadline to be extended in many jurisdictions.[47] On the other hand, the agreed start date for banks to begin disclosing their leverage ratios and for the phase-in of Basel III liquidity requirements is 1 January 2015, but many members have already made steps towards introducing these new requirements, including Canada, China, India, the Russian Federation and the United States.

Concerning global systemically important banks (G-SIBs), by 2013, their common equity capital increased by about $500 billion, or close to 3 per cent of their risk-weighted assets, as compared to 2009,[48] while two jurisdictions—Canada and Switzerland—have begun to enforce final regulatory rules, with an internationally agreed start date of 1 January 2016.[49] However, apart from these new capital requirements, examples of translation of these recommendations into national legislations have been limited. Two exceptions are the Dodd-Frank Wall Street Reform and Consumer Protection Act in the United States, which incorporates living wills into its framework, and the European Union (EU) Bank Recovery and Resolution Directive. However, there is the risk of a delay in the implementation of these legislations and, moreover, additional legislative measures would be necessary to implement all requirements and ensure the creation of arrangements for cross-border cooperation on resolution measures.

Overall, there are significant differences between countries in the extent of their implementation of banking regulatory frameworks.[50] Similarly, many differences exist in the interpretation of the legislation into national guidelines. For example, countries have very different requirements on risk weightings used in calculating risk-weighted assets[51] as part of capital requirements. Figure III.5 shows risk-weightings for corporate lending across regions and countries. As shown, these weightings can vary substantially. For example, weightings on average for corporate loans vary from 85 per cent in North America to 50 per cent in Europe. There are some who argue that these differences can lead to a watering down of standards, while others argue that differences are necessary given different institutional country frameworks.

Implementation of banking reforms has been slow and uneven across countries

---

[47] By August 2013, out of the 27 jurisdictions of the Basel Committee members, 11 had issued final Basel III capital rules that were legally in force. Fourteen jurisdictions had issued final rules but not yet brought them into force (Argentina, Brazil, the Republic of Korea, the Russian Federation, the United States and the nine EU member States that are members of the Basel Committee on Banking Supervision), while the remaining two – Indonesia and Turkey – were at the stage of issuing draft rules. See Basel Committee on Banking Supervision, "Report to G20 leaders on monitoring implementation of Basel III regulatory reforms" (Basel: Bank for International Settlements, August 2013).

[48] Financial Stability Board, "Progress and next steps towards ending 'too big to fail': report of the Financial Stability Board to the G20" (Basel, 2 September 2013).

[49] Basel Committee on Banking Supervision 2013, "Report to G20 leaders on monitoring implementation", op. cit.

[50] Christine Lagarde, "The global financial sector: transforming the landscape", op. cit.

[51] A risk-weighted asset is a bank's assets or off-balance sheet exposures, weighted according to risk. This way of calculating assets is generally used in determining the capital requirement or Capital Adequacy Ratio (CAR) for a financial institution.

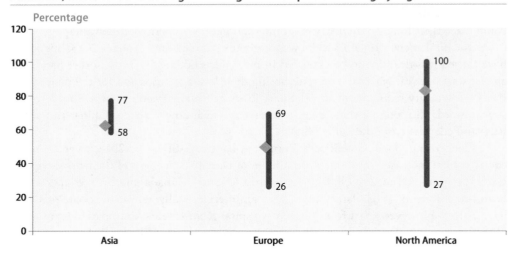

Figure III.5
Minimum, maximum and average risk-weights for corporate lending by region

Source: Vanessa Le Leslé and
Sofiya Avramova, "Revisiting
risk-weighted assets: why do
RWAs differ across countries and
what can be done about it?", IMF
Working Paper, No. WP/12/90
(March 2012), p. 22.
Note: Diamond indicates the
average risk-weight.

The Basel III framework
may not be fully suitable for
developing countries

There are also some debates on the extent to which Basel regulations should be implemented in emerging market and developing economies, many of which fall outside of the Basel Committee on Banking Supervision member jurisdictions. The FSB has pointed out that some countries are hampered in implementing the Basel III framework as a result of inadequate resources and lack of capacity.[52] Outreach activities by international financial institutions and the Basel Committee, as well at the Basel Committee's increased emphasis on emerging markets are aimed at addressing these issues.[53] However, the actual relevance of these rules to developing and emerging countries has been questioned as Basel III was designed for financial institutions in developed countries, and is not necessarily fully appropriate for the rest of the world. For instance, as required by the Liquidity Coverage Ratio, banks need to hold corporate and government bonds, which can be in shorter supply and not particularly liquid, in countries with thinner, less liquid capital markets. In this respect, it has been argued that Basel III should not necessarily aim to cover all jurisdictions in all aspects because of major differences in national institutional arrangements.[54] This does not imply that developing and emerging countries should not be regulated, but rather that regulatory frameworks could be more effective when adapted to national circumstances.

Implications of new regulations for financing sustainable development

Basel III may have the effect
of limiting long-term lending
and SME financing

While Basel III is in the early stages of implementation and its full impact is not yet clear, there has been some concern that the Basel capital adequacy rules might have the effect of limiting riskier lending by raising the cost of lending. In particular, Basel III imposes higher

---

52   Financial Stability Board, "Monitoring the effects of agreed regulatory reforms on emerging market and developing economies (EMDEs)", 12 September 2013.

53   Ibid., p. 6.

54   Stephany Griffith-Jones, Shari Spiegel and Matthias Thiemann, "Recent developments in regulation in light of the global financial crisis", op. cit.

costs on risky activities of banks to internalize the costs of risky behavior and incentivize banks to reduce risky activities. Indeed, this is considered an implicit goal of the Basel Accord.[55] In other words, by construction, the regulatory framework incentivizes a reduction in areas of high-risk investment. Yet, some of these higher-risk sectors are precisely those that need investment for achieving sustainable development. In the light of this trade-off, regulation needs to strike a balance between limiting risky lending while at the same time ensuring that investments in sustainable development enhancing activities are not unduly stifled. For example, as mentioned earlier, a key aspect of the Basel III regulations concerns the capital requirement ratio (ratio of capital to risk-weighted assets). This ratio incorporates higher risk weights for longer-term and/or higher-risk lending. It also implies higher risk weightings for areas without sufficient data on default histories, such as trade finance and green investments. As a result, there has been particular concern regarding the impact of Basel rules on long-term lending, including infrastructure lending, trade finance, innovation, and SME financing.

Recognizing the risk of lower SME lending, as shown in table III.2, the EU has allowed small companies to be incorporated into the retail category, which has a lower risk weighting (75 per cent) than unrated corporates. In addition, the Capital Requirement Directive IV reduced the risk weights for SMEs by further reducing the weights by a factor of 0.7169, bringing the risk weighting down to 57 per cent, in line with higher-rated corporate loans.

There are similar questions regarding trade financing, which is a particularly important form of credit for the developing world. Trade finance could be constrained in some cases by the leverage rule, which incorporates off-balance sheet items, such as letters of credit used in trade finance, at what many consider to be a high risk factor.

Table III.2

Summary of Basel corporate risk weights for banks using the standardized approach in the European Union

Loan Type		Risk Weight
Retail portfolios	These are exposures to individuals or small businesses. Includes revolving credits, loans and leases	75%
Mortgages on residential property—owner occupied or rented	National regulators should ensure that strict prudential criteria are applied to residential mortgage lending, such as substantial margin of additional security over the amount of the loan based on strict valuation rules	35%
Commercial real estate	50% risk weighting may be granted in well-developed and long-established markets for mortgages on office and/or multi-purpose commercial premises where the loan does not exceed 50% of the market value	100%
Past due loans	May be less than 50% if bank holds specific provisions > 20% of the loan amount	150%
Corporate Loans	Use external (Moody's, S&P) or mapped internal ratings	
	AAA to AA-	20%
	A+ to A-	50%
	BBB+ to BB-	100%
	B+ and below	150%
	not rated	100%

Source: Financing for Development Office, UN/DESA.

---

55 IMF, *Global Financial Stability Report: Restoring Confidence and Progressing on Reforms* (Washington, D.C., October 2012).

The different requirements
of the Basel III rules
create incentives that
can potentially impact
investment across sectors

More broadly, the different requirements of the Basel III rules (such as capital, leverage and liquidity requirements) create implicit incentives for investment, which differ across different types of banks as well as across jurisdictions. This is illustrated by the Global Financial Markets Association's Basel III leverage ratio survey, which covers 26 banks across Canada, Japan, United States and Europe (including 18 out of 28 G-SIBs).[56] For more than half the banks surveyed, the leverage ratio was cited as the binding constraint rather than the risk-based capital requirement ratio. Indeed, for larger banks, the leverage requirement is likely to constrain their lending before the capital requirement takes effect. By contrast, smaller banks are likely to be less constrained by leverage rules in comparison with the capital requirement rules. The interplay of these different requirements may have stronger consequences in regions that are most reliant on bank financing, such as Asia and Europe.

Despite these concerns, not all jurisdictions are focusing sufficiently on the extent of the incentive implications of the new regulations across sectors. One argument often made is that regulations should focus on reducing risks while other policy measures should focus on incentivizing investment. In this regard, the broader discussion on financing sustainable development includes other policy measures, including direct investment through development banks, low-interest loans, subsidies, and different forms of private public partnerships. Yet, in the current economic context, in many countries public funds for such measures are limited. Furthermore, it can be argued that there is a need to view economic policymaking outside of a silo approach, including appreciating the underlying incentives implicit in policies, including in the regulatory structure.

Overall, the goal should be to maintain strong capital buffers, while at the same time reducing negative incentives or even promoting positive incentives for investment. There are two potential approaches. First, rules can be adjusted as necessary when access to credit in important sectors is seen as restricted. This can be cumbersome and slow, but is likely the preferred route for countries already implementing Basel III. Alternatively, a regulatory framework could be based on broad-based simple regulations, such as high capital ratios and low leverage ratios, with simple countercyclical rules built in.[57] This could encourage safety and stability while allowing banks intermediate credit in ways that are conducive to sustainable development.

Progress in regulating shadow banking

Risky activities could shift
from the regulated banking
system to the shadow
banking sector

In the wake of the new banking regulations, there is concern that risky activities that require higher capital could shift from the regulated banking system to shadow banking practices, representing a form of regulatory arbitrage. Shadow banking is defined as "credit intermediation involving entities and activities (fully or partially) outside the regular banking system",[58] and includes derivatives, money market funds, hedge funds, structured finance vehicles and other investment funds. Despite this wide range, these entities have two common elements: they are not subject to the banking sector regulatory framework

---

56　Global Financial Markets Association and others, "Comments in response to the consultative document on the revised Basel III leverage ratio framework and disclosure requirements", 20 September 2013, available from http://gfma.org/correspondence/item.aspx?id=536.

57　It may still be appropriate to have some specific regulations in particular areas, but only when they are areas that are relatively self-contained and for which regulators have access to full information.

58　For a more detailed discussion and critique of these measures and policy implications for emerging market countries, see Stephany Griffith-Jones, Shari Spiegel and Matthias Thiemann, "Recent developments in regulation in light of the global financial crisis", op. cit.

and they lack direct access to a liquidity backstop through a public lender of last resort, which makes them riskier than banks. Moreover, most of these entities are subject to mark-to-market accounting, thus amplifying procyclicality—an effect exacerbated by both a lack of transparency and the complexity of many shadow banking products. This in turn leads to mispricing of securities, potentially worsening boom and bust cycles.

In the past decade, the value of shadow banking has increased substantially, from an estimated $26 trillion in 2002 to $67 trillion in 2011 (the most recent estimate to date), while its share of total financial intermediation decreased since the onset of the crisis from 27 per cent in 2007 to 25 per cent in 2009-2011. According to the FSB, the aggregate size of the shadow banking system is about half the size of banking system assets.[59] The FSB has spearheaded the process of designing a framework for managing systemic risks in the shadow banking system. The latest policy recommendations issued in September 2013 focus on five thematic areas: (i) mitigating the spillover effect to the regulated banking system; (ii) reducing the susceptibility of money market funds to "runs"; (iii) assessing and aligning incentives associated with securitization; (iv) mitigating risks and procyclical incentives associated with specific securities; and (v) assessing and mitigating systemic risks posed by other shadow banking entities and activities.

The FSB has established an annual monitoring exercise to assess the global trends and risks of the shadow banking system; this system now includes jurisdictions covering 90 per cent of global financial system assets, and has put forward a calendar for national implementation of these new regulations with a peer review set for 2015.[60] In September 2013, the G20 endorsed both this exercise and the bid to identify global systemically important non-bank non-insurance financial institutions by end-2013.[61] The recognition of the need to regulate shadow banking is an important step forward. However, without implementation of regulatory measures at the national level, recommendations made by the FSB are unlikely to prevent the systemic risks of shadow banking from impacting the regulated banking sector.

Derivatives

In 2008, the crisis exposed several risks associated with unregulated derivatives, which dramatically increased leverage in the system. Risks were noted particularly in the over-the-counter derivatives market, including a lack of transparency regarding counterparty exposures, insufficient collateralization, uncoordinated default management, and concerns about market misconduct. The G20 responded by agreeing to improve transparency, mitigate systemic risk and prevent market abuse, with several measures to be taken by the end of 2012.[62] Overall, the FSB reported some progress on this agenda, with three quarters of FSB member jurisdictions intending to have relevant legislation by the start of 2014, and the creation of central clearing requirements in most derivatives markets. However, at the

The regulation of the derivatives market remains behind schedule

---

59 Financial Stability Board, "Global shadow banking monitoring report 2012", 18 November 2012.

60 Financial Stability Board, "Strengthening oversight and regulation of shadow banking: an integrated overview of policy recommendations", 18 November 2012.

61 See the G20 Leaders' Declaration at the St. Petersburg Summit, September 2013, p. 17.

62 All over-the-counter derivatives contracts should be reported to trade repositories; all standardised contracts should be traded on exchanges or electronic trading platforms; and non-centrally cleared contracts should be subject to higher capital requirements with the establishment of minimum margining requirements. See Financial Stability Board, "OTC derivatives reforms progress: report from the FSB Chairman for the G20 Leaders' Summit", 2 September 2013.

time of writing, the FSB had not reported on any legislative reform actually implemented at the national level to regulate the derivatives market, implying that derivatives are not necessarily regulated more effectively than in 2008.

Regulating the credit rating agency industry

Credit ratings play an important role in financial markets by reducing informational asymmetries between lenders and borrowers. In theory, credit ratings should support economic and development activities by lowering the cost of intermediation. However, the rating agencies were strongly criticized for failing to correctly rate the risks of securitized products prior to the financial crisis.

In particular, ratings on certain structured products have proven to be highly inaccurate. Indeed, the failure of credit rating agencies (CRAs) to properly assess the inherent risk of collateralized debt obligations and related products contributed to the subprime mortgage crisis and the ensuing world financial and economic crisis. There have also been questions of the accuracy of sovereign debt ratings, particularly in ratings prior to recent sovereign debt problems in some European countries. In general, the current process for sovereign ratings tends to incorporate more of the analysts' judgement on political and other issues than other rating sectors. On the other hand, evidence appears to indicate that ratings on corporate debt, for which there is a significant amount of historical data, have been relatively accurate.

Lack of competition in the ratings industry contributed to the failings of CRAs

There are several underlying issues that have been identified with regard to the failings of CRAs, both with regard to the structure of the industry and the business model and the ratings methodologies. First, there is a high level of concentration in the industry, which is dominated by the three main CRAs (Standard and Poor's, Moody's and Fitch). This has resulted in a lack of competition in the industry. In addition, there are significant conflicts of interest since it is the borrowers who pay the agencies to obtain their ratings. Ratings have also exhibited considerable procyclicality, with many ratings being raised during boom periods and lowered during slowdowns when financing is most needed, as discussed below. This has exacerbated volatility in credit flows.

There are also issues of transparency, which make it difficult for investors to assess the accuracy of ratings. This is particularly the case with sovereign ratings, which often involve qualitative and quantitative analysis, and should be seen as more of a tool for evaluation than a standard. At the same time, sovereign debt ratings can wield considerable influence on the ability of countries to borrow and finance development.

In addition, there has been an over-reliance on many ratings on the part of some market participants. First, ratings have been built into regulatory frameworks, such as Basel capital requirements. Many investors also rely on credit ratings in a mechanistic fashion, without doing internal credit screening. To that extent, investors should perform their own research and risk management, while regulators need to reduce reliance of ratings in regulations.

In response to these problems, policymakers have begun to develop new regulations for CRAs. The FSB has published "Principles for reducing reliance on credit rating agencies" along with a road map for their implementation, which were approved by the G20. These principles aim to reduce the "hard wiring" of credit ratings in standards, laws and regulations, and to provide incentives for financial institutions to develop their own capacity to assess credit risk.[63] The International Organization of Securities Commis-

---

63   Financial Stability Board, "Roadmap and workshop for reducing reliance on CRA ratings", FSB report to G20 Finance Ministers and Central Bank Governors, 5 November 2012.

sions, a trade group, has also established a code of conduct for credit rating agencies and is carrying out a peer review.

The response of Governments has been varied. A number of countries have implemented reforms, such as Argentina, China and the United States, and the EU.[64] In the United States, the implementation of the Dodd-Frank Act (2010) requires the complete removal of references to CRA ratings from the Securities and Exchange Commission (SEC) regulations and empowers the SEC with an Office for Credit Ratings to oversee credit ratings agencies. As a result, the new capital rules for banks eliminate ratings from the standardized approach, as discussed above. In the EU, the latest CRA III regulation approved in June 2013 requires the relevant regulatory agency—the European Securities and Markets Authority—to draft regulatory technical standards on the European Rating Platform, on the disclosure of requirements for structured finance instruments, and on the periodic reporting on fees charged by CRAs.

Potential proposals to further address weaknesses in the rating system include: the establishment of a global rating platform, based on a uniform rating scale, to compile information and give investors access to ratings; increased transparency in ratings methodologies and assumptions; mechanisms to increase competition, notably the creation of domestic rating agencies, whether public or private; and, to reduce conflicts of interest, the creation of alternative structures (such as investor organizations that collectively request ratings) under new business models where the investors would pay for the rating, or whereby investors maintain the power to choose which CRA is hired.

> Consideration should be given to proposals for addressing underlying weaknesses in the structure, business models and methodologies of the ratings industry

In addition, there have been calls for mechanisms to reduce the procyclicality of ratings. For example, rating agencies often describe their process as being "forward looking". This can imply that ratings are based on analysts' predictions. However, based on private sector performance, analysts are rarely correct more than 40 per cent of the time.[65] Rather than tying ratings to specific predictions based on macroeconomic cycles, an alternative approach would be to assess ratings throughout a cycle, so that the rating would reflect how well different borrowers could withstand different degrees of economic slowdown, as well as liquidity crises. Such steps could be taken by CRAs themselves, but given the role of ratings in the financial system, there is an important role for Governments in working with the industry to strengthen the ratings process.

Financial inclusion

One of the primary goals of an effective financial system, which has not been fully incorporated into the reform agenda, is the importance of access to finance and financial services for all. Most recently, the Basel Committee on Banking Supervision, the Financial Action Task Force, and the International Association of Insurance Supervisors have revised their normative standards to strengthen financial inclusion through the proportionality principle—that is, the balancing of risks and benefits against costs of regulation and supervision. Further guidance is required on how to apply proportionality in the design of regulatory and supervisory frameworks to promote responsible financial inclusion at the country level. At the same time, there is no one-size-fits-all approach for building an inclusive financial system. Some countries have placed priority on building a nationwide electronic payment

---

64   Financial Stability Board, "Credit rating agencies: reducing reliance and strengthening oversight", Progress report to the St. Petersburg G20 Summit, 29 August 2013.

65   United Nations, *World Economic and Social Survey 2011*, op. cit.

system, while others have focused on access to credit for SMEs, and still others have focused on the need to improve the quality of usage, financial education and consumer protection. In all cases, coordination among a wide array of public and private actors is vital in order to arrive at a regulatory framework conducive to inclusive finance.

International development cooperation and official flows

Official development assistance

In addition to private flows, public resources play an important role in the international financial system. Public and private flows should be viewed as complements, not as substitutes for each other, as each has very different objectives. Despite small (but growing) pockets of socially conscious investors, most private capital remains driven by the profit motive. As a result, the private sector will under-invest in public goals when the expected return is lower than the expected return on other investment opportunities (on a risk-adjusted basis). Hence, it is important to recognize that public financing and public sector policies will remain essential.

International public financing is indispensable in two key areas. First, it remains essential for countries that do not have sufficient resources to fulfil development goals, such as the LDCs, where ODA accounts for approximately half of all external financing.[66] In addition, international public finance is needed for areas that the private sector does not finance sufficiently, such as global public goods, including climate change mitigation and adaptation. International public finance thus mirrors the main purposes of public finance more broadly—first, for equity (the distributive function of public finance, motivated by ethical concerns), and second, for allocative efficiency (addressing market failures and the provision of national and global public goods).[67]

ODA has been falling for two years owing to economic difficulties in donor countries

Nonetheless, despite increasing needs, the most recent ODA figures published by the Organization for Economic Cooperation and Development (OECD) indicate that ODA has now been dropping for two years. Following a sustained increase in ODA from 2000 to 2010, ODA fell by 4 per cent in real terms in 2012, after a 2 per cent drop the previous year. ODA dropped particularly sharply in the poorest countries. Bilateral ODA to East, West, Central and Southern Africa fell by 7.9 per cent between 2011 and 2012 to $26.2 billion, while ODA to the African continent as a whole fell by 9.9 per cent. Likewise, bilateral ODA to LDCs fell by 12.8 per cent to $26 billion.[68]

Excluding 2007, which saw the end of exceptional debt relief operations, the recent fall in ODA is the largest since 1997. The OECD has attributed this fall to the continuing financial crisis and euro area turmoil, which caused austerity measures to be implemented in Europe and weak fiscal positions across the developed world. Indeed, the sharpest drops in ODA, which were observed in Greece (-17 per cent), Italy (-34.7 per cent), Portugal (-13.1 per cent) and Spain (-49.7 per cent), tend to confirm this interpretation.

These negative developments represent a clear retreat from the internationally agreed aid targets. OECD Development Assistance Committee (DAC) donors' ODA represents

---

66   UNCTAD, *Least Developed Countries Report 2012* (United Nations publication, Sales No. E.12. II.D.18).

67   The third purpose of public finance is stabilization. For further detail see United Nations, "The variety of national, regional and international public sources for development finance", Report of the UNTT Working Group on Sustainable Development Financing, chap. 2 (New York, 2013).

68   OECD, "Aid to poor countries slips further as governments tighten budgets", 3 April 2013.

0.29 per cent of their gross national income (GNI), well short of the United Nations target of 0.7 per cent. OECD DAC donors also fell short of LDC ODA targets of between 0.15 and 0.20 per cent of GNI.

As concerns about environmental degradation have grown, aid targeting environmental sustainability has increased. Between 1997 and 2010, aid that had environmental sustainability as a principal objective has grown more than threefold, reaching $11.3 billion in 2010. More broadly defined environmental aid—the sum of all activities that have environmental issues as main or principal objectives—now represents a quarter of all bilateral aid. This represents a shift in aid allocation in favour of issues of international concern and global public goods. While these often have large developmental benefits, it is important that they do not crowd out traditional ODA.

Looking forward, while country programmable aid[69] is expected to bounce back in 2013, it is expected to remain flat between 2014 and 2016, although the uncertainty of the current economic environment means that such longer-term trends are difficult to predict.[70]

South-South and regional cooperation

At the same time, South-South flows have been increasing. While a number of DAC countries, such as the United Kingdom of Great Britain and Northern Ireland, went against the above-mentioned trend and saw an increase in ODA, the sharpest increase for 2012 was recorded in two non-DAC donor countries, Turkey (98.7 per cent) and the United Arab Emirates (30.6 per cent).[71]

The dramatic increase in aid originating from Turkey and the United Arab Emirates reflects the increasingly important role of South-South aid and other forms of cooperation. South-South cooperation—concessional loans, grants and technical cooperation, specifically—was estimated to have reached between $12.9 billion and $14.8 billion in 2010 and it is expected to continue growing in the near future with increases planned by China, India and the Bolivarian Republic of Venezuela.[72] However, the term South-South cooperation is often understood more broadly to cover other forms of exchange and cooperation between developing countries, including trade, loans, technology sharing and direct investment. Such investment is often integrated into packages that include commercial transactions as well as grants and loans at concessional rates.

While South-South cooperation may thus help cushion the concurrent fall in ODA from DAC members, it cannot be considered a substitute. As acknowledged in the Global Partnership for Effective Development Cooperation—established in June 2012 in a follow-up to the Fourth High-Level Forum on Aid Effectiveness, held in Busan, Republic of Korea from 29 November to 1 December 2011—South-South cooperation can work in concert with traditional ODA, which has had a tendency to focus on humanitarian assistance, social interventions, and climate change mitigation and adaptation.

South-South cooperation is increasing but cannot be considered a substitute for ODA

---

69 Country programmable aid is an alternative indicator to ODA for international public financing for development which has the advantage of indicating future trends with the publication of forward spending plans by OECD.

70 OECD, "Outlook on aid: survey on donors' forward spending plans 2013-2016", 3 April 2013.

71 OECD, "Aid to poor countries slips further", op. cit.

72 United Nations, "The variety of national, regional and international public sources for development finance", op. cit., pp. 6-7.

Innovative sources of international finance for development

In the light of growing needs, there has been a search for new sources of international public financing for development, leading to increased interest in new and innovative sources of finance. However, the ability of such sources to mobilize sizeable new and additional financing has not yet materialized.

Proposals for new innovative mechanisms are technically feasible, but face substantial political difficulties

Existing innovative financing mechanisms can be categorized into three groups: those that raise new resources, those that intermediate existing resources, and those that disburse traditionally raised funds in innovative ways. Measures to raise new resources include international taxes, such as financial and currency transaction taxes, carbon taxes, and non-tax revenues, such as the IMF Special Drawing Rights for financing development. Such mechanisms have the potential to raise considerable amounts of financing. For example, the European financial transaction tax proposed by the European Commission and adopted by 11 EU member States, is expected to raise between €30 billion and €35 billion a year. It was originally supposed to enter into force on 1 January 2014, but will likely be delayed by at least six months.[73] Likewise, the World Bank estimated that a carbon tax of $25 per ton on developed countries would raise $250 billion annually by 2020.[74] This and other proposals are technically feasible, but face substantial political difficulties.

There have also been innovations in the intermediation and disbursement of existing resources, with a view to improving both the efficiency of flows and disbursement mechanisms. Existing intermediate mechanisms of innovative development finance are designed to restructure existing flows to better match financing with needs, reduce risk, pool philanthropic funds with official resources, or leverage official flows with private resources. To date, these mechanisms—such as the International Finance Facility for Immunization or Advance Market Commitments in the health sector—have been of relatively small size, but have often been effective at the task they have set for themselves. Innovations in disbursement have most prominently taken place through purpose-specific funds such as the Global Fund to Fight HIV/AIDS, Tuberculosis and Malaria and the GAVI Alliance. They have successfully brought together donor and recipient governments, philanthropists, the research community, civil society and the private sector into the health sector. However, the vast majority of contributions to such funds have come from existing ODA budgets and, to a smaller degree, from philanthropic organizations. Evidence to date therefore suggests that innovative financing mechanisms have so far created only limited resources additional to ODA (box III.1).

Box III.1
Innovative sources of financing: the case of forests

Innovative mechanisms have also increasingly been used in forest financing. However, similar to the broader experience with innovate development finance, they have largely relied on a sharp increase in public financing and official development assistance (ODA) in particular, rather than mobilizing additional public or private sources of financing.

Beginning in the late 1980s, ODA played a leading role as a source of financing for sustainable forest management. In the early 2000s, however, two innovative forms of forest financing appeared. The first of these was the establishment of a large number of national forest funds in different countries. Despite the mixed record of already established funds, such as the Indonesian Dana Reboisasi, national funds have

---

73 Tom Fairless, "European financial transaction tax delayed", *Wall Street Journal*, 25 June 2013.

74 World Bank Group and others, "Mobilizing climate finance", paper prepared at the request of the G20 Finance Ministers, 6 October 2011, p. 6.

been perceived as an innovative means of allocating international funds specifically for forests, while still respecting national sovereignty. Moreover, they have been put forward as a way of helping to leverage additional sources of financing and in particular attracting private sector financing, although evidence for this continues to remain scarce.

One example is Brazil's Fundo Amazônia (Amazon Fund), open to international funds and set up in 2008 by the Brazilian National Development Bank to finance the conservation and sustainable management of Brazil's share of the Amazon biome. As of August 2013, close to $150 million has been donated to the Amazon Fund. While the fund is open to financing from both public and non-government sources, the vast majority of funding has so far been provided by the Governments of Norway (88 per cent) and Germany (8 per cent), with only 4 per cent coming from private sources, namely Petrobras, which is a semi-public company itself. The Amazon Fund has thus not been successful in tapping into the complementarity of public and private funds. This is characteristic of the majority of national forest funds, which have been successful in attracting public funds but not in mobilizing private financing other than from philanthropic organizations.

Reducing Emissions from Deforestation and Forest Degradation, or REDD, is the second type of innovative forest financing. First developed in 2005 during climate change negotiations under the United Nations Framework Convention on Climate Change (UNFCCC), REDD was quickly embraced by donors, not only because it promised to simultaneously reduce deforestation while mitigating climate change, but also because many saw in it a means of leveraging private sector financing through a carbon market-based mechanism. Protracted intergovernmental negotiations and disagreements on the creation of such a market since then have not dampened the enthusiasm of donors, who continue to see REDD as an economical means of financing both forests and climate.

In short, innovative sources of forest financing have not yet delivered in their promise to raise private sources of financing. Instead, their success comes from the enthusiasm they raised among international public donors, which has translated into an almost threefold increase in ODA allocated to forests in just two years, from $515 million in 2009 to $1,459 million in 2011 (figure III.1.1). This has raised concerns about the stability of forest financing especially during a period of overall falling aid. As the growth in financing is largely attributable to the popularity of REDD, there is also a risk that access to such financing will be tied to the ability to demonstrate a reduced rate of carbon stock depletion. This focus on a single function of forests (stocking carbon to mitigate climate change, that is) could come at the expense of local and indigenous rights and the multiple values of forests, including biodiversity, providing clean water for people and agriculture, and being the source of livelihood to 1.6 billion people, which together make sustainable forest management a major building block of sustainable development.

Source: UN/DESA.

Figure III.1.1.
Forestry sector ODA, 2000-2011

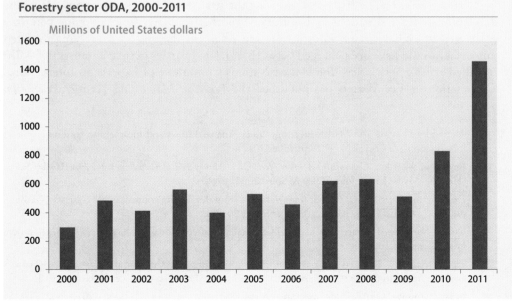

Millions of United States dollars

Source: OECD StatExtracts database 2013.

Illicit capital flows and international tax cooperation

In the light of the increasingly urgent need to mobilize finance for sustainable development, the issue of responding to illicit financial flows, including those related to tax evasion and avoidance, has been at the forefront of high-level policy discussions. There is no universal definition of what constitutes illicit financial flows; in the context of this report, the concept refers to money that is illegally earned and/or illegally utilized and, in either case, transferred across borders.[75] Estimates of the total amount of illicit financial flows vary dramatically, in part because of definitional differences and in part because such flows are clandestine by nature. Amounts range from a 2005 estimate of $540 billion[76] to a more recent estimate of $858.8 billion to $1,138 billion—for developing countries alone—for the year 2010.[77]

Estimates of the total amount of illicit financial flows vary dramatically but are in the hundreds of billions

Two categories of illicit financial flows can be distinguished: tax-related flows, such as tax evasion and avoidance, and the funds resulting from illegal activities, such as the manufacturing, trading and selling of illegal narcotics. Concerning taxes, money illegally earned through tax evasion and then transferred abroad is illegal, but tax avoidance (exploiting the gaps in tax systems between countries) is often not defined as illegal in itself, and there is debate as to whether funds derived through tax avoidance should be considered illicit. However, Governments generally consider tax avoidance activities to be violating the will of national legislation and, as such, should result in policy and administrative responses.[78] In any case, the term "tax avoidance" is not used consistently to refer to purely legal activities;[79] anti-abuse provisions are often termed "General Anti-Avoidance Rules" or "Specific Anti-Avoidance Rules" that deny the intended legal effect of such avoidance arrangements.[80] The terms are used together in this report in the light of these issues.

Transfer pricing—the mechanism by which intragroup transactions are priced—can be done in a way representing one very specific and very complicated form of tax evasion or avoidance. Transfer mispricing most often makes use of differences in corporate tax rates by minimizing profits apparently made by group members in high tax jurisdictions and maximizing profits apparently made in low- or no-tax jurisdictions.

This issue is best addressed by ensuring that transfer pricing legislation is adapted to developing-country situations and priorities. Another challenge for developing countries is the gap in available data, information and resources they face when trying to determine what would have been charged between unrelated parties in such a transaction—the so-called arm's length price. The United Nations Committee of Experts on International Cooperation in Tax Matters has published the *Practical Manual on Transfer Pricing for*

75   Alessandra Fontana and Martin Hearson, "Illicit financial flows and measures to counter them: an introduction", U4 Brief, No. 9 (September 2012).

76   Raymond W. Baker, *Capitalism's Achilles Heel: Dirty Money and How to Renew the Free Market System* (Hoboken, New Jersey: John Wiley & Sons, 2005).

77   Dev Kar and Sarah Freitas, "Illicit financial flows from developing countries: 2001-2010" (Washington, D.C.: Global Financial Integrity, December 2012).

78   United Nations, "The variety of national, regional and international public sources for development finance", op. cit., p. 5.

79   See, for example, "Tempted by tax avoidance?: a warning for people thinking about avoidance schemes", available from http://www.hmrc.gov.uk/avoidance/tempted.htm, accessed 15 November 2013.

80   Ernst & Young, "GAAR rising: mapping tax enforcement's evolution", February 2013, p.2.

Developing Countries, [81] which offers practical guidance for administrations and taxpayers on addressing mispricing of intragroup transactions.

Curbing illicit financial flows is dependent on capable customs administrations, financial intelligence and the availability of anti-money-laundering experts. Moreover, political will from developed and developing countries is needed. Illicit financial flows affect each country in a different way, but they impact both developed and developing countries. At the St. Petersburg Summit in September 2013, G20 leaders advocated greater transparency and flows of information between jurisdictions to tackle this problem. The details of this proposal are being worked out currently; how it benefits and/or burdens developing countries will depend on the final form of the proposal, including its administrative requirements, the preconditions for accessing such information and the extent to which assistance is provided for both making and responding to information requests.

The G20 has advocated greater transparency and information flow between jurisdictions in order to curb illicit financial flows

Additional measures to enhance international financial stability

Global liquidity mechanisms and a financial safety net

One essential element in ensuring global financial stability is the capacity of the multilateral financial system to provide liquidity in times of systemic crises. Such a safety net could also reduce the incentive for countries to build up reserves as a form of self-insurance against potential external shocks, which has the adverse effect of exacerbating global imbalances.

The IMF plays a central role in the global financial safety net. It has established new flexibility facilities in its lending framework, notably with the creation of the Flexible Credit Line, providing upfront access to the IMF for members with a strong track record, as well as the Precautionary and Liquidity Line, aimed at countries with sound policies but moderate vulnerabilities. The IMF Rapid Financing Instrument was also created as a consolidation of different instruments for emergency assistance. This comes in addition to existing instruments such as the Standby Credit Facility, the Extended Credit Facility and the Rapid Credit Facility, which provides disbursements with limited conditionalities for low-income countries. Despite this, the IMF is facing a prospective drop in lending capacity after 2014—especially in the lending of the Poverty Reduction and Growth Trust—which is likely to pose a challenge to its capacity to fund low-income countries. [82]

Over time, the global financial safety net has evolved into a complex and multilayered structure composed of global, regional and bilateral components. Central banks provided the bulk of liquidity needed to ease funding pressures during the financial crisis. Their involvement is likely to remain crucial for a well-functioning safety net, prompting the United Nations to join the call for the creation of a more permanent framework of liquidity lines between central banks. [83]

A more permanent framework of liquidity lines between central banks is needed

Regional financing arrangements are another increasingly important component of the global financial safety net. In October 2012, the European Stability Mechanism was

---

81 United Nations, *Practical Manual on Transfer Pricing for Developing Countries* (United Nations publication, ST/ESA/347), available from http://www.un.org/esa/ffd/documents/UN_Manual_Transfer-Pricing.pdf.

82 United Nations, Report of the Secretary-General on international financial system and development, op. cit., p. 14-15.

83 Ibid.

established, with a maximum lending capacity of €500 billion, replacing two temporary mechanisms. To date, it has approved two financial assistance facility agreements—one with Cyprus, the other with Spain. Earlier in 2012, the existing liquidity programme for the Association of Southeast Asian Nations plus China, Japan and the Republic of Korea doubled the size of funds to $240 billion. In Latin America and the Carribean, regional development banks, including the Inter-American Development Bank, and the Andean Development Bank, are playing increasing roles in this respect, although they act as development banks rather than monetary funds. No comparable mechanism exists in Africa.

Increased multilateral surveillance

The international architecture of multilateral surveillance is based on collaboration between the IMF, the FSB, the G20 and a number of standard-setting bodies. However, global policy coordination continues on an ad hoc and piecemeal basis, with the G20 taking the lead on promoting initiatives set up by different bodies, including the IMF. Given that many countries, particularly developing countries, are not represented within it, the G20 would need to continue strengthening collaboration with the United Nations for greater efficiency in this regard.

The IMF has implemented a range of measures to improve the quality of its surveillance work

In response to the 2008 financial crisis, the IMF has implemented a range of measures to increase the quality of its surveillance activities for early warnings on economic and financial risks. In particular, greater emphasis has been placed on cross-border and cross-sectoral linkages as well as the spillover effects of economic policies in the world's largest economies. The latest Triennial Surveillance Review in 2011 showed continued fragmentation and lack of depth in existing surveillance activities, as well as insufficient focus on interconnections and transmission of shocks. In January 2013, the Fund responded by implementing the Integrated Surveillance Decision that defines the scope and modalities of multilateral surveillance, including a framework for potential multilateral consultations.[84] At its latest Summit in September 2013, the G20 endorsed this decision and called for further proposals on how to incorporate global liquidity indicators more broadly into the Fund's surveillance work.

A pilot External Stability Report prepared by the IMF on the world's largest economies has also proved to be an additional building block of the surveillance system, particularly important in the light of increasingly interconnected economies and financial systems as well as the need to carry out external sector evaluations. The Fund also increased surveillance of the role of the financial sector in generating risks to global stability. The new Financial Surveillance Strategy acts as a basis for developing a framework that takes into account the interdependencies of financial sectors and of interactions between macroeconomic and macroprudential policies in the medium term.

Sovereign debt distress

After a hiatus of over a decade, the ongoing debt crisis in the euro area has once again highlighted gaps in the international financial architecture with regard to timely and effective solutions to problems of debt distress. Debates on sovereign debt restructuring have direct implications for financing sustainable development, as countries with unsustainable debt burdens spend a large proportion of public resources for debt servicing, which could other-

---

84   Ibid., p. 16.

wise be spent on development goals. In addition, uncertainty surrounding sovereign debt restructurings increases both country-specific and systemic risks.

For the first time, debt overhangs in developed economies are more pronounced than in developing countries. Public debt as a percentage of GDP in OECD countries jumped from about 70 per cent in the 1990s to almost 110 per cent in 2012. The increase in debt levels was accompanied by downgrades of credit ratings in some countries. Debt problems in Europe have once again highlighted the interlinkages between sovereign debt problems and the financial sector. Given the size of sovereign debt generally held by the banking system, sovereign debt crises can trigger bank runs and/or banking crises, potentially leading to regional or global contagion. Similarly, given the prevalence of too-big-to-fail institutions which can entail government bailouts, banking crises can trigger sovereign debt distress, with potential systemic implications due to regional and international holdings of debt.

In contrast to developed countries, developing countries are currently running historically low public debt-to-GDP ratios, with public debt at about 46 per cent of GDP for developing countries as a whole in 2012.[85] Many low-income countries in sub-Saharan Africa benefited from comprehensive debt relief programmes over the past two decades, including Heavily-Indebted Poor Countries (HIPC) and Multilateral Debt Relief Initiative (MDRI). Nonetheless, sovereign debt challenges remain in some small states and low-income countries. The problem is most acute among countries in the Caribbean, which were negatively impacted by the financial crisis. As a result, since 2013, Belize, Grenada, Jamaica and Saint Kitts and Nevis all sought to restructure portions of their debt.

In addition, increased borrowing by HIPCs—including bond finance, lending from non-traditional creditors and concessional finance—is filling the newly created borrowing space. For example, over the last couple of years, ten African countries, including three low-income countries, have issued sovereign bonds on international capital markets, raising a total of $8.1 billion (box III.2). However, despite this increased borrowing, the external risk of debt distress in low-income countries, as assessed in individual countries' IMF-World Bank debt sustainability analyses, has improved or remained stable in 90 per cent of low-income countries since 2009.[86]

The composition of public debt has been changing for all categories of developing countries. In particular, there has been an increase in the share of domestic debt denominated in local currencies, which reduces currency mismatch risk for countries. At the same time, there has been an increase in short-term debt as a proportion of GDP, possibly reflecting the shift in financing in domestic capital markets, which often lack longer-term bond markets.

In order to enhance the role of foreign borrowing for growth and development, efforts are needed to strengthen three pillars: responsible lending and borrowing, debt management, and a framework for sovereign debt restructuring. A central issue for domestic and international economic policy is how to reduce the occurrence of sovereign debt problems in both developing and developed countries. First and foremost, responsible lending and borrowing to reduce the chance of debt distress is crucial. Governments need to make regular use of analytical tools to assess alternative borrowing strategies, better manage their

> Debt problems in Europe potentially have global systemic implications, while debt problems in developing countries are, on average, at historical lows

> A number of developing countries, particularly in the Caribbean, see an increase in short-term debt as a proportion of GDP

---

85   United Nations, *The MDG Gap Task Force Report 2013—Global Partnership for Development: The Challenge We Face* (United Nations publication, Sales No. E.13.I.5).

86   IMF, "Review of the policy on debt limits in Fund-supported programs" (Washington, D.C., 1 March 2013).

Box III.2

Sub-Saharan African sovereign bonds: an alternative source of development finance or a looming debt crisis?

In December 2009, Senegal made history as the first least developed country to issue a dollar denominated sovereign bond, popularly known as the Eurobond. Given Senegal's B+/B1 below investment grade credit rating, the $200 million bond carried a high coupon of 8.75 per cent, at a time when Senegal's other external borrowing was concessional, with an average interest rate of 1.2 per cent and maturity of 34.6 years. Senegal was not the first sub-Saharan economy to join the bandwagon of expensive borrowing from international capital markets. Since Ghana's debut Eurobond issue in 2007, 11 sub-Saharan countries—Angola, Côte d'Ivoire, Gabon, Mozambique, Namibia, Nigeria, Rwanda, Senegal, the United Republic of Tanzania and Zambia—borrowed $11.5 billion through international bonds, making it the most important source of external finance for these economies, and exceeding the total $7.9 billion concessional International Development Association (IDA) loans that they received during 2007-2011.

Figure III.2.1

Eurobond issues and coupon rate in sub-Saharan Africa, 2007-2013

Average coupon rate (right-hand scale) —

Total issues (left-hand scale) ■

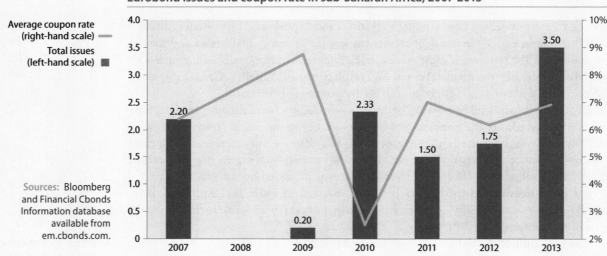

Sources: Bloomberg and Financial Cbonds Information database available from em.cbonds.com.

    Why would countries like Senegal or Rwanda borrow at interest rates that are 6-7 times higher than concessional rates and with far shorter maturity? First, concessional funds from bilateral and multilateral sources have been drying up for many of these economies. Second, even when available, concessional funds are often inadequate to meet the growing infrastructure development needs of these countries. Third, strict conditionalities, long gestation, and high transaction costs associated with concessional loans often render them unattractive to many Governments striving to develop their priority projects quickly. Unending dependency on concessional loans is neither possible nor desirable, and the recent spate of borrowing with sovereign bonds perhaps signals the inevitable transition to borrowing on commercial terms.

    However, a risk for these economies is that they may lose eligibility for IDA concessional credit from the World Bank. Article V 1(c) of the IDA Articles of Agreement states, "The Association shall not provide financing if in its opinion such financing is available from private sources on terms which are reasonable for the recipient or could be provided by a loan of the type made by the Bank." The cost of losing access to concessional funds may be very high for Governments seeking to increase public sector investments in health, education and other social sectors. While commercial term loans may be feasible for infrastructure projects, they may be far too costly for building schools or extending social protection to the poor.

There is also the risk of rising borrowing costs. Similar to other international markets, yields on these African bonds have witnessed significant volatility since May 2013. For example, yields on Ghanese, Senegalese and Zambian bonds jumped from 4.7 per cent, 5.5 per cent, and 5.625 per cent, respectively in April or May, to over 7.0 per cent, 8.4 per cent, and 7.136 per cent between June and August, and could potentially rise further if global interest rates increase. These higher yields are likely to raise the overall cost of external finance and adversely affect growth and development of these economies.

Sub-Saharan Africa needs additional external resources to finance its development. It is encouraging that the international capital market has responded positively to meet the financing gap. There is nevertheless growing concern that although the current level of external debt of these economies is moderate, their debt burden may grow amid increasingly high borrowing costs, a possible collapse of commodity prices, and international volatility. The sub-Saharan Eurobond issuers could then be forced to cut fiscal spending to maintain their credit ratings and keep yields from rising further in a countercyclical manner, just when government spending is most needed. Countries will need robust growth to ensure that these newfound sources of finance do not lead them to yet another crisis.

Source: UN/DESA.

assets and liabilities, and restrain from irresponsible borrowing. At the same time, lenders need to better assess credit risk, improve credit screening and reduce irresponsible lending to high-risk countries.

Nonetheless, debt distress does occur, and can be costly. When debt burdens become excessive, there is a need for an effective mechanism that minimizes economic and social costs and allows countries to restructure their obligations in an effective and fair manner and that also gives countries a clean slate to be able to resume growth and investment. For low-income countries, HIPC and MDRI, while important initiatives, accounted for debt relief as development assistance, which side-stepped the broader challenge of how to address issues of debt overhang in a comprehensive manner. The international community has agreed to certain broad principles for debt restructuring, including fair burden-sharing between debtors and creditors agreed in the Monterrey Consensus, and the legal predictability called for in the Doha Declaration. However, these have yet to be institutionalized in concrete practices.

The lack of an international bankruptcy procedure for sovereign debt restructuring has implications for the cost and speed of resolving of debt problems. Historically, it has been shown that this delay in restructuring can be extremely costly.[87] Lack of legal predictability creates uncertainties for both debtors and creditors, and raises important issues of equity. Recently, the issue of hold-out creditors has elicited international concern, with litigation against Argentina having the potential to increase the leverage of hold-out creditors, thereby undermining the sovereign debt restructuring process.

The international community should more actively pursue the development of an agreed rules-based approach to sovereign debt workouts to increase predictability and the timely restructuring of debt when required, with fair burden-sharing. Such an approach would reduce risk in the global financial system and free up resources for investment in sustainable development.

---

[87]   Barry Herman, José Antonio Ocampo and Shari Spiegel, eds., *Overcoming Developing Country Debt Crises* (Oxford and New York: Oxford University Press, 2010).

Chapter IV
Regional developments and outlook

Developed market economies

A majority of the developed market economies have finally entered a period of growth, more than five years into the aftermath of the global financial crisis. Gross domestic product (GDP) for developed countries as a whole is estimated to have grown by a subdued rate of 1.0 per cent in 2013, but is expected to strengthen to 1.9 and 2.4 per cent in 2014 and 2015, respectively. A variety of policies have effectively promoted growth and stability in these economies. The United States of America weathered the fiscal headwinds generated by the sequester, helped to some extent by the continued large-scale purchasing of long-term assets by the United States Federal Reserve (Fed). Japan's new, bold stimulus policies have so far worked to boost growth and end deflation. The euro area, as well as the rest of Western Europe, finally exited recession, buttressed by the European Central Bank's (ECB) policies for stabilizing confidence in the region. But economic activity remains weak in most developed countries, as high unemployment persists. These economies are also facing a number of different uncertainties and risks in the prospects: for the United States, a continued political wrangling on budget issues and a possible uneven process of tapering the quantitative easing; for the euro area, continued fiscal tightening and a fragmented banking system, with many banks remaining fragile; and for Japan, an anxiously awaited package of structural reforms.

North America

The United States: improved growth prospects, but downside risks remain

The economy of the United States is estimated to grow at a meagre pace of 1.6 per cent in 2013, significantly lower than the 2.8 per cent of 2012. Fiscal tightening and a series of political gridlocks over budget issues have weighed on growth. As this report is being written, uncertainties over the debt ceiling and the budget are still looming. Although monetary policy has been extremely accommodative, long-term interest rates started to increase in the second half of 2013 owing to concerns about the tapering of the quantitative easing (QE) programme (figure IV.1). Looking ahead, GDP is expected to grow by 2.5 and 3.2 per cent in 2014 and 2015, respectively, based on the assumption that the debt ceiling will be raised and the future unwinding of the monetary easing will be smooth (see annex table A.1). However, risks remain on the downside, particularly because the political wrangling over the budget may continue to linger in the coming years if public finance is not placed on a path that is sustainable.

Figure IV.1
Daily yields of United States Treasury Bonds, 3 January 2006-8 November 2013

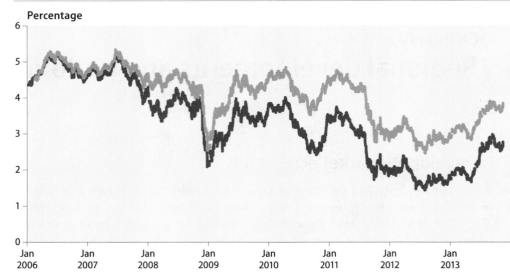

10-Year ——
30-Year ——

Source: UN/DESA, based on data from the Federal Reserve Bank of St. Louis, available from http://research.stlouisfed.org/fred2, accessed on 13 November 2013.

Consumer spending is expected to strengthen moderately

Private consumption is expected to expand by 1.9 per cent in 2013, slightly lower than the previous two years. Supportive factors include wealth effects from recovering housing prices and rising equity prices. In addition, the modest increase in disposable income generated by the continued, albeit slow, growth in employment has contributed positively. On the negative side, consumer confidence has frequently been disturbed by uncertainties associated with the political fights over fiscal issues. Fiscal tightening, including higher income taxes, the expiration of the relief on payroll taxes and the sequestration on government spending, have adversely curbed consumption spending. Moreover, many households are still undertaking financial deleveraging by reducing mortgage loans relative to income. During the forecast period, some of these adverse effects are expected to lessen, with consumer spending expanding by about 2.5 and 2.7 per cent in 2014 and 2015, respectively.

Business investment has experienced a marked deceleration in 2013, growing only 2.4 per cent, less than half of the 7.3 per cent growth in 2012. Uncertainties associated with fiscal policy have delayed business decisions on capital spending and project planning, but the pace of fixed investment is expected to pick up slightly in 2014-2015.

The housing recovery has slowed

The recovery in the housing sector was hampered in mid-2013, as mortgage interest rates increased by about 100 basis points, triggered by the expectation of QE tapering. The Standard and Poor's Case-Shiller National Home Price Index has recovered about 12.0 per cent since 2011, but it is still about 20.0 per cent below the pre-crisis peak registered in 2006. The housing sector is expected to continue its recovery, supported by low inventories and the easing of lending standards for construction and land development loans.

The unemployment rate is projected to decline slowly

The labour market in the United States is still on a path of slow recovery. Payroll employment has increased at an average monthly rate of 184,000 jobs in the past year. The unemployment rate declined to 7.3 per cent in late 2013, from a peak of 10.0 per cent in 2010 (see annex table A.7). Part of the decline, however, is due to a continuous drop in the labour participation rate, resulting from several factors, including an aging population, higher school enrolment, and the number of discouraged unemployed workers no longer seeking work. The unemployment rate is projected to decline slowly, reaching 6.5 per cent by mid-2015.

Inflation has been benign, with the consumer price index (CPI) increasing at an average rate of 1.5 per cent in 2013, and expected to stay below 2.0 per cent in the 2014-2015 period (see annex table A.4).

Real exports of goods decelerated notably during 2013, growing at about 2.0 per cent, down from 3.8 per cent of 2012. Exports of food and computer equipment declined, but exports of aircraft and consumer goods increased solidly. Real imports of goods also moderated, from 2.2 per cent in 2012 to 1.7 per cent in 2013. Imports of petroleum products and computers decreased while consumer goods grew at a reasonable pace. Real exports and imports are expected to grow at a similar pace, about 5-6 per cent in 2014-2015. The trade deficit is estimated to be about $420 billion in 2013. Both the trade deficit and the current-account deficit are expected to stay at their current ratios relative to GDP in 2014-2015.

The Fed has maintained an extremely accommodative monetary policy stance in 2013 through two instruments: keeping the federal funds interest rate at zero and increasing the purchases of long-term government bonds and mortgage-backed securities. The target range for the federal funds rate will be kept at exceptionally low levels, as long as the unemployment rate remains above 6.5 per cent, or inflation between one and two years ahead is projected at no more than half a percentage point above the 2.0 per cent longer-run target. Therefore, it is expected that the federal funds interest rate will remain within the range of 0.0 per cent to 0.25 per cent until mid-2015. The Fed is expected to gradually reduce the amount of its purchases during 2014.

A gradual tapering of QE is expected

Fiscal policy in the United States has been tightened during 2013, through two channels: the expiration of the two-percentage-point reduction in payroll taxes and an increase in income taxes for the top one per cent of high-income households; and the activation of across-the-board automatic spending cuts (sequestration), worth $85 billion in 2013. As a result, government spending in real terms is estimated to decline by about 5 per cent in 2013. During the forecast period 2014-2015, fiscal policy is expected to remain restrictive, but less severe than in 2013. Government spending in real terms will be flat in 2014-2015.

Major risks for the economy of the United States are associated with both monetary policy and fiscal policy. The Fed is facing a dilemma: purchasing long-term assets for too long could cause asset bubbles, but tapering off too soon might choke the economic recovery and destabilize financial markets. The risks related to fiscal policy may be even more acute, as the political divide continues on the debt ceiling and budget issues.

Risks for the United States are associated with monetary and fiscal policies

Canada: in tandem with the United States

The Canadian economy is estimated to grow at 1.6 per cent during 2013, slightly lower than in 2012. In 2014 and 2015, GDP is expected to grow by 2.4 per cent and 2.8 per cent, respectively.

Residential construction has been a positive contributor to GDP growth in 2003, but the pace of construction is near a maximum. Excess inventory accumulations have been worked off, but the contributions of inventory growth to GDP are not expected until the second half of 2014. Recent increases in the personal savings rate, although related to the revisions to the national accounts, may indicate that households are becoming more anxious about their debt levels and are increasing their savings in response, curbing consumption in the near term.

Households are becoming more anxious about their levels of debt

The unemployment rate has improved marginally, dropping to an average of 7.1 per cent in 2013, from 7.3 per cent in 2012, and is expected to improve further to 7.0 and 6.8

in the next two years. Inflation has been running at about 1.0 per cent during 2013 and is expected to remain well below 2.0 per cent in 2014-2015.

Net exports were a negative contribution to growth in early 2013 and are not projected to add significantly to GDP growth for several quarters to come. Real exports are estimated to grow by 1.0 per cent in 2013, before increasing gradually by 2.5 per cent to 3.0 per cent in 2014-2015. Real imports are expected to follow a similar pattern.

Real government spending has been growing more slowly than real GDP growth for the past three years. All levels of government are trying to cut deficits, inevitably affecting GDP growth. Expenditure restraint and low interest rates on government debt will permit the federal budget deficit to decline and possibly turn the fiscal balance to surplus by 2016. Monetary policy in Canada is largely influenced by United States monetary policy. Interest rates in Canada will therefore rise with those of the United States, but not before; Canadian interest rates are already higher by 100 basis points.

Developed Asia and the Pacific

Japan: out of deflation, but high public debt remains

A new set of bold stimulus policies adopted since late 2012 has boosted economic growth in Japan and ended the decade-long deflation. GDP is estimated to grow by 1.9 per cent in 2013 and the annual change in the CPI has turned from negative to slightly positive. However, the government budget deficit remains significant and the public debt, which is the highest among all developed countries in terms of GDP, continues to rise. The Government is expected to introduce another set of policies targeting structural reforms, along with implementing the planned increase in the consumption tax rates over the next two years. While the effects of the anticipated structural reforms remain uncertain, higher consumption tax rates can curb demand. GDP growth is projected to moderate to 1.5 per cent and 1.2 per cent in 2014 and 2015, respectively.

The fiscal stimulus included a 10.3 trillion yen supplemental budget for the fiscal year ending in March 2013. The consumption tax rate will increase from the current level of 5 per cent to 8 per cent in April 2014 and further to 10 per cent in October 2015. Later this year, the Government will introduce another budget act of about 5 trillion yen to compensate for the negative impacts of the higher tax. The deficit for 2014 will not change much from the level of 10 per cent of GDP for 2013.

The Bank of Japan (BoJ) announced the new Quantitative and Qualitative Monetary Easing policy (QQME) on 4 April 2013. It targeted a doubling of the monetary base in two years through the purchase of Japanese government bonds (JGB) and other financial securities at the rate of 60-70 trillion yen per year. The scope of bond purchases was also expanded to include longer-maturity JGB. The BoJ expects to bring down the yields of longer-term securities and to boost the inflation expectations of consumers, firms, and investors. The ultimate goal is to increase the annual CPI inflation rate to 2 per cent within two years. The early impact of QQME on JGB yields has been noticeable and seems to be sustainable. QQME has also had a significant impact on the Japanese yen, which depreciated vis-à-vis the United States dollar by 21 per cent in one year as of October 2013 (see figure I.5 in chapter I).

Japan had experienced deflation for 15 consecutive years since 1998. QQME has changed the inflation expectations of economic agents, as revealed by the surveys conducted about mid-2013. The sharp depreciation of the Japanese yen has also put upward pressure on the prices for imported goods. Headline inflation rates for the first three quarters of 2013 are consistent with an annual increase in the CPI by 0.3 per cent. The annual inflation rate is forecast to increase further to 2.0 per cent for both 2014 and 2015, partly as a result of the higher consumption tax rate. However, core inflation is expected to remain lower.

Export volumes have not returned to their pre-crisis levels. Weakened external demand and the appreciation of the Japanese yen have both hampered export growth. After the recent depreciation of the yen, it is projected that real exports will grow by 2.2 and 3.6 per cent in 2013 and 2014, respectively. Import volumes will also be growing, but at a much slower pace. The balance of merchandise trade will remain in deficit but will stop being a drag on growth in 2014. The current-account balance is projected to remain positive, although at a much lower level than the pre-crisis period (figure IV.2).

The external surplus is shrinking

In 2013, private consumption is expected to grow by 1.8 per cent, supported by strengthened consumer confidence and also in part by the bringing forward of durable goods purchases to avoid the higher consumption tax. Correspondingly, private consumption growth will slow down to about one per cent in later years. In 2013, fixed investment was given a boost by the continued growth of public construction projects financed by the supplemental budget, as well as the residential investment brought forward in response to the higher consumption tax. It is predicted that investment will grow by 2.0 per cent and 1.3 per cent in 2013 and 2014, respectively.

Policy choices are shifting the dynamics of consumption and investment

Given the mild growth prospects, employment is expected to grow very slowly in the outlook. The labour force is likely to continue declining, owing to the drop in the working-age population. Assuming no major changes in the structure of the labour market, the average unemployment rate is predicted to fall from 4.0 per cent in 2013 to 3.7 per cent in 2014 before returning to 4.0 per cent in 2015.

Figure IV.2
Japan: Quarterly current-account balance and major components

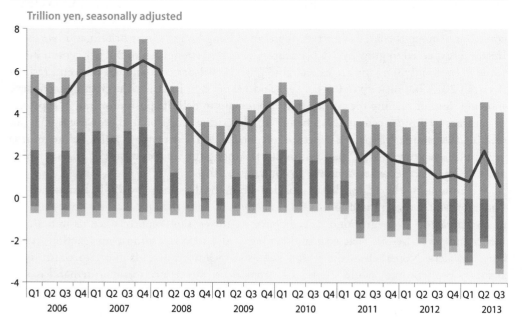

Trillion yen, seasonally adjusted

Legend:
— Current-account balance
▪ Income
▪ Trade balance
▪ Services balance
▪ Current transfers

Source: UN/DESA, based on data from the Japanese Ministry of Finance, available from http://www.mof.go.jp/english/international_policy/reference/balance_of_payments/ebpnet.htm, accessed on 11 November 2013.

Australia and New Zealand: solid growth driven by exports and investment

In Australia, after strong growth in 2012 driven by exports and intensive investment in the mining sector, export growth remains solid. Investment in the mining sector, however, is expected to peak, partly owing to weakened international prices for Australia's major mining products. The GDP growth rate is estimated to be 2.6 per cent in 2013 and projected to be 2.8 per cent in 2014. CPI inflation has been low and will likely remain so. Against this backdrop, on 6 August 2013, the Reserve Bank of Australia decided to cut its policy rate further by 25 basis points to 2.50 per cent, the eighth cut since November 2011.

In New Zealand, the initiation of delayed reconstruction to repair damage caused by the earthquakes in 2010 and 2011 boosted GDP growth to 2.7 per cent in 2012—the best performance since 2007. Fixed investment is expected to remain solid and export growth is predicted to remain stable. GDP growth is estimated to be 2.6 per cent in 2013 and is expected to be 2.8 per cent in both 2014 and 2015. The Reserve Bank of New Zealand has kept its policy rate at a historically low level; it has also decided to impose a restriction on the mortgage loan-to-value ratio starting in October 2013, based on macroprudential concerns.

Europe

Western Europe: recession ends, but growth remains weak

Western Europe emerged from recession in the second quarter of 2013, after six consecutive quarters of declining GDP. Economic activity is expected to continue to expand in the second half of the year, but at a weak pace. Annual growth rates will be negatively affected by the very strong downturn at the end of 2012 and beginning of 2013. GDP in the EU-15 is therefore expected to decline by 0.1 per cent in 2013, but projected to strengthen to 1.4 and 1.8 per cent in 2014 and 2015, respectively (see annex table A.1). The continuous weak recovery from the Great Recession has caused the output level of the European Union (EU) to be 2.8 per cent below the potential.[1] There are, however, considerable differences across countries. Among the large countries, the United Kingdom of Great Britain and Northern Ireland is expected to grow by 1.4 per cent in 2013 and strengthen to 2.2 per cent in 2014, while France and Germany are expected to grow by 0.1 per cent and 0.4 per cent, respectively, in 2013, but pick up to 0.8 per cent and 1.9 per cent in 2014. The crisis countries are showing signs of turning the corner, but they remain in delicate positions. Italy is expected to contract by 1.8 per cent in 2013 before finally exiting recession and growing by 0.8 per cent in 2014; similarly, Spain is expected to contract by 1.2 per cent in 2013, before returning to positive growth of 0.9 per cent in 2014. Among the smaller crisis countries, Cyprus and Greece are expected to continue to contract in 2014.

Tensions in the region have subsided dramatically since the ECB announced its Outright Monetary Transactions (OMT) facility. Despite the fact that the policy has yet to be activated, sovereign bond spreads have narrowed significantly since its announcement, and several crises that occurred earlier in the year saw almost no reaction in the bond markets. Nonetheless, the region faces significant headwinds going forward: fiscal austerity programmes, while less intense, remain in force; intraregional demand is still

---

[1]   European Commission, "European Economic Forecast Autumn 2013", p. 138.

exceptionally low, while extraregional demand has slowed; balance sheet repair is still an ongoing process for banks, non-financial corporations and households, placing a significant drag on consumption and investment spending; and lending conditions are heterogeneous, with bank credit amply available in some countries, while conditions in others remain extremely tight. The sharp deceleration of inflation at the end of 2013 points to some risks of deflation.

Consumption expenditure remains weak and is estimated to have declined marginally in the euro area in 2013, as it did in 2012. It has been held back by a number of factors: deleveraging by households, which is a continuing legacy of the Great Recession; the generally poor state of labour markets; low consumer confidence, which has been badly impacted following each episode of the euro area crisis; fiscal austerity programmes; and high energy prices, which have depressed real, disposable income. Going forward, consumption spending is expected to pick up moderately, as many of these factors diminish in their intensity or, in some cases, turn around. In particular, consumer confidence has stabilized and climbed steadily since the easing of tensions in the region; household deleveraging is expected to diminish; and oil prices have stabilized and are expected to retreat slightly in the outlook. The intensity of government austerity programmes and the state of labour markets have varied tremendously across the region, explaining to some extent the more robust consumption expenditure in Austria, France and Germany, as well as in those countries that are not members of the Economic and Monetary Union. But labour markets are stabilizing in general and austerity programmes in many cases are lessening in intensity. More countries in the region will therefore see some improvement.

Investment expenditure has been a major weak spot, dropping sharply in most countries in both 2012 and 2013, and is expected to make only a weak rebound going forward. Weak demand, continuing uncertainty, deleveraging, and funding difficulties in the crisis countries have been key constraints, and commercial loans to non-financial corporations continue to contract. Investment is expected to increase in 2014 and 2015 as demand picks up gradually, deleveraging eventually runs its course, and funding conditions begin to turn more favourable. But the rebound will be weak. Capacity utilization has increased since the beginning of the year, but remains low by historical standards. Industrial confidence has also improved significantly, but is now only at its long-term average. Funding conditions vary tremendously across the region; interest rates on loans, particularly to small- and medium-sized enterprises (SMEs), are much higher in the crisis countries, than elsewhere in the region. This situation will take a long time to normalize. Housing investment has started to turn around, but remains a drag on activity in some countries.

Export volume growth remains exceedingly low. In the euro area, export volumes are expected to grow by only 1.2 per cent in 2013 as a consequence of extremely weak intraregional demand, coupled with the slowing of extraregional demand, particularly from East Asia. The appreciation of the euro during the year further dampened exports. As regional and global demand pick up, exports are expected to follow suit, supported by the assumed depreciation of the euro for the rest of the forecast period. Import volumes were even weaker in 2013, estimated to have declined for the second consecutive year. Some rebound is seen for 2014 and 2015, as regional growth improves. Although the depreciation of the euro could negatively affect imports, the evolution of demand will be the dominant factor.

The relentless increase in unemployment—experienced by most countries in the region following the Great Recession—tapered off during 2013 with the rate of unemployment in the euro area increasing 0.2 percentage points during the year, to reach a new

Consumption is picking up but still faces headwinds

Investment remains a weak spot

High rates of unemployment will persist for many countries

historical high of 12.2 percent. There is tremendous diversity across the region, however. In Germany the rate of unemployment is at an historical low of about 5 per cent, while Greece and Spain are facing extraordinarily high unemployment rates of nearly 27 per cent, with youth unemployment rates more than double that amount.

Going forward, the unemployment situation is expected to improve, but at a glacial pace. The growth outlook for the region is simply not strong enough to impart much dynamism to labour markets. In addition, as discouraged workers dropped out of the labour force during the recession, they will re-enter as conditions improve, delaying the improvement of the headline unemployment rate. Some discouraged workers will transition to the long-term unemployed as their skills deteriorate, or will be subject to skills mismatch due to the sectoral reallocation of resources, making their re-integration into the labour force even more challenging. In the euro area, the rate of unemployment is estimated to average 12.0 per cent in 2013 and expected to stabilize during 2014 with an average rate of 12.1 per cent before finally starting to decline to 11.8 per cent in 2015 (see annex table A.7).

Inflation decelerates but raises new fears

Headline inflation in the euro area decelerated from 2.5 per cent in 2012 to 1.5 per cent in 2013 as oil prices eased, the euro appreciated, and base effects from the previous year's high oil prices exerted negative pressure—all against a backdrop of very weak economic activity. The impact of the weak activity was evident in the movement of core inflation (abstracting from energy, food, alcohol and tobacco), which ran close to 1.5 per cent throughout 2012, but has subsequently drifted down to below 1.0 per cent during 2013.

In the outlook, growth is expected to pick up only slightly, causing the output gap to remain significant. Wages will be held back by weak labour markets. Oil prices as well as other commodity prices are assumed to remain contained, but some upward pressure will come from the depreciation of the euro. Headline inflation is expected to tick up marginally to 1.6 per cent in 2014, after an estimated 1.5 per cent in 2013 and again in 2015 to 1.7 per cent (see annex table A.4). The very low rate of inflation envisaged means that the region will be close to deflation—particularly those countries that are in the process of improving competitiveness, which requires them to experience lower-than-average rates of inflation (figure IV.3).

Fiscal austerity eases somewhat, but policy remains committed to deficit reduction

Fiscal policy remains dominated by the need to reduce deficits, despite progress made since the end of the Great Recession—the euro area deficit-to-GDP ratio came down from 4.2 per cent in 2011 to 3.7 per cent in 2012, and is expected to come close to 3 per cent in 2013. However, the majority of the euro area countries remain under the Excess Deficit Procedure of the Stability and Growth Pact. Under these circumstances, fiscal consolidations of at least 0.5 per cent per annum and a two-year timetable for completion are required. Thus, the pressure remains for further austerity, although there is some recognition that its terms will need to ease in the short run. In June 2013, the Economic and Financial Affairs Council granted some countries extensions of their deadlines (to 2014 for the Netherlands and Poland, 2015 for France, Portugal and Slovenia, and 2016 for Spain). At a longer horizon, however, pressure for austerity will remain. The euro area's "fiscal compact" entered into force in 2013. This adds additional fiscal targets: the structural deficit should now be less than 0.5 per cent of GDP (with some caveats) and remedial action will now be required for countries with debt-to-GDP ratios above 60 per cent.

In the forecast period, it is assumed that fiscal policy will still be focused on reducing fiscal imbalances and that the debt crisis countries will continue with their adjustment programmes. The timetable for achieving targets will, however, be extended in some cases. In addition, it is assumed that no countries will ask for formal assistance under the European Stability Mechanism and the OMT will not be activated.

Figure IV.3
Inflation in the euro area: January 2012-October 2013

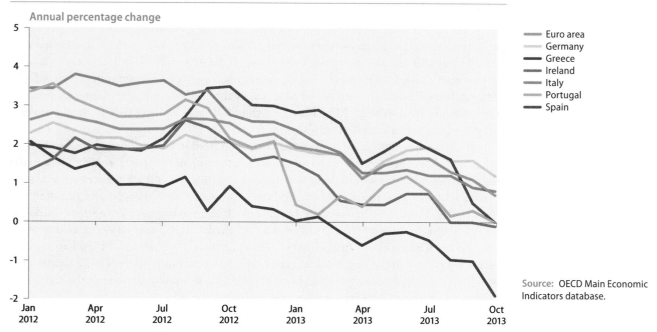

Annual percentage change

Euro area
Germany
Greece
Ireland
Italy
Portugal
Spain

Source: OECD Main Economic
Indicators database.

Monetary policy has been dominated by various types of unconventional policies since the Great Recession, but the ECB returned to conventional measures in May and November 2013 when it cut both its main refinancing rate and marginal lending rate by a cumulative 50 basis points, bringing them to 0.25 and 0.75, respectively. In each case, the Deposit Facility Rate was left at zero, avoiding the adoption of a negative interest rate and narrowing the corridor bounded by the Deposit and Marginal Lending Rates.

Unconventional policies continue to be the policies used most effectively and most often to combat the sovereign debt crisis and the slow growth across the region. The ECB has pursued QE via a number of different long-term refinancing operations (LTROs). The ECB balance sheet expanded by more than 1 trillion euro to reach more than 3 trillion euro, particularly through the two three-year refinancing operations in December 2011 and February 2012. However, in contrast to the QE programmes of the Fed, the Bank of England (BoE) or the BoJ, the QE programme of the ECB is endogenous (passive rather than active), with liquidity being provided to banks on demand. Since January 2013, banks have been allowed to repay these loans and the ECB balance sheet has shrunk to close to 2 trillion euro.

The other major unconventional policy, introduced in September 2012, was the OMT facility. Under this policy, the ECB can potentially make unlimited purchases of selected country bonds to reduce their yields, but only if a country formally requests assistance and accepts conditionality. These purchases would not be QE, as they would be fully sterilized and have no impact on the ECB balance sheet. So far the policy has not actually been deployed, but it has acted as a powerful circuit breaker, keeping bond yields contained after a number of crises at the beginning of 2013.

In July 2013, the "forward guidance" policy was unveiled, under which the ECB committed itself to maintain policy interest rates at a low level for an extended period of time, following a similar path as that of the Fed and the BoE. However, the ECB did not

Monetary policy maintains an accommodative bias

link this policy to the achievement of explicit targets—unlike the BoE, which stated that it would not consider raising interest rates until the jobless rate falls to 7% or below, a similar target to that of the Fed.

During the forecast period, it is assumed that the ECB will not cut its policy interest rates further. Given the outlook for low inflation and weak growth, it is assumed that interest rates will remain at current levels through the end of 2015. It is also assumed that the existence of the OMT will keep government bond yields within appropriate bounds. In addition, it is expected that further LTROs will be introduced to smooth the winding down of the existing three-year LTROs. However, the ECB balance sheet will gradually unwind as the banking sector's needs diminish.

Risks remain to the downside

Risks to the outlook are more evenly balanced than in the past few years, but remain to the downside. There are ample possibilities for a flare-up of the sovereign debt crisis in the affected countries. This would depress consumer and business confidence across the region, or more seriously, lead to renewed turmoil in the sovereign debt markets and test the ECB OMT policy. Vulnerable banks could become insolvent, forcing more government bailouts. The Asset Quality Review being undertaken by the ECB in anticipation of assuming its new role as chief regulator in the region will likely reveal a number of banks in need of re-capitalization. On the positive side, external demand may pick up with more vigour than anticipated, giving a boost to exports and investment. In addition, some of the structural policies may begin to bear fruit sooner than anticipated.

The new EU members: tentative green shoots of recovery

In many of the new EU member States from Eastern Europe, the negative economic trends continued in the first half of 2013, with output shrinking year on year and consumer and business confidence depressed. These economies continued to feel the impact of the protracted weakness in the EU-15 trading partners, with whom their business cycles are largely synchronized, and the ongoing deleveraging by foreign banks present in the region (although deleveraging is occurring at a more modest scale). The outlook for the new EU members, however, has improved with the return of the euro area economy to positive growth in the second quarter of 2013, as reflected by more optimistic forward-looking indicators in the second half of 2013.

In 2013, the aggregate GDP growth for the region is estimated at 0.5 per cent, marginally lower than 0.6 per cent registered in 2012. The speed of economic expansion should strengthen in 2014 and 2015, in line with the improving external environment and a gradual recovery in domestic demand, to 2.1 per cent and 2.7 per cent, respectively (see annex table A.1). A more robust growth is needed, however, to return these countries to the path of sustainable convergence with the income levels of their EU-15 peers.

Croatia, the Czech Republic and Slovenia have registered a contraction in GDP in 2013. Croatia joined the EU in July 2013 and will therefore face tougher fiscal spending requirements. Its exports will become subject to tariffs in some of the important trading partners, as the result of leaving the Central European Free Trade Agreement. On the other hand, the country will receive more aid from the EU.

Prospects for the new EU members improve and growth should accelerate in 2014

For most of the region, with the exception of the Baltic States and Hungary, growth in 2013 was driven predominantly by net exports. Domestic demand in most of the countries in the first half of the year remained suppressed by high unemployment and stagnant real wages, as well as by the ongoing fiscal consolidation. Investment was held back by low foreign direct investment (FDI) inflows and stagnation in the construction sector. By contrast, the export-oriented manufacturing sector was able to benefit from the slightly improved economic situation in the EU-15, and, in the case of the Czech Republic, Hungary, Poland and Romania, also by the modest depreciation of the respective currencies versus the euro in 2013. The automotive industry—the backbone of manufacturing in Central Europe—showed signs of an upturn, and the increasing exports should have a multiplier effect, although with some lag. During the summer, both business sentiment and household economic confidence visibly strengthened. The prospects for 2014-2015 can therefore be considered with cautious optimism.

However, while private consumption may pick up in the near-term, investment is likely to remain subdued, except in the Baltic States. Most of those economies still operate below full capacity, which deters businesses from undertaking risks and investing; for many new EU members, the annual figure for investment growth in 2013 is expected to be negative. The recovery in investment will depend, among other factors, on the resumption of FDI inflows; however, capital flows to the region remain volatile (box IV.1).

Inflationary pressures in the new EU member States have continuously weakened over the course of 2013, held back by fragile domestic demand and lower prices for food and energy, as well as administrative price reductions, such as the utility price cuts in Hungary. Annual inflation reached record-low levels in Croatia, the Czech Republic, Poland and Hungary, with core inflation estimated to be virtually zero. In 2014 and 2015, a modest acceleration of inflation is possible, in line with the pickup in economic activity and changes in indirect taxes, but inflation is expected to remain in the low single digits in most of those countries

Inflation subsided to record-low levels in parts of the region

For the new EU member States, countercyclical fiscal policy actions remain limited. In 2013 conventional and unconventional monetary policy measures were the main macroeconomic tool used to bolster economic activity in the countries with flexible exchange

Interest rates are cut to record-low levels...

Figure IV.4
Policy rates for the Eastern European countries with flexible currencies, January 2011-October 2013

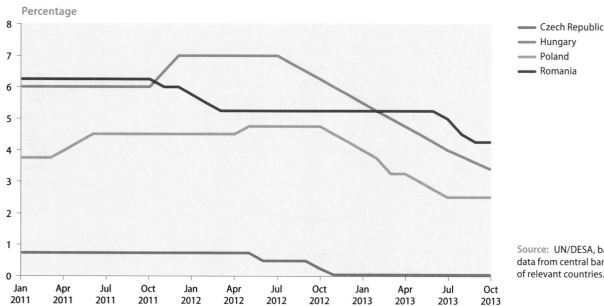

Source: UN/DESA, based on data from central bank websites of relevant countries.

rates.[2] Policy interest rates were kept near zero in the Czech Republic and cut, within the course of the year, to record-low levels in Hungary, Poland and Romania (figure IV.4). In addition, the Hungarian National Bank announced the "Funding for Growth Scheme", offering funds at zero interest rates for commercial lenders, in order to help SMEs to obtain low-cost credits and to convert their foreign currency loans into the domestic currency. The Czech National Bank announced direct interventions into the currency market, in order to weaken the exchange rate and to support exports, and to prevent deflation. The scope for further interest-rate cuts in those countries will depend on the timing of tapering of the Fed bond-buying programme. The large share of foreign currency loans in some of those countries is another hurdle on further monetary easing,[3] but the low-interest-rate environment is likely to continue in 2014.

...credit growth, however, stagnates

Despite accommodative monetary policy, credit growth in the region remains either anaemic or negative. Cross-border deleveraging by the parent EU-15 banks continues, as those banks face tighter capital requirements in line with new EU banking regulations and Basel III regulatory requirements, but the magnitude of deleveraging is smaller than in the previous years. However, as banks increasingly rely on a domestic deposit base, credit supply constraints are becoming less prevalent. Low demand for loans is a larger obstacle to recovery in private credit, as households and businesses still continue to rebuild their balance sheets. Credit standards remain tight, as the share of non-performing loans remains high, exceeding 15 per cent in Hungary and Slovenia.

Fiscal policies remain conservative, but are becoming less austere

On the fiscal policy side, most Governments continued their efforts at reducing budget deficits in 2013 in order to rebuild their public finances and, for a number of countries, to exit the excessive deficit procedure of the EU. While this trend is set to continue in 2014-2015, Governments are nevertheless gradually moving away from the tight austerity path of the past few years. Provided the revenue intake improves along with economic strengthening, a slightly more expansionary fiscal policy may be expected in the region in 2014 and in 2015, especially in those countries that already have or will achieve fiscal deficits below 3 per cent of GDP.

Marginal improvement exists in the labour markets

The labour markets in the Baltic States, where the post-crisis reduction in the unemployment rate was the most noticeable, continued to improve steadily in 2013. In Latvia, the registered unemployment rate stood at 9.3 per cent in mid-2013, down from 11.6 per cent a year earlier. However, this reduction in the unemployment rate may be attributed not only to increased employment figures, but also a labour force that is shrinking as a result of the large outward migration from all three Baltic countries.

In Central Europe, the labour market situation deteriorated in late 2012, but has improved somewhat since the second quarter of 2013. In the third quarter, however, the rate of registered unemployment in the Czech Republic, Poland and Slovakia was still about a percentage point higher than a year ago. Public employment projects contributed to a reduction in the unemployment rate in Hungary, although creating jobs that require low skill and offer low pay. Unemployment may slightly decline in 2014 and in 2015, but its structural nature in the region and the continuing skill mismatch will impede serious employment gains. Some countries, such as Slovenia, still have to undertake cuts in public sector employment to meet their fiscal deficit targets, adding to unemployment in the near term.

---

2   Estonia, Slovakia and Slovenia are members of the euro area; Latvia will join the euro area in January 2014; Bulgaria and Lithuania have currency board regimes, with their currency pegged to the euro.

3   In Hungary, about 57 per cent of all retail loans (valued at over $15 billion) were denominated in foreign currencies in 2013.

The near-term outlook is still subject to risks from a renewed slowdown in the EU-15, but also to certain domestic risks in several countries. In particular, the Slovenian banking system and the country's large current-account deficit remain a serious risk for macroeconomic stability. Although countercyclical policy measures are limited, the countries should adopt pro-growth policies and aim to improve the labour market situation, including improving participation rates. In addition, absorption of the available EU funding, especially for infrastructure, should improve significantly.

Both external and internal risks remain

Economies in transition

Growth of the Commonwealth of Independent States (CIS) and South-Eastern Europe noticeably slowed in 2013, largely reflecting a sharp deterioration of growth in the Russian Federation. In other energy-exporting countries of the CIS, robust growth continued or resumed, while some small economies of the area also experienced moderation. South-Eastern Europe returned to positive growth in 2013, although insufficient to address the region's long-standing structural problems and reindustrialization needs. In line with the improved global economic outlook, growth in aggregate GDP of the transition economies is expected to gain momentum, accelerating to 3.3 per cent in 2014 and 4.0 per cent in 2015. Both country groups continue to face serious economic risks, owing to the composition of their exports or concentration of their export markets, and have to overcome structural challenges, such as diversification of output in the CIS economies away from the energy and primary commodities sectors. In addition, the volatility of FDI and portfolio capital flows constitute a risk factor for those economies (box IV.1).

Box IV.1
Capital flow volatility in the transition economies and new EU member States

Private capital flows into the economies in transition and the new EU member States have fluctuated considerably over the last decade and have been a significant factor behind the overall volatility that these regions have experienced (table IV.1.1). Prior to the global crisis in 2008-2009, capital inflows into these economies were among the highest of any region of the world. During the financial crisis, capital flows declined more for this region than any other and, largely as a result of this, this region's gross domestic product (GDP) decline was the largest in the world. Although global capital inflows have largely rebounded during the recovery of the last several years and even become excessive for some economies, they have remained depressed in this region during 2010-2012 at levels of less than one third of those prior to the global crisis (2005-2007).

There are numerous factors responsible for the recent depressed levels of capital inflows into these economies; these include a reduction in the availability of funds from both the traditional external sources of supply and from a reduced domestic demand for borrowing, due to slower growth and stricter lending standards. Historically, a significant proportion of inflows to the region have been channelled through Western European banks directly or through their local branches and subsidiaries. However, the parents of these banks suffered large losses during the financial crisis, the subsequent euro area sovereign debt crisis, and through the recent stricter regulatory capital requirements. As a result, these multinational banks have been attempting to deleverage by reducing loans to this region. In addition, the supply of funds available for lending by Western European banks also declined during this period when solvency concerns about these banks led to withdrawals by U.S. money market funds. For these reasons, western banks have reduced their loans in the transition economies and new EU member States. Thus, while foreign direct investment (FDI) inflows to these economies were down (as a percentage of GDP) by 51 per cent in 2010-2012 compared with 2005-2007, the category of "other capital flows", largely composed of bank loans, was down by 88 per cent. In the earlier period, bank loans were slightly greater than FDI, but in the more recent period they equal less than one third of FDI.

Box IV.1

Capital flow volatility in the transition economies and new EU member States (*continued*)

Prior to the crisis, the very large capital inflows (14.3 per cent of GDP, annually) were largely matched by outflows (8.1 per cent of GDP) and reserve accumulation (6.1 per cent of GDP). In the period after the crisis, the foreign exchange provided by much smaller inflows (4.7 per cent of GDP) was consumed primarily by capital outflows (4.4 per cent of GDP); reserve accumulation declined to only 1.3 per cent of GDP in the recent period and was financed by current account surplus (1.0 per cent of GDP) (table IV.1.1). In addition, instead of purchasing reserves from domestic savings, several of the non-energy exporters have resorted to borrowing additional international reserves through an increased use of official financing. For example, Belarus received $440 million from the Eurasian Economic Community in mid-2012, and $1.3 billion in 2013.

Aggregate figures for the region hide important country differences. Nevertheless, these basic trends of much smaller capital inflows matched by smaller capital outflows and less reserve accumulation have been observed in most of the economies in the region. For example, 22 economies experienced a decline in capital inflows, only 4 showed an increase, and 2 saw no change; 24 had a decline in capital outflows and 4 an increase; and 25 experienced a decline in the rate of reserve accumulation or an actual loss while only 3 had an increase. Despite a similarity in trends, the levels of these flows do vary. Historically and presently, the nature of capital flows varies significantly between those economies with extensive energy exports—such as Azerbaijan, Kazakhstan and the Russian Federation, which have been net capital exporters—and the rest of the economies in transition and the new EU member States, which have been net importers. Another notable difference is that the current-account balances of Azerbaijan, Kazakhstan, the Russian Federation and the economies in transition have deteriorated in the recent period, while those in the new EU member States have improved significantly. Given these differences, data for each of these three groups are provided in table IV.I.I below. (Energy-rich Turkmenistan and Uzbekistan are not considered because of the lack of appropriate data.) Although the levels and net signs on some of the balance-of-payments categories differ between the three groups, each group has observed the basic trend changes discussed above—that is significant declines in inflows, outflows and reserve accumulation.

An important concern about this decline in capital inflows is that it would lead to a decline in domestic investment and thereby reduce the prospects for long-term growth. However, since the decline in inflows was largely neutralized by the decline in outflows and reserve accumulation, the resources available for domestic absorption (consumption plus investment) did not change appreciably for the region overall. Nevertheless, there is a significant distinction between the three groups: the decline in current-account positions of the economies in transition has provided more resources for domestic use and, as a result, the investment share of national income in most of these economies was similar or even larger during 2010-2013 than during the 2005-2007 period. In contrast, the improvement in the current accounts of the new EU member States has meant that fewer resources have been available for domestic use. The investment share of GDP has therefore declined in all of these economies—by over 5 per cent of GDP in 8 of 11 cases, which will have very significant implications for their longer-term growth.

The implications of the decreased rate of reserve accumulation are more difficult to assess. There are now less reserves available (than if previous trends had been maintained) to cover imports and/or current-account deficits, which is troublesome. However, since there were less capital inflows, the amount needed to protect against capital-account reversals is less, which is favourable. This latter consideration is proving to be important; the expectation that advanced economies will scale back their quantitative easing programmes has already led to large capital outflows from many emerging markets (see chapter 1), and more are expected. Given the region's smaller inflows in 2010-2012, the current outflows and those expected in 2014-2015 are also likely to be somewhat smaller. The region may thus largely avoid the financial disturbances associated with higher global interest rates that may affect other emerging economies recently impacted by larger capital inflows. However, there are several countries where these outflows have nevertheless been quite large and the reserve losses have become problematic. For example, from May through July of 2013, Ukraine used almost 10 per cent of its international reserve assets in an attempt to stabilize the currency. Table IV.I.I also reveals that despite the large decline in inflows, declining outflows remain quite significant in Azerbaijan, Kazakhstan and the Russian Federation, showing their continued susceptibility to capital flight.

Table IV.1.1
Capital flows to new EU member States and economies in transition, 2005-2012

Region	Period	Percentage of GDP			
		Inflows	Outflows	Change in reserves[a]	Current-account balance
Azerbaijan, Kazakhstan and Russian Federation	2010-2012	4.3	7.1	1.5	5.0
	2005-2007	11.8	9.0	9.6	8.1
	Change	-7.5	-1.9	-8.1	-3.2
Other economies in transition	2010-2012	10.6	4.1	-0.1	-8.0
	2005-2007	15.8	7.5	4.8	-4.0
	Change	-5.2	-3.4	-4.9	-4.0
New EU member States	2010-2012	3.8	0.4	1.4	-2.7
	2005-2007	16.7	7.4	2.5	-6.6
	Change	-12.9	-7.0	-1.1	3.9
Economies in transition and new EU member States	2010-2012	4.7	4.4	1.3	1.0
	2005-2007	14.3	8.1	6.1	0.6
	Change	-9.6	-3.7	-4.8	0.4

Source: UNECE, based on IMF Balance of Payments Statistics and International Financial Statistics database.
a Positive number indicates cumulation of reserves.

South-Eastern Europe: moderate growth, but high unemployment and possible financial vulnerabilities

Real economic activity in South-Eastern Europe turned positive in 2013 after experiencing a decline in GDP of almost 1 per cent in 2012. All economies in the region registered positive GDP growth in 2013. Growth should pick up slightly in 2014, thanks largely to the improving growth prospects in the EU with which it is highly integrated both in terms of trade and financial flows. The aggregate GDP of South-Eastern Europe increased by 1.8 per cent in 2013, after contracting by 0.9 per cent in 2012. Growth is projected to accelerate to 2.6 per cent in 2014 to 3.1 per cent in 2015, along with a gradual recovery in FDI flows and in domestic demand (see annex table A.2).

However, growth at these subdued rates will not be sufficient to address the region's long-standing needs of reindustrialization, to significantly lower the exceedingly high rates of unemployment that have plagued the region since the 1990s, or to increase the labour force participation ratio. Growth at these rates is also not sufficient to warrant the large current-account deficits in these economies.

Projected growth is still too low to address problems in the region

There has been fairly limited variation in the economic performance of the South-Eastern European economies, as all of them grew in the 1.5 to 2.0 per cent range in 2013 except for Bosnia and Herzegovina, whose GDP has yet to return to its pre-crisis level. In Serbia, growth was driven by export-led manufacturing and improved agricultural output, but domestic demand remains lack-lustre and the economy is likely to remain heavily dependent on exports in the near term. In Albania, by contrast, where recession was avoided altogether in 2009, modest growth was driven both by exports and by a recovery in construction output. In the former Yugoslav Republic of Macedonia, activity was supported by large-scale public investment projects. In the outlook period, the external environment for those countries is expected to improve, including the terms of access to external finance.

Most economies in the region grew about 2 per cent in 2013

As credit conditions ease, investment is set to recover gradually in 2014-2015, along with strengthening private consumption.

Labour markets in the region remain weak and require serious policy efforts

Currently, unemployment is well above ten per cent in the entire region and, given the anticipated growth rates, is likely to stay elevated for many years (see annex table A.8). In Bosnia and Herzegovina, the former Yugoslav Republic of Macedonia and Serbia, labour force surveys estimate unemployment at over 25 per cent.[4] Unemployment in South-Eastern Europe is mostly structural and predates the financial crisis. The capital stock in much of the region was destroyed by the conflicts in the 1990s and insufficient investment in new facilities and education has resulted in a situation where the region lacks necessary production facilities and skilled labour. The situation in the region's labour markets was further aggravated by the cyclical economic downturn. Some positive trends have emerged in the former Yugoslav Republic of Macedonia, where the registered unemployment rate dropped to 28.8 per cent in the second quarter of 2013, from 31.2 per cent a year earlier, and the activity rate also increased, thanks in part to publicly financed large-scale construction projects. However, this is still a marginal improvement, and in the outlook, the unemployment rates in the region are expected to remain high. Serious efforts are needed to address them, including reductions in unit labour costs, reforms in labour market policy, improved education and training facilities, better public infrastructure, and more incentives for private sector investment.

Inflation remains moderate

Inflation has been quite moderate in South-Eastern Europe, with rates in the 2-4 per cent range (with the exception of Serbia) and should stay in the same range in 2014-2015 (see annex table A.5). Many of these economies have fixed exchange rates with the euro so that monetary policy is quite constrained. Although inflation rates in most cases are slightly higher than in the euro area, this differential appears generally consistent with productivity and price convergence trends. Albania and Serbia have more flexible exchange rates and thus slightly more monetary flexibility. Inflation in Serbia has been in double-digits in early 2013, in particular, because of higher food prices, but has gradually subsided over the course of the year. Still it is likely to be 8.4 per cent in 2013, but is expected to decline in 2014.

Fiscal policies remain tight

Fiscal policies in South-Eastern Europe remain tight, as the countries struggle to reduce their budget deficits or to comply with loan requirements by the IMF—as in the case of Bosnia and Herzegovina. In Serbia, the budget deficit is likely to approach 6 per cent of GDP in 2013. Since the Government aims to achieve a balanced budget by 2016, fiscal policy will remain tight in the medium-term. In the former Yugoslav Republic of Macedonia, however, fiscal policy will not be tightened significantly in the near-term, as large-scale public investment projects need to be completed. Formal or informal currency pegs in turn constrain the conduct of monetary policy in the region. Among the countries with flexible currencies, the National Bank of Serbia repeatedly increased its key policy rate until April 2013 in response to accelerating inflation, before cutting it several times as inflationary pressures tapered. Facing increasing risk aversion among investors, the monetary authorities are likely to put further interest-rate cuts on hold in the near-term. By contrast, the Bank of Albania brought its policy rate to a record-low level in July 2013 amid rapidly falling inflation.

Current-account deficits may become a source of vulnerability

Some countries in the region run high current-account deficits. Those deficits are likely to reach 6 per cent of GDP in Serbia, 9 per cent of GDP in Albania, and 15 per cent

---

4   In some countries, there are substantial differences between monthly registered unemployment rates and labour force surveys, which are only conducted on a yearly basis.

of GDP in Montenegro in 2013. Given the relatively slow rates of economic growth, deficits of this size pose vulnerability, as they are only covered in part by FDI inflows and the remainder is often financed by short-term capital flows. Pegged exchange rates or high levels of debt denominated in foreign currency limit the ability of using depreciation to address these deficits. The level of public debt in South-Eastern Europe is moderate, with four economies having public (gross) debt-to-GDP ratios of over 50 per cent, and only Albania's and Serbia's being over 60 per cent. The debt of the former Yugoslav Republic of Macedonia is relatively low at about 35 per cent of GDP.

The major risks to the forecast are to the downside. The region has strong financial, trade and remittances linkages with the euro area (especially Greece and Italy), making it vulnerable should growth not materialize there. The region could also be negatively impacted if there are large capital reversals related to any pressure on the EU parent banks or the unwinding of the unconventional monetary policies in the advanced economies.

Risks are on the downside

The Commonwealth of Independent States: slowdown follows tepid recovery

The post-crisis economic expansion began to moderate in 2012 and further slowed down in 2013 throughout the region.[5] The global economy continues to provide a challenging environment for these economies, characterized by weak external demand and difficulties in accessing external finance. Sluggish growth in the Russian Federation, the largest economy in the CIS, has had a dampening effect on economic activity throughout the CIS through trade, investment and remittance channels. Nevertheless, all of the CIS, especially the other energy-exporting countries, have sustained growth—except for Ukraine which flatlined in 2013. The aggregate GDP of CIS and Georgia expanded at about 2.0 per cent in 2013, a slowdown compared with the 3.4 per cent growth achieved in 2012. Economic activity is expected to strengthen modestly in 2014 with aggregate output expanding by 3.4 per cent, and to recover more solidly in 2015 with a growth rate of 4.1 per cent.

Growth slows down

In the Russian Federation, where GDP growth has already slowed to 3.4 per cent in 2012, the slowdown has been driven by weak investment growth, despite public support for infrastructure development. By contrast, consumption remained resilient as a result of a strong labour market, rapid nominal wage growth and fairly moderate inflation. In the outlook, structural problems—such as sluggish energy sector expansion, capacity constraints and weak investment—will prevent an acceleration of growth to the pre-crisis levels. Net private capital outflows persisted in 2013. In 2014, a partial freeze on tariffs of the natural monopolies may lead to a squeeze in their investment plans. While strong real wage growth supported consumption in Ukraine, the lack-lustre performance of investment resulted in stagnating domestic demand. Moreover, the country is facing a large external financing gap and may need to sign a loan agreement with the IMF in order to avert a possible balance-of-payments crisis. (In 2013, the country suffered several credit-rating downgrades). Ukraine faces high costs of external borrowing and in September the country's foreign-exchange reserves dropped to a level covering just 2.5 months of imports. The slowdown in China and the Russian Federation has led to weaker demand for steel, one of the main Ukrainian exports, and low growth rates are expected for the forecast period. In Belarus, economic growth markedly slowed, dragged down by plummeting exports as prices of

Investment drives down domestic demand in several countries

---

5   Georgia's performance is discussed in the context of this group of countries for reasons of geographic proximity and similarities in economic structure.

potash, one of the main exports of Belarus, fell on international markets. In the Caucasus, robust expansion in Azerbaijan was driven by the non-oil economy, which received a boost from continued public investment and pre-electoral fiscal stimulus. Growth slowed in Armenia and Georgia, however.

Among the countries of Central Asia, rapid growth in the oil sector boosted economic expansion in Kazakhstan despite the unresolved problems of the banking sector (non-performing loans constitute about 30 per cent of total loans and the banks are deleveraging). The Kyrgyz economy bounced back strongly from the decline driven by problems in gold production in 2012, thanks to a recovery in gold production and a strong expansion in the other sectors of the economy. Infrastructure development and rising hydrocarbons output supported growth in Turkmenistan. Despite the economic slowdown in the Russian Federation, employment dynamics have prompted large remittances benefiting the poorest countries in the region.

Unemployment falls

Despite the deceleration in growth, unemployment in most of the economies remained relatively stable or declined slightly, with the notable exception of Ukraine. In the Russian Federation in particular, the unemployment rate reached historical lows amid strong wage growth and labour shortages in some areas. By contrast, unemployment remains elevated in the low-income countries particularly in the Caucasus. Kazakhstan continued to generate new jobs for a growing, economically active population and has a relatively stable unemployment rate. Migration, predominantly to the Russian Federation, remains an important mechanism to alleviate labour market tensions in the low-income countries of the CIS.

Inflation trends diverge

Similar to 2012, inflationary trends in the CIS area diverged in 2013, with inflation rates recorded at close to double-digit figures in Central Asia and a near-zero inflation rate registered in Georgia and Ukraine. Belarus registered the highest annual inflation rate in the CIS at over 20 per cent. This followed the Government's marked increase in public sector wages and its attempt to stimulate private credit growth as the currency further depreciated. In the Russian Federation, World Trade Organization tariff reductions and increased agricultural production helped to stabilize inflation; however, it remained above the central bank's target range, thus constraining the use of monetary policy in addressing the slowing economy. A proposed freezing of prices for natural monopolies and wages for certain public sector workers could restrain inflation in 2014. In Ukraine, the possibility of a sharp exchange-rate adjustment threatens renewed inflationary pressures, but a good harvest and a sluggish economy have kept inflation down. In Kazakhstan, higher utility prices have offset the disinflationary gains resulting from declining food prices. Currency depreciation contributed to inflationary pressures in Uzbekistan. Sharp price increases in electricity and imported gas prompted the acceleration of inflation in Armenia. Lower food and oil prices and improved competitive practices have fuelled deflationary pressures in Georgia. Diverging inflation trends are expected for 2014-2015, with inflation in the Central Asian countries remaining above the CIS average.

Monetary loosening remains on hold

In the Russian Federation, inflation that is slightly over the target has prevented the central bank from loosening policy, despite the slowing economy. Amid accelerating household consumption and continued economic expansion, interest rates remained unchanged in Kazakhstan. Ukraine cut interest rates in an attempt to revive the economy, but the desire to support the exchange rate has prevented a more aggressive pace of loosening. A more flexible exchange rate would allow more room for monetary easing. However, the large share of foreign-currency denominated debt in the economy requires caution regarding possible balance sheet effects. Fears over stagnant economic growth prompted further monetary loosening in Belarus, despite fast wage increases and a depreciating currency. In

Armenia, where inflation accelerated beyond the central bank's target range, the policy rate was increased to keep rising prices in check.

In the Russian Federation, slower than anticipated growth impacted revenues and resulted in tighter spending control as the country continued to adhere to a path of fiscal prudence, despite low sovereign debt. This fiscal tightening, with a declining non-oil deficit, has been a drag on economic expansion; further budget cuts and a freeze on public sector wages is proposed for 2014. On the other hand, the Government also announced plans to spend part of the National Wealth Fund on three major transport projects in a bid to provide a stimulus to the economy. By contrast, other energy-producing countries, such as Azerbaijan and Turkmenistan, have provided a fiscal stimulus that has added to inflationary pressures. The fiscal deficit in Ukraine remained high, being compounded by the large financial gap at Naftogaz, the state oil and gas company. In Kazakhstan, continued economic expansion improved fiscal balances. In Armenia and Georgia, lower-than-planned spending has contributed to the observed deceleration of economic growth.

Fiscal prudence prevails

The energy-exporting countries of the CIS continued to register current-account surpluses. However, those surpluses continued to shrink in the Russian Federation and in Azerbaijan (figure IV.5). By contrast, there was little adjustment in the large deficits observed in the low-income energy-importing economies, which remain vulnerable to any shortfalls in raising finance. In Ukraine, falling gas imports from the Russian Federation contributed to a limited correction in the elevated current-account deficit; however, the external liquidity situation remained fragile, amid large external and fiscal deficits and very precarious access to financing, with the high cost of external debt. Current reserve levels are low relative to short-term foreign debt. In Kazakhstan, the impact of rapid oil growth on external balances has been partly offset by large dividend payments to international oil companies.

Current-account surplus in the Russian Federation shrinks further

Some improvement in the external environment will support a better economic performance in the region in 2014, but lagging reforms aimed to increase productivity and

Vulnerabilities remain

Figure IV.5
Current-account balances of the energy-exporting CIS countries

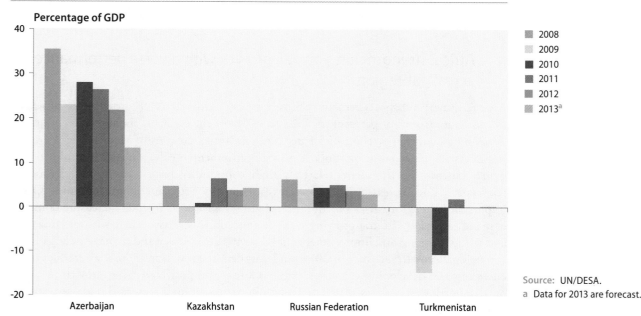

Source: UN/DESA.
a Data for 2013 are forecast.

competitiveness, and weak investment will constrain the pickup in growth in the CIS European countries. By contrast, a more solid performance is likely in energy-producing countries, with the exception of the Russian Federation, due to a sustained investment effort. With linkages to a still fragile global economy, the region would suffer if external conditions were to deteriorate. While weak linkages shelter the low-income countries in the region from global financial turbulences, the large deficits in Belarus and Ukraine make them vulnerable to any deterioration in capital market access. Lack of economic diversification exposes the region to reductions in commodity prices that result from a worsening global economy. While the Russian Federation and other energy-producing countries have some policy space to offset these negative trends, other economies have fewer resources with which to face these challenges.

Developing economies

Developing economies registered a growth of 4.6 per cent in 2013, only slightly less than 4.7 percent achieved in 2012. Among the subregions, East and South Asia and Southern Africa as well as South America showed moderate increases in their growth rates. By contrast, the most pronounced decrease in growth occurred in North Africa, due to political unrest and disruptions to oil production, as well as Mexico and the Caribbean, due to structural constraints. In the outlook, developing economies will see a steady acceleration in growth to 5.1 per cent in 2014 and 5.3 per cent in 2015. However, despite these positive headline numbers, numerous developing economies continue to face significant challenges—including high unemployment, a lack of diversification into higher-value-added production and a lack of infrastructure, especially in the energy sector. At the same time, the forecast is subject to a number of risks and uncertainties. For example, the rebound in North Africa is based on the assumption of a return to a more stable political environment. In the area of monetary policy, the looming reduction in QE by the Fed holds the potential to have major effects on capital flows and exchange rates. For many developing countries with a dominant role in the agricultural sector, adverse weather conditions pose a major risk, with potentially severe impacts in the form of higher food prices or outright food shortages.

Africa: strengthening overall growth with diverse performance across subregions

Growth will accelerate, owing to improving infrastructure, still solid commodity prices and stronger domestic demand

Africa's growth prospects remain relatively strong, with the GDP growth rate projected to accelerate from 4.0 per cent in 2013 to 4.7 per cent in 2014, slightly lower than the developing countries' average of 5.1 per cent (see annex table A.3). Medium-term growth prospects are expected to be supported by improvements in the global economic and regional business environment, relatively high commodity prices, easing infrastructural constraints, and increasing trade and investment ties with emerging economies. Other important factors for Africa's medium-term growth prospects include increasing domestic demand, especially from a growing class of new consumers associated with urbanization and rising incomes, and improvements in economic governance and management. A moderate global growth recovery in 2014, underpinned by growth in industrial production in emerging and developing countries, led by China, and projected faster growth in developed countries should also stimulate growth in Africa through increased trade, investment and capital flows.

Figure IV.6
Africa: GDP growth performance by trade structures

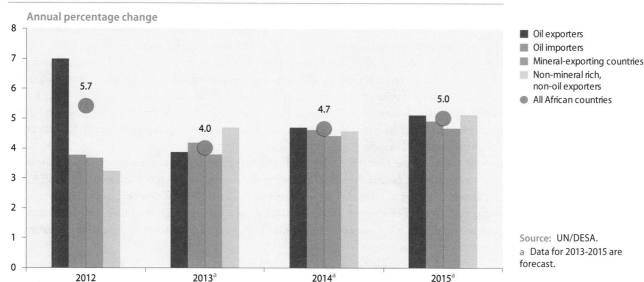

Annual percentage change

Legend:
- ■ Oil exporters
- ▥ Oil importers
- ▨ Mineral-exporting countries
- ░ Non-mineral rich, non-oil exporters
- ● All African countries

Source: UN/DESA.
a Data for 2013-2015 are forecast.

Disruptions in oil production and political unrest in parts of North and West Africa (Central African Republic, Libya and Mali) slowed growth in Africa's oil-exporting economies[6] to 3.9 per cent in 2013 (figure IV.6). Growth is expected to rise to 4.7 per cent in 2014 as some stability returns. Growth in mineral-rich economies[7] is also expected to accelerate from 3.8 per cent in 2013 to 4.4 per cent in 2014, thanks mainly to increased investments and new mineral discoveries in countries such as Sierra Leone (in iron ore and diamond production), Zambia (in copper mining), Botswana (in copper, coal and diamonds), Namibia (in uranium and diamonds), Angola (in coal mining) and Ghana and Liberia (in gold mining). Growth in Africa's non-oil and non-mineral-rich economies[8] is forecast to moderate slightly from 4.7 per cent in 2013 to 4.6 per cent in 2014, mostly driven by strong expansion in services and agriculture in countries such as Ethiopia.

At the subregional level, growth in West and East Africa is expected to increase from 6.7 per cent and 6.0 per cent in 2013 to 6.9 per cent and 6.4 per cent in 2014, respectively. Growth is also projected to increase from 2.3 per cent and 3.6 per cent in 2013 to 3.3 per cent and 4.2 per cent in 2014 in North and Southern Africa, respectively. Central Africa's growth is expected to recover moderately in 2014 to 4.7 per cent from a slight decrease to 4.2 per cent in 2013, mainly due to political instability and violence in the Central African Republic, deceleration in oil production in the Congo (Brazzaville) and Equatorial Guinea, and reduction in oil exports from Gabon.

---

6 This includes Algeria, Angola, Cameroon, Chad, the Congo, Cote d'Ivoire, Equatorial Guinea, Egypt, Gabon, Libya, Nigeria, South Sudan and Tunisia.

7 This includes Botswana, Central African Republic, Democratic Republic of the Congo, Ghana, Guinea, Mali, Mauritania, Mauritius, Mozambique, Niger, Rwanda, Sierra Leone, South Africa, United Republic of Tanzania, Zambia and Zimbabwe.

8 This includes Benin, Burundi, Burkina Faso, Cabo Verde, Comoros, Djibouti, Gambia, Guinea-Bissau, Lesotho, Liberia, Madagascar, Morocco, Senegal, Sao Tome and Principe, Somalia, Swaziland, Togo and Uganda.

West Africa will continue to attract investments in the oil and minerals sector, a key source of growth in the subregion, especially in countries such as Burkina Faso, Ghana, Guinea, Liberia, Niger, Nigeria and Sierra Leone. Real GDP growth in East Africa will benefit from several positive factors including, for example, increased consumer spending in Kenya, increased consumption and investment in the natural gas sector in Tanzania, increased activity in construction, transport, telecommunications, financial services, exploration and construction in the burgeoning oil industry in Uganda, and improved agricultural and service sector growth spearheaded by the wholesale and retail trade sector performance in Ethiopia. Growth in Kenya will also benefit from an expected rebound in 2014, after a cut in growth in 2013 in key sectors (such as tourism) due to after-effects of the Westgate Mall attacks.

Growth in the Central African subregion is expected to remain strong despite decelerating as a result of political instability and violence and an expected fall in oil production in the absence of new discoveries in the Central African Republic, where growth is projected to decline to 0.8 per cent in 2014. Gabon's growth is also expected to decelerate from 5.7 per cent in 2013 to 5.4 per cent in 2014, as the country's oil fields are maturing, leading to a decline in output.

Political instability and disruptions in oil output continue to weaken growth prospects in North Africa, especially in Egypt, Libya and Tunisia. Growth in the subregion is expected to improve from 2.3 per cent in 2013 to 3.3 per cent in 2014, contingent on the assumption that some stability returns to the affected economies. Growth prospects in Southern Africa are improving, largely because of projected increases in South Africa's growth rate from 2.7 per cent in 2013 to 3.3 per cent in 2014, declining labour market unrest, increased investments, and rising mineral output. The subregion is likely to attract increased foreign investment thanks to huge coal deposits and offshore gas discoveries in Mozambique, increased oil output in Angola, and the increased investment in the copper sector in Zambia and uranium mining in Namibia.

Africa's recent relatively robust growth is heavily driven by commodity production and exports; it remains far below the continent's potential, however. Growth is still failing to translate into meaningful job creation and the broad-based economic and social development needed to reduce the high poverty and rising inequality rates seen in many countries. It is therefore essential that African countries embark on strategies to transform their economies through increased value addition in the primary commodity sector and diversification into higher productivity sectors, especially manufacturing and modern services (box IV.2).

Inflation across Africa is expected to decelerate slightly from an average of 8.0 per cent in 2013 to 7.8 per cent in 2014. A variety of factors will contribute, including subdued global demand, moderating international food and fuel prices, and tighter monetary policy in most African countries, despite the increased investment in infrastructure (see annex table A.6). For example, in Central Africa, inflation is expected to remain low and decelerate from 3.9 per cent in 2013 to 3.3 per cent in 2014. Monetary policy in most of the countries in the region is managed by the regional central bank, Banque des Etats de l'Afrique Centrale, and will remain focused on controlling inflation and maintaining the CFA franc's peg to the euro. South Africa is expected to tighten its monetary policy in 2014 in order to control inflation and to ensure that real interest rates return to positive territory. Exchange-rate depreciation and falling foreign reserves will be major concerns for monetary policy in a number of countries—Burundi, Egypt, Kenya, Malawi, Sudan, Uganda and the United Republic of Tanzania—although the gravity of the situation varies from country

Inflationary pressure will decrease in the light of moderating changes in food and fuel prices

Box IV.2
Fostering the interface between mining and manufacturing in Africa to accelerate and sustain growth

Increasing the role of mining in Africa's economic performance

The recent strong performance of Africa's mineral sector demonstrates both the importance of mining to the continent's economic growth, and the potential for greater linkages between mining and the economy as a whole. Africa's recent commodity- and minerals-based growth has not translated into sufficient or quality job creation. With a rapidly growing working-age population, a challenge to African policymakers and mining stakeholders is to ensure that mineral endowments play a role in accelerating inclusive growth and sustainable development for the continent, particularly through the interface with manufacturing.

Estimates show that activities related to resources (excluding agriculture) accounted for 24 per cent of Africa's gross domestic product (GDP) growth over 2002-2007.[a] The importance of mineral and fuel resources is most evident in the external sector, with mining and fuel exports to the rest of the world increasing from $250 billion in 2009 to $382 billion in 2011 (figure IV.2.1), an increase from 17 per cent to 20 per cent of GDP. Hydrocarbon and metals exports account for more than half of exports in 14 African countries, which together make up 39 per cent of the continent's population.[b] In 2011, mining exports represented a significant proportion of GDP in a variety of selected mineral-rich African countries (table IV.2.1).

Figure IV.2.1
African exports by commodity, 2009-2011

Billions of United States dollars

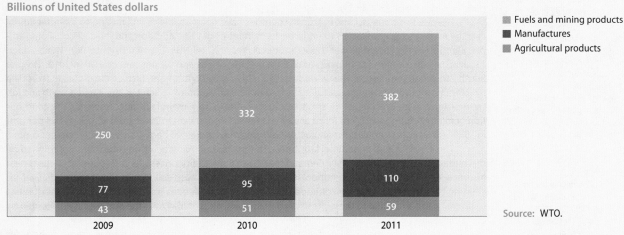

Legend:
- Fuels and mining products
- Manufactures
- Agricultural products

Source: WTO.

Table IV.2.1
Share of mining sector in GDP for selected African countries, 2011

| | Percentage | | Percentage |
Country	Share	Country	Share
Botswana	2.8	Niger	11.1
Gabon	1.3	South Africa	7.4
Guinea	17.6	United Republic of Tanzania	4.5
Mauritania	43.6	Zambia	36.5
Morocco	2.8	Zimbabwe	13.1
Mozambique	14.3		

Box IV.2
Fostering the interface between mining and manufacturing in Africa to accelerate and sustain growth (*continued*)

a Charles Roxburgh and others, "Lions on the move: The progress and potential of African economies", McKinsey Global Institute Report, June 2010.

b Emerging Markets Forum, "Africa 2050: Realizing the Continent's Full Potential".

c *Economic Report on Africa 2013: Making the Most of Africa's Commodities: Industrializing for Growth, Jobs and Economic Transformation* (United Nations publication, Sales No. E.13.II.K.1).

d Ibid.

e See "Africa continues to grow strongly despite global slowdown, although significantly less poverty remains elusive", World Bank press release, 15 April 2013.

f See *Africa's Pulse*, vol. 6 (October 2012).

g See presentation by Jorge Maia on "The interface between mining and manufacturing in South Africa: the context" held at the Industrial Development Corporation in South Africa on 22 August 2013, available from http://www.idc.co.za/interface.

h OECD, "Export restrictions on raw materials: experience with alternative policies in Botswana", Working Paper TAD/TC/WP(2013)17, September 2013.

i *Economic Report on Africa 2013*, op. cit.

j See, *Economic Development in Africa Report 2011: Fostering Industrial Development in Africa in the New Global Environment* (United Nations publication, Sales No. E.11.II.D.14).

Source: UNECA.

Africa's mining outlook is strong despite falling metals prices, which are expected to pick up modestly over the outlook period, owing to continued demand from developing countries. There is significant untapped potential as well, adding to the positive outlook. Africa is home to 40 per cent of global gold reserves and 80-90 per cent of chromium and platinum group metal reserves.[c] Gold production is robust, due to South Africa's dominant role in global gold output; also, output in West Africa, which accounted for 8 per cent of global gold output as of 2011, is increasing, with Ghana the strongest performer.[d] Recent discoveries of titanium and rare earths in Kenya, lead, copper and zinc in Ghana, and upgraded mining in Mozambique, Niger, Sierra Leone and Zambia[e] are among the developments that underpin the positive outlook of mining and overall growth in Africa. While in 2010 only one third of countries had mineral rents accounting for more than 5 per cent of GDP, increasing mineral discoveries such as these have raised expectations that by 2020 nearly all African countries will be involved in mineral extraction.[f]

The need for an enhanced interface between mining and manufacturing

As demonstrated in South Africa in 2012, policies that support a conducive business environment for mineral-based value addition can lead to large income and employment multipliers in both mining and manufacturing. For example, mining's direct impact of 267 billion rand and 524,000 jobs turned into an overall economy-wide impact of 536.1 billion rand and 1.35 million jobs.[g] In the case of Botswana, an economic diversification strategy and local content policies that focus on diamond beneficiation provided the framework for the country to create jobs and reach upper-middle-income status; diamond cutting and polishing employ more than 3,000 workers directly.[h]

Despite this potential, most African countries have been unable to link mining to manufacturing, and the mining sector continues to underperform in terms of value addition and job creation. For example, Zambia is a significant global copper producer. Yet, this industry, characterized by non-value-added exports, only accounted for 10 per cent of formal employment and 9.9 per cent of GDP in 2010.[i] Despite South Africa holding most of the world's manganese, it only controls one fifth of the global market. The development of a healthy manufacturing base is vital for an economy to achieve sustained growth and job creation, and there is evidence for strong multiplier effects from manufacturing. However, the contribution of manufacturing to GDP in Africa as a whole fell to 10.5 per cent in 2008, from a peak of 15.3 per cent in 1990.[j] Africa's share of global manufacturing exports has remained negligible at below two per cent.

The need for a stronger interface between mining and manufacturing is further underpinned by the outlook for global commodity demand. Although commodity prices are anticipated to remain near historical highs, the flat growth outlook will adversely affect those economies that depend on ever-increasing revenues from primary commodity extraction. If Africa does not capitalize on its opportunities to diversify and add value to these presently lucrative activities, it may miss the opportunity presented by the commodities boom.

In order to enhance the interface between mining and manufacturing, transformative policies for creating development linkages must be institutionalized in national development visions and continental plans in order to ensure a broad-based approach. Upstream and downstream activities should be geared towards both domestic production (for job and income creation and economy-wide knock-on effects) and to exports (to garner foreign-exchange earnings). Knowledge networks, innovation and entrepreneurship are vital for development of linkages and must be promoted, particularly since value-addition requires more complex processes to transform raw materials. As envisaged by the African Union and Economic Commission for Africa's African Mining Vision, now is the time to transform Africa's economies by capitalizing on high demand and investment, and enhancing linkages between mining and manufacturing.

to country. Loose monetary policy, high fiscal deficits, domestic currency depreciation and relatively high energy costs are among the factors that are expected to strengthen inflationary pressure in 2014 in some of the countries in East and Southern Africa. Efforts to rein in rising costs for subsidies, particularly fuel subsidies, in North Africa will put some upward pressure on inflation.

Africa's average fiscal deficit increased from 1.35 per cent in 2012 to 1.80 per cent of GDP in 2013. This is caused in part by there being a number of Governments across the continent under continuous pressure to increase spending on public services like education, health and infrastructure, and to increase wages in the public sector and provide subsidies on food and fuel. However, this deterioration was largely due to lagging revenues in oil-importing countries. Oil-exporting and mineral-rich countries recorded fiscal surpluses of 4.72 per cent and 4.97 per cent, respectively, in 2013. The fiscal outlook is brighter for the region's large economies of Equatorial Guinea, Ghana, Kenya, Morocco, Nigeria and South Africa, as considerable improvements are expected in their respective fiscal balances in 2014. Among these countries, Angola, Equatorial Guinea and Gabon continue experiencing relatively large fiscal surpluses, thanks to sustained increases in oil production and exports. Other countries, such as Egypt and Morocco, have taken steps this year to address significantly rising deficits created by the rising costs of subsidies.

Africa's overall current-account deficit is expected to slightly decline from 1.8 per cent of GDP in 2013 to 1.7 per cent in 2014. External balances will remain positive, despite deceleration, in oil-exporting African countries, but will be negative and improving in oil-importing countries, mineral-rich countries, and non-mineral-non-oil-rich countries.

Africa's total exports are expected to decline in 2014 to 29.6 per cent of GDP from 30.9 per cent in 2013, mainly due to the weakening global commodity markets, although oil and other commodity exports will continue to dominate. At a subregional level, exports are expected to decline in all the regions except East Africa, where exports will slightly increase from 15.5 per cent of GDP in 2013 to 15.7 per cent in 2014. This increase can be accounted for by a rise in non-traditional exports, such as floriculture and trade in services, especially in Ethiopia, Kenya and the United Republic of Tanzania. Along with exports, total imports are expected to decline as a percentage of GDP across all subregions, with the largest decline occurring in Southern Africa, from 29.5 per cent of GDP in 2013 to 27.3 per cent of GDP in 2014. This significant drop in imports is associated with an expected decline in Botswana, South Africa and Zambia, some of the regions' larger economies.

Despite the positive growth picture for many countries, the employment situation remains a major problem across the region, both in terms of the level of employment as well as the quality of jobs that are generated, especially in North Africa (see annex table A.8). High youth unemployment remains a concern for the region and continues to contribute to social pressures. Wide gender disparities in employment and earnings are also a significant issue. Women face unemployment rates at least double that of men in countries such as Algeria and Egypt. With the labour force growing at a rapid pace, the solid rates of GDP growth have proven far from sufficient to absorb all new labour market entrants, given the current pattern of production and employment generation. The lack of economic diversification away from the heavy dependence on resource extraction or agriculture is a key reason why labour demand is not more dynamic, but continued growth in other sectors such as telecommunications, financial services, transport and construction in countries such as Ghana, Kenya and Nigeria is helping to change this situation.

Despite the expected robust medium-term growth prospects, some significant internal and external downside risks and uncertainties exist in the region. On the external front, a global economic slowdown encompassing the euro area and the emerging economies would have a significant negative impact on Africa's performance through the impact on trade, FDI and ODA flows, tourism, and remittances to the region. Changes in global commodity prices and terms of trade are among the key risk factors Africa will face in the medium-term.

Budget balances will deteriorate in oil-importing countries

The overall current-account deficit will decline slightly

Unemployment continues to be a pressing issue

Downside risks and uncertainties include a global economic slowdown, lower commodity prices, political instability and adverse weather conditions

Declining global oil prices, while having a significantly positive impact on current-account balances in oil-importing countries, are expected to further reduce current-account surpluses in oil-exporting countries, exerting pressure on their fiscal balances as their export revenues decline. Political, civil and labour unrest still pose a significant threat to production in several African countries (such as Central African Republic, the Congo, Democratic Republic of the Congo, Egypt, Libya, Mali, Somalia, South Africa and Tunisia), especially through their negative effects on investment, trade and tourism. Developments in these countries continue to pose a significant downside risk to Africa's overall economic outlook. Furthermore, since most of the economies in the region are agriculture-based, weather-related shocks represent a key downside risk for economic growth and a key upside risk for agricultural prices in Africa.

East Asia: growth projected to pick up slightly

After slowing markedly in 2011 and 2012, economic growth in East Asia has stabilized over the past year. While East Asia remained the fastest-growing region in the world in 2013, economic activity was adversely affected by continued sluggish external demand in developed economies and an adjustment to lower growth in China. In addition, domestic demand weakened in several of the region's economies, including Indonesia, Malaysia and Thailand. Average GDP growth in the region stood at 6.0 per cent in 2013, slightly up from 5.9 per cent in 2012. A further mild pickup in regional growth to 6.1 per cent is projected for 2014 and 2015, mainly driven by a gradual recovery in exports amid improving conditions in developed countries. In most East Asian economies, private consumption and investment will continue to expand robustly, supported by stable labour market conditions, low inflation and fairly accommodative monetary policies. Fiscal policies will remain moderately expansionary, providing support for growth.

Consumption demand remains a main driver of growth; mild recovery in exports is expected

Slow export growth persisted across East Asia in 2013 as demand in its major trading partners—particularly Europe and the United States—remained sluggish. In most economies, net exports did not contribute significantly to overall growth (figure IV.7). Household consumption remained the main growth driver, whereas the contribution from investment declined moderately. While no significant change to this growth pattern is expected in 2014 and 2015, a gradual pickup in external demand is likely to provide some support.

After weakening in the first half of 2013, China's economy gained momentum in the second half, driven by stronger domestic demand. Investment was supported by minor fiscal stimulus measures, including tax breaks for small businesses and accelerated construction spending. Full-year growth in China is estimated at 7.7 per cent in 2013, the same pace as 2012. Looking ahead, a further gradual slowdown to 7.5 per cent in 2014 and 7.3 per cent in 2015 is projected, in line with the Government's objective of a more sustainable growth path.

The high-income and strong export-oriented economies of Hong Kong Special Administrative Region of China, the Republic of Korea, Singapore and Taiwan Province of China saw a moderate recovery over the past year, which is expected to continue in 2014 and 2015. However, the strength of this recovery depends heavily on global conditions as well as specific domestic factors. Household debt, for example, has steadily increased since the global financial crisis and could weigh on growth if monetary conditions are tightened.

After a strong performance in 2012, growth in Indonesia, Malaysia and Thailand decelerated markedly in 2013, mainly owing to a moderation in consumption and invest-

Figure IV.7
Contributions to growth by demand component in selected East Asian countries, 2013

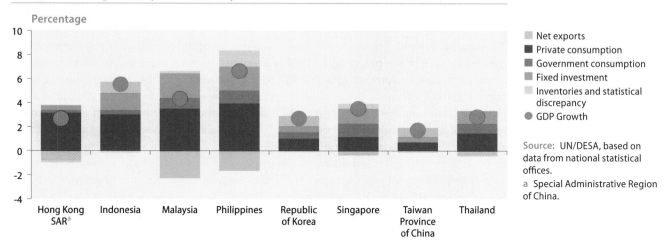

Percentage

Legend:
- Net exports
- Private consumption
- Government consumption
- Fixed investment
- Inventories and statistical discrepancy
- ● GDP Growth

Source: UN/DESA, based on data from national statistical offices.
a Special Administrative Region of China.

ment demand. Stronger exports should support a mild pickup in growth in Malaysia and Thailand in 2014. In Indonesia, growth is forecast to weaken slightly further in 2014 as lower commodity prices and the recent monetary tightening—introduced in response to rising inflation, a widening current-account deficit and large capital outflows—weigh on economic activity. The economy of the Philippines continued to expand at a robust pace of close to 7 per cent over the past year, driven by strong consumption and a boom in construction. In November 2013, the country was hit by a severe storm and flooding, which caused many deaths and widespread destruction. In economic terms, the effect is a small reduction in growth in 2013, with reconstruction possibly adding to growth in 2014.

East Asia's labour markets have remained broadly stable in 2013. Unemployment rates are generally low, although considerable differences between and within countries exist. In the high-income economies, unemployment rates range from about 2.0 per cent in Singapore to 4.2 per cent in Taiwan Province of China. In the Republic of Korea, the unemployment rate declined to 2.7 per cent in September 2013, down from 2.9 per cent in 2012, mainly owing to expansion in service sectors. Over the same period, however, the jobless rate for those aged 25 to 29 increased from 6.7 per cent to 7.7 per cent. Official unemployment rates are also relatively low in China, Malaysia, Thailand and Viet Nam. In China, the unemployment rate for urban registered workers declined marginally to 4.04 per cent in September 2013. Conversely, translating economic growth into employment opportunities remains a significant challenge in the Philippines. Despite growth of 7.6 per cent in the first half of 2013, the unemployment rate rose to 7.3 per cent in July as the economy failed to create sufficient full-time jobs to accommodate the rapidly growing labour force. In Indonesia, the positive trend of the past few years continued in early 2013, supported by employment growth in manufacturing, construction and services. However, after dropping to 5.9 per cent in the first quarter of 2013, the unemployment rate rose to 6.3 per cent in the third quarter amid slowing economic growth and increased labour supply. In 2014 and 2015, unemployment rates across East Asia are expected to remain fairly stable, given the expected moderate growth in most countries. A pressing concern, particularly in some South-East Asian countries, is continuing widespread informal employment, which tends to suffer from low wages, weak productivity, and lack of benefits and job security.

Labour markets have remained broadly stable

Consumer price inflation continues to be mild

Consumer and producer price inflation is generally mild across East Asia, owing to reduced pressure from international commodity prices. Food prices remained fairly stable in 2013, thanks to favourable weather conditions and robust agricultural production. Average consumer price inflation is projected at 2.5 per cent in 2013, slightly down from 2.8 per cent in 2012. In most countries, inflationary pressures will likely remain muted as commodity prices are projected to further ease. In line with a gradual pickup in growth, average inflation is forecast to accelerate to 3.1 per cent in 2014, ranging from 1.8 per cent in Taiwan Province of China to 7.1 per cent in Viet Nam. In China, consumer price inflation stands at about 3 per cent and producer prices remained in deflationary territory in 2013, despite persistent increase in both food prices (particularly pork and vegetables) and private-sector wages. Falling commodity prices, significant overcapacities and weakening domestic demand put downward pressure on prices in China. Conversely, inflation accelerated sharply in Indonesia in the third quarter of 2013 after the Government hiked the administered prices of gasoline and diesel significantly. The sharp depreciation of the rupiah since June further spurred inflation, which is estimated to average about 7 per cent in 2013, before easing slightly in 2014 and 2015. Malaysia's Government also reduced fuel subsidies, but the impact on overall prices was more limited, with year-on-year inflation projected at about 3 per cent in late 2013.

Monetary policy remains fairly accommodative; some tightening is expected in 2014-2015

Monetary policy remains generally supportive of economic growth across East Asia, in line with low inflation and subdued external demand. Several central banks (including those of Papua New Guinea, the Republic of Korea, Thailand and Viet Nam) reduced their policy interest rates during the first half of 2013 in response to decelerating domestic demand and lower inflationary pressures. Further easing is, however, unlikely, and some central banks may tighten monetary conditions in 2014, provided that growth picks up and the Fed tapers its large-scale asset purchase programme. The Bank of Indonesia already hiked interest rates four times by a total of 175 basis points between June and November 2013, while also strengthening macroprudential measures. These policies were implemented to control inflation, maintain financial stability, halt the depreciation of the rupiah and reduce the current-account deficit. Financial stability has also gained increased attention in other East Asian economies. The People's Bank of China (PBC) responded to a temporary liquidity squeeze in June by providing additional liquidity to financial institutions that faced funding shortages and complied with macroprudential requirements. Going forward, the PBC will likely maintain its focus on adjusting liquidity in the banking system and ensuring steady credit growth. Continued financial reform, especially further liberalization of interest rates, and increased regulation of the shadow banking sector will have a significant impact on the liquidity conditions in the economy. In addition to national measures, East Asian countries are also increasingly looking to regional monetary and financial cooperation, such as the extension of bilateral swap arrangements, in response to financial market volatility.

Fiscal policy remains supportive of growth

Fiscal policy has continued to support growth across East Asia as many Governments are trying to counter the slowdown in domestic demand. The Chinese Government implemented several targeted measures, including scrapping taxes for small firms and boosting investment in infrastructure and railways. The Government in the Republic of Korea passed a supplementary budget in May 2013, which includes expenditure on public-sector jobs, business start-ups, mortgage subsidies and trade financing for small exporters. Malaysia, the Philippines and Thailand are pushing for large infrastructure projects, although delays in implementation have so far limited their impact. These expansionary fiscal policies, combined with costly subsidy schemes in some countries, have led to a slight dete-

Box IV.3

Social welfare programmes to promote inclusive development in the Asia-Pacific region

Despite rapid growth and a steady decline in extreme poverty, a large number of countries in the Asia-Pacific region are experiencing greater levels of economic and social inequality. However, since the beginning of the Great Recession, the region has unveiled several economic and social policy measures aimed at boosting domestic consumption and aggregate demand, while also reducing inequality.

The 2013 ESCAP survey[a] cautioned that if the current economic growth slowdown continues, the region would face stalled progress towards reaching the Millennium Development Goals (MDGs).[b] Faced with a new normal of lower growth, several countries in the region have initiated targeted social welfare enhancing policies and programmes to promote inclusive economic growth and sustainable development. For instance, the region has witnessed initiatives of welfare programmes addressing health in Indonesia, food security in India, employment in the Republic of Korea and Thailand, and more generally, economic and social development in China.

By implementing the universal health care coverage plan on 1 January 2014, Indonesia has embarked on a road map that seeks to provide access to health care for the entire population by 2019. This will be important in targeting poor segments of the society. Similarly, India's National Food Security Act, 2013, an attempt to ensure food and nutritional security, is expected to provide an entitlement of food grains at highly subsidized prices to about two thirds of the population. The Republic of Korea has implemented several new employment and labour market policies in 2013 as part of its employment-for-all agenda. These policies seek to improve the quality of jobs by setting up institutions for upgrading skills, knowledge and training programmes, especially for young people, and to enhance labour productivity and wage stability. China is implementing a national development policy agenda to boost social welfare programmes that will improve levels of social security benefits. This agenda is expected to stimulate economic transformation by promoting a targeted emphasis on productive employment generation. Thailand further increased the minimum national wage in January 2013 to 300 Thai baht (about 10 dollars) per day. This increase is expected to help reduce inequalities by increasing the incomes of low-wage workers.

These policies and measures constitute an important step towards a more inclusive development model, which ensures that the benefits of rapid growth are shared more equitably than in the past.

a See *Economic and Social Survey of Asia and the Pacific 2013: Forward-looking Macroeconomic Policies for Inclusive and Sustainable Development* (United Nations publication, Sales No. E.13.II.F.2).

b Asian Development Bank, United Nations Economic and Social Commission for Asia and the Pacific and United Nations Development Programme, "Asia-Pacific Aspirations: Perspectives for a Post-2015 Development Agenda", Bangkok, August 2013.

Source: UN/ESCAP.

rioration of fiscal positions in 2013. In most economies (except Malaysia and Viet Nam) budget deficits and government debt levels as a share of GDP are still low. However, debt levels of local governments and state-owned enterprises, which are generally not recorded in government balance sheets, have been rising rapidly in some cases, most notably in China. Accordingly, total debt might exceed official government statistics and vulnerability to international monetary conditions is probably higher. In 2014 and 2015, fiscal balances are likely to improve slightly in most economies, given fairly robust growth expectations. In Indonesia and Malaysia, a gradual reduction of fuel subsidies will help narrow the budget shortfall. Several Governments (for example those in Malaysia and the Republic of Korea) have also developed tax reform plans with a view to widening the tax base and diversifying the revenue sources.

East Asia's trade and current-account surpluses have narrowed since the global financial crisis. In 2013, the region's combined current-account surplus stood at about 3 per cent of GDP, compared with a high of 8.3 per cent in 2007. This significant decline can be attributed to the protracted weak demand in developed economies and the robust growth in consumption and investment demand across East Asia during the initial recovery from the crisis. In 2013, East Asia's exports and imports grew slowly, in line with the subdued conditions in the key destination markets, notably Europe and the United States, and the less dynamic expansion in the region. Looking ahead, trade growth is projected to recover mildly in 2014 and 2015, but will remain well below the pre-crisis level. In some economies,

Exports and imports projected to pick up mildly in 2014

such as Indonesia and Malaysia, export sectors may benefit in the short run from the recent depreciation of the national currencies. Current-account balances as a share of GDP are expected to remain relatively stable in most countries. China's current-account surplus is forecast to further narrow gradually from about 2.0 per cent in 2013 to 1.6 per cent in 2014 and 1.2 per cent in 2015. This can be attributed to a steady decline in the trade surplus and a widening service balance deficit.

Significant capital flow and exchange rate volatility were widespread in the region in 2013

Many East Asian economies experienced significant capital flow and exchange-rate volatility in 2013—particularly in the middle of the year, when fears among investors of reduced global liquidity led to massive capital outflows and a sharp depreciation of some national currencies against the dollar. Between May and September 2013, the Indonesian rupiah depreciated by about 17 per cent, the Malaysian ringgit by 7 per cent, and the Philippine peso and Thai baht by about 5 per cent against the dollar. In September, the decision by the Fed to delay the tapering of its asset-purchasing programme temporarily eased the pressures on the region's capital markets, but significant risks of further financial turbulence remains.

Fed tapering and sharper-than-expected slowdown in China pose considerable downside risks

In some cases, renewed strong capital outflows may add pressure on central banks to raise domestic interest rates, thereby dampening economic growth. Tighter liquidity conditions and higher global and regional interest rates could pose considerable challenges, particularly for countries with high levels of household debt, such as Malaysia, the Republic of Korea and Thailand. At the regional level, a sharper-than-expected slowdown in China could severely impact growth across East Asia.

South Asia: lack-lustre growth in 2013, but gradual recovery projected

Economic growth in South Asia remained lack-lustre in 2013 as a combination of internal and external factors hampered activity, particularly in the region's large economies (India, the Islamic Republic of Iran and Pakistan). The region's total gross domestic product grew by 3.9 per cent in 2013, after increasing by 4.2 per cent in 2012, the slowest pace in almost two decades. Growth is forecast to pick up gradually to 4.6 per cent in 2014 and 5.1 per cent in 2015, supported by stronger external demand, a mild recovery in domestic demand in India and improved economic conditions in the Islamic Republic of Iran. The region's economic performance will greatly depend on the progress in tackling growth bottlenecks—such as energy and transport constraints and volatile security conditions—and macroeconomic imbalances. The room for monetary and fiscal policies to stimulate domestic demand is limited by elevated inflation, large fiscal and current-account deficits, and volatile global financial conditions.

India's economic woes continued in 2013

South Asia's subdued growth performance masks significant differences between individual countries. India's economy, which accounts for over 70 per cent of total output in South Asia, slowed further in 2013, held back by weak household consumption and sluggish investment. Full-year growth decelerated from 5.1 per cent in the calendar year 2012 to 4.8 per cent in 2013. External conditions continued to be challenging as the economy experienced significant capital outflows, particularly between June and August 2013. These outflows, which led to a sharp depreciation of the rupee, were triggered by expectations of an upcoming tapering of the Fed bond-buying programme, combined with concerns over India's large current-account deficit. While India's slowdown may have bottomed out, the recovery is likely to be slower than previously expected. Economic activity is forecast to expand by 5.3 per cent in 2014 and 5.7 per cent in 2015. This gradual pickup in GDP growth is likely to be supported by a good monsoon season, a mild recovery in investment, and stronger export growth on the back of improved global conditions and a weaker rupee. The Islamic Republic of Iran continues to face severe international sanctions, which have led to a sharp drop in oil exports and serious supply shortages. As a result, economic activity contracted further in 2013. The economy is expected to emerge from recession in 2014, with the possibility of a more pronounced recovery should the sanctions be gradually lifted. Nepal and Pakistan also continue to face significant macroeconomic challenges and subpar growth as political uncertainty, volatile security conditions and severe supply-side bottlenecks hamper household consumption and investment. In Pakistan, the newly elected Government finalized a loan agreement with the IMF in the third quarter of 2013 that aims at stabilizing macroeconomic conditions and solving the balance-of-payments problems; the programme comes with several conditions attached. Increased fiscal consolidation efforts and monetary tightening by the State Bank of Pakistan may weigh on activity in the short run, but some improvement is expected for 2015. The current economic situation and the outlook are more favourable in Bangladesh, where growth has remained fairly robust at about 6 per cent, and in Sri Lanka, the region's fastest growing economy in recent years. In both countries, household consumption will remain the main driver of growth, fuelled by rising incomes and remittance inflows.

Recent employment surveys in South Asian countries suggest that the economic slowdown has taken its toll on the region's labour markets. The latest figures for India, the Islamic Republic of Iran and Pakistan indicate that unemployment increased in the past year and the labour force participation declined slightly. According to India's Employment-Unemployment Survey, the average unemployment rate rose from 3.8 per cent in the fiscal year 2011/12 to 4.7 per cent in 2012/13, with large differences by region, gender and age group. Unemployment is estimated to be higher among women (7.2 per cent) than men (4.0 per cent), higher in urban areas (5.7 per cent) than rural areas (4.4 per cent) and much higher for the age group 15-29 (13.3 per cent) than for those 30 and above (1.0 per cent). Similar unemployment patterns prevail in other South Asian countries. In Pakistan, the structural weakness of the economy seems to have exacerbated the employment gaps. In the second quarter of 2013, an estimated 18.7 per cent of women living in urban areas were unemployed compared to only 6.3 per cent of men. Moreover, the female labour force participation rate in urban areas was only 7.3 per cent, down from 8.4 per cent two years earlier. However, available unemployment data only provide a partial picture of the actual situation as the majority of South Asian workers are employed in the informal sector. The share of vulnerable employment (defined as unpaid family workers and own-account workers) in total employment is estimated to range from about 40 per cent in the Islamic Republic of Iran and Sri Lanka to about 60 per cent in Pakistan and 80 per cent in Bangladesh and India. Given that economic growth in South Asia is expected to remain below potential and the labour force will increase rapidly, the labour market pressures are likely to further intensify in the years ahead.

In most South Asian countries, consumer price inflation moderated slightly over the past year as aggregate demand pressures declined and international commodity prices eased. Inflation remains, however, significantly higher than in other world regions and, in most cases, well above the respective central bank's comfort zone. The continued strong upward pressures on prices can be attributed to several factors, including persistent supply bottlenecks, entrenched inflationary expectations, ongoing weakness of local currencies (particularly in India, the Islamic Republic of Iran and Pakistan), and the attempts by several Governments (India and Pakistan, for example) to reduce their food and fuel sub-

The economic slowdown has taken its toll on labour markets

Inflation trends diverge across South Asia

sidy bills. Because of a surge in inflation in the Islamic Republic of Iran, average annual consumer price inflation in South Asia increased from 12.5 per cent in 2012 to an estimated 13.9 per cent in 2013. A gradual moderation to 11.3 per cent in 2014 and 9.4 per cent in 2015 is forecast. In the Islamic Republic of Iran, severe supply shortages and a sharp devaluation of the rial pushed consumer price inflation sharply up to about 40 per cent in 2013. Inflation is projected to decelerate slowly in 2014 and 2015, but an easing of the sanctions could lead to a more rapid decline. In India, consumer price inflation has remained stubbornly high at close to 10 per cent, even as domestic demand weakened further. By contrast, inflation slowed moderately in Bangladesh, Nepal, Pakistan and Sri Lanka during 2013, with full-year averages ranging from 7 per cent to 9 per cent. While the baseline scenario foresees a gradual decline in inflation across South Asia in 2014 and 2015, upside risks remain. Those include poor harvests, further depreciation of national currencies, and pressures stemming from significant subsidy reductions (particularly in India, Pakistan and Sri Lanka).

Monetary policy focus in India and Pakistan has shifted towards lowering inflation

Recent monetary policy actions in South Asia reflect the considerable differences in macroeconomic conditions between countries. On the one hand, the monetary authorities in India and Pakistan recently hiked their benchmark interest rates. In doing so, they have shifted the policy focus towards lowering inflation and easing external pressures amid volatile global financial conditions. The Reserve Bank of India (RBI) raised its main policy rate by 50 basis points, although GDP growth hit a multi-year low in 2013. This marks a turnaround from the first half of the year, when policy rates were cut three times. The RBI also recently rolled back the exceptional liquidity tightening measures introduced in July and August 2013 in response to the massive capital outflows and the sharp drop in the value of the rupee. While the RBI is expected to maintain its focus on inflation, it is unlikely to raise policy rates considerably given the ongoing weakness in investment and growth. Should inflationary pressures ease in 2014 and the external financial environment stabilize, the RBI is likely to loosen monetary conditions. The State Bank of Pakistan also changed course in the second half of 2013, raising its benchmark interest rates in September and November. The path of Pakistan's monetary policy in the quarters ahead will be mainly determined by the trend in inflation, which has recently accelerated again. The central banks in Bangladesh and Sri Lanka, by contrast, have maintained their accommodative monetary policy stances as consumer price inflation moderated and exchange rates were fairly stable. In both countries, monetary conditions are expected to remain unchanged over the next few quarters, with the possibility of some tightening later in the forecast period.

Economic slowdown puts further strains on government finances

The current economic slowdown in South Asia put further pressure on government finances, which were already strained by very low tax bases and rising expenditure needs as the authorities confront many development challenges. In recent years, the Governments regularly missed their deficit-reduction targets by a wide margin. Growth projections proved too optimistic and expenditures on food, fuel and fertilizer subsidies were significantly higher than anticipated. In the past fiscal year, the budget deficit reached nearly 5.0 per cent of GDP in Bangladesh, India and the Islamic Republic of Iran, 6.7 per cent in Sri Lanka and 8.0 per cent in Pakistan. Given the weak growth momentum in the region and the difficulties in raising tax revenues and curbing expenditure growth, fiscal deficits will remain substantial in the near term. In India, the Government is unlikely to meet its target of reducing the deficit to 4.8 per cent of GDP in the current fiscal year 2013/14, since growth is below projections and the depreciation of the rupee pushes up the subsidy bill. In Pakistan, the new agreement between the Government and the IMF includes a strong commitment to consolidate public finances. The programme envisages a gradual decline in the deficit from about 8.0 per cent of GDP in 2012/13 to 5.8 per cent in 2013/14 and 3.5 per cent in 2015/16.

South Asia's merchandise exports continue to be affected by relatively weak demand in key destination markets, including the EU and the United States. However, several countries, notably Bangladesh and India, saw external demand improve significantly in the course of 2013. This positive trend is likely to persist in the quarters ahead as demand in developed economies strengthens. In addition, the export industries in India, Pakistan and Sri Lanka may benefit from the recent depreciation of national currencies, which lost significant value against the dollar in mid-2013 (figure IV.8). In Bangladesh, garment exports rose rapidly in the second and third quarter of 2013, even as the domestic currency appreciated gradually against the dollar and several deadly industrial accidents exacerbated international concerns over workers' rights. Exports from the Islamic Republic of Iran, by contrast, contracted further over the past year owing to the ongoing international sanctions. South Asia's imports have been weighed down by slowing domestic demand, depreciating national currencies and lower international commodity prices. Accordingly, trade and current-account balances as a percentage of GDP improved in 2013, especially in India. Workers' remittance inflows have continued to grow strongly in most economies, providing support for household consumption and current-account balances.

Downside risks to the economic outlook for South Asia are related to a likely tightening in global liquidity conditions and to regional or domestic vulnerabilities. The tapering of QE by the Fed could lead to renewed turbulence in financial markets and significant capital outflows, particularly for India. This, in turn, could require monetary tightening and emergency measures that would weigh on economic growth. Protracted sluggish growth in India would likely have a negative impact on some of its neighbour countries. On the domestic front, higher consumer price inflation, resulting, for example, from subsidy cuts and weaker currencies, could constrain household spending and limit room for monetary policy easing.

Moderate improvement in export performance projected

Tighter global liquidity could prove challenging, particularly for India

Figure IV.8
Daily exchange rates in selected South Asian countries, 3 January 2012-1 November 2013

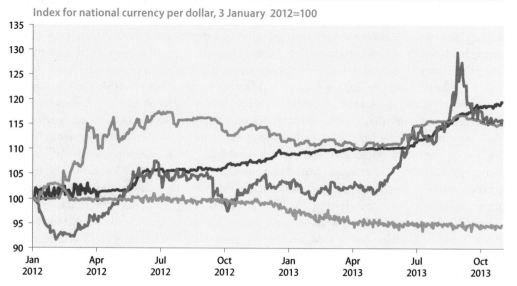

Index for national currency per dollar, 3 January 2012=100

Legend:
— Bangladesh
— India
— Pakistan
— Sri Lanka

Sources: For India and Sri Lanka: the United States Federal Reserve System; for Pakistan: ForexTicket, available from http://www.forexticket.co.uk/en/histo/USD-PKR; for Bangladesh: Investing, available from http://www.investing.com/currencies/usd-bdt-historical-data.

Note: Upward movement indicates depreciation of the currency against the dollar.

Western Asia: solid growth overall despite the fallout from military conflicts

Western Asia has seen slightly slower aggregate growth of 3.6 per cent in 2013 than in 2012, projected to accelerate to 4.3 per cent in 2014, but moderating to 3.9 per cent in 2015 (figure IV.9). However, Arab countries in Western Asia (Western Asia excluding Israel and Turkey) exhibited further divergence in their economic performances. While the member countries of the Gulf Cooperation Council (GCC), namely Bahrain, Kuwait, Oman, Qatar, Saudi Arabia and the United Arab Emirates, have been on a stable recovery path, the economies of Iraq, Jordan, Lebanon, Syrian Arab Republic and Yemen have been hampered by continuing political instability, social unrest, security incidents and geopolitical tensions. For example, the Syrian crisis has led to a severe refugee crisis across the subregion, leading to population increases of 25 per cent in Lebanon and 15 per cent in Jordan. Growth in GCC member countries is expected to have tapered off in 2013 mainly owing to the moderate decline in oil export revenues, which marked a historical high in 2012. Non-oil sectors, particularly the real estate sector, regained their strength, partly owing to active fiscal policy in the subregion. Iraq's growth is also expected to decline moderately in line with its oil export revenues, while growth in Jordan, Lebanon and Yemen remains relatively weak, ranging from 1.3 per cent to 4.8 per cent during 2013-2014.

In Turkey, financial markets have been under pressure since May 2013, with the currency depreciating and interbank interest rates rising as a result of a reversal in international capital inflows. This was triggered by the anticipated tapering in global liquidity, as well as concerns about the large public debt and the current-account deficit in the country. The devaluation of the currency has in turn added to inflation pressures, with CPI inflation running at about 8 per cent. These unfavourable factors are expected to weigh on real economic growth in the near term. GDP is estimated to grow by 3.2 per cent in 2013 and by 5.0 per cent in 2014, before decelerating to 3.0 per cent in 2015. The GDP of Israel is estimated to grow at a pace of 3.2 per cent in 2013, driven mainly by consumer demand and net exports. In the outlook, GDP is forecast to grow by 2.2 per cent in 2014 and 3.3 per cent in 2015.

High unemployment remains a major policy challenge in many countries in Western Asia

The GCC countries have seen a recovery in employment in line with the consistent growth of non-oil sectors, while employment creation was subdued in other economies in the region. However, the issue of employment has remained one of the region's most important policy challenges, including in GCC countries, given high chronic unemployment among nationals. Several GCC countries, most notably Saudi Arabia, shifted to a more stringent labour nationalization policy, rigorously promoting employment of nationals in the private sector where the labour force consists mostly of foreign expatriates. Since March 2013, the Saudi Government has encouraged foreign expatriates to rectify their sponsorship status or to voluntarily leave the country. A significant number of foreign workers have left Saudi Arabia voluntarily, which especially affected the parts of the private sector with low skill requirements. In Iraq, Jordan, Lebanon, the State of Palestine and Yemen, chronic high unemployment was exacerbated by low domestic demand growth. Where official statistics are available, the unemployment rate stood at 12.6 per cent in Jordan in the second quarter of 2013, compared to 12.5 per cent in 2012. In the same period, the unemployment rate of the State of Palestine was 20.6 per cent, compared to 23.0 per cent in 2012. Although no official statistics were released, a large portion of the labour force in the Syrian Arab Republic is estimated to have become unemployed, underemployed or economically inactive. Most Syrian refugees competed with domestic low-skilled workers for jobs in the informal sector in host countries.

Figure IV.9
Western Asia: GDP growth by subregion

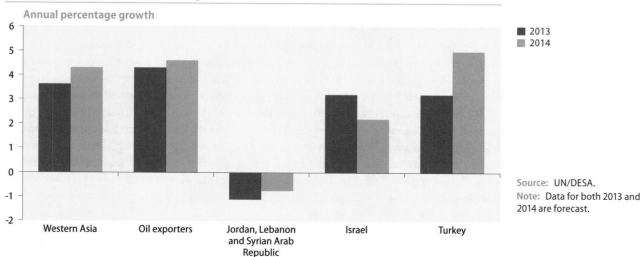

Source: UN/DESA.
Note: Data for both 2013 and 2014 are forecast.

Although international commodity prices were stable, the inflation rate crept up in the region. For GCC countries, the upward trend in the inflation rate is due to recovering domestic demand. The price of housing-related items, including property rents, showed a robust recovery. Wage increases were observed in several high-skill sectors in GCC countries, but its impact on the general price level is projected to be limited. For Iraq, Jordan and Lebanon, upward creeping inflation stems from modestly binding foreign-exchange constraints and a significantly increased number of residents, including Syrian refugees. The depletion of foreign reserves and a substantial devaluation of the national currency caused a state of hyperinflation in the Syrian Arab Republic. According to estimates, the consumer inflation rate went beyond the 100 per cent mark in August 2013. In the area of monetary policy, Arab countries in Western Asia utilize the stable exchange rate as a main monetary anchor. Therefore, monetary policy is rather passive as it follows that of the Fed. In Turkey, despite depreciation pressure on the currency, the central bank has refrained from raising interest rates. Instead, it adopted an unorthodox policy scheme by creating an interest-rate corridor between 6.75 per cent and 7.75 per cent without increasing the policy interest rate. In Israel, with inflation subdued, the central bank has been cutting interest rates during 2013, but monetary policy is expected to tighten in late 2014.

> Inflation is increasing due to recovering domestic demand

The GCC countries and Iraq retained active fiscal policies, following growing oil export revenues in the fiscal year covering 2013. This trend is projected to continue in 2014. The focus has been on a shift to capital expenditure and large public-sector led infrastructure projects, although the actual fiscal impact on respective economies depends heavily on the implementation rate of budgeted fiscal items. A case in point is Kuwait, where the postponement of planned large, public-sector-led projects negatively affected overall economic growth. A tightened fiscal policy stance continued in Jordan, Lebanon and Yemen, owing to decreasing revenues and increasing deficits.

> Oil exporters maintain active fiscal policy, while the non-oil exporters face more pronounced fiscal constraints

In Turkey, fiscal policy has been somewhat restrictive, with government expenditure growing at a much slower pace than government revenue. In Israel, fiscal policy is neutral, with the budget deficit standing at above 3 per cent of GDP. Government spending is expected to grow only moderately in 2014-2015 in order to curb the deficit further.

External balances are decreasing in the oil-exporting countries due to weaker oil export revenues and robust domestic demand for imports

The current-account surpluses of GCC countries and Iraq are estimated to have declined moderately in 2013. Oil export revenues edged down, while imports increased because of robust domestic demand growth. Meanwhile, the current-account deficits of Jordan, Lebanon and Yemen are estimated to have narrowed. Without any sign of improvement in export performances, the level of imports declined owing to weak domestic demand. In Turkey, real exports decelerated significantly in 2013 to a growth rate of about 3.0 per cent, compared with growth of 16.7 per cent in 2012. Export growth is expected to improve in the outlook, as external demand from Europe starts to recover. Real imports have accelerated from zero growth in 2012 to 8 per cent growth in 2013, but the pace of growth is projected to moderate in the outlook, partly owing to the recent depreciation. In Israel, both exports and imports declined in 2013, but the drop in the former was less than in the latter, leaving the current account in moderate surplus. The start of natural gas output is expected to boost exports further.

Risks during the outlook period include a fall in oil prices and the impact from a change in monetary policy in the United States

A rise in geopolitical tensions can easily affect the region's economic prospects. Nevertheless, as the region's geopolitical tensions are projected to remain focused around the situation in the Syrian Arab Republic, GCC countries are projected to be less affected. The division is to a large extent reflected in the different performance among stock markets in the region: in dollar-adjusted terms, stock price indices rose significantly in all GCC countries over the first three quarters of 2013, while those of the Syrian Arab Republic and its neighbouring countries declined. For GCC countries, the risk lies more in a sudden plunge in oil prices, as in 2008. Oil prices are crucial not only for export revenues, but also for economic sentiment and confidence of non-oil sectors in GCC countries. If oil prices fell below $80 per barrel, it would dent the growth of domestic demand. As the source of revenues depends on oil, countercyclical fiscal measures may not be sufficient for such contingency. With exchange rates pegged mostly to the United States dollar, the region will be impacted by any change in the monetary policy stance of the Fed. The looming reduction of bond purchases by the Fed will affect the yields of United States Treasury bonds; any rise in yields will affect the borrowing costs in the region, particularly in GCC countries.

Latin America and the Caribbean: growth to accelerate in 2014-2015

In Latin America and the Caribbean, economic growth is estimated to be 2.6 per cent in 2013. All economies in the region achieved positive growth, mainly supported by resilient domestic demand, although weak global economic conditions have indeed hampered the region's growth. In 2014 and 2015, GDP growth is expected to pick up to 3.6 per cent and 4.1 per cent, respectively, underpinned mainly by a gradual recovery in developed economies, sound macroeconomic policies, and resilient domestic demand.

South America registered the strongest GDP growth in 2013, while Mexico and Central America are expected to rebound more strongly in 2014

The economic expansion has been uneven across the region. In South America, economic growth is estimated to have accelerated in 2013 to 3.2 per cent, up from 2.5 per cent in 2012, owing to a rebound in Argentina and Brazil, and also supported by growing domestic demand, which partially compensated for the bleak external environment. Other agricultural exporters (Paraguay and Uruguay) also recorded higher growth rates in 2013, fostered by the recovery of the agricultural harvests so hard hit during 2012. In 2014 and 2015, the subregional economy should benefit from stronger external demand, along with the economic recovery in the United States and Europe. In 2014 and 2015, GDP growth in the subregion is expected to accelerate to 3.4 per cent and 4.1 per cent, respectively.

In Mexico and Central America, economic activity in 2013 is estimated to slow down to 1.5 per cent from 4.0 per cent in 2012. The Mexican economy has faced structural constraints and GDP growth decelerated significantly. In 2013, the economy is expected to have expanded only by 1.2 per cent, but the economic outlook is positive for the period covering 2014-2015. The Mexican Government has announced a set of reforms that should address part of the current structural weakness—including inefficient technology in the energy sector—and should potentially stimulate private investment. By contrast, several Central American economies will continue to grow at a fast pace, particularly Guatemala, Nicaragua, and Panama. In the forecast period, Mexico, and also Central America, should benefit from anticipated higher growth rates in the United States economy, their main economic partner. The Mexican economy is expected to expand by 4.0 per cent in 2014 and 4.2 per cent in 2015.

The Caribbean region is still struggling to recover from the impact of the global financial crisis in 2008, experiencing relatively low GDP growth and large current-account deficits. External demand has been subdued, in particular for the tourism sector, given the relatively slow economic recovery in the United States and Europe. Weaker commodity prices have also affected net exporters of commodities in the region, while domestic demand has been relatively weak following fiscal austerity measures and high levels of unemployment. Public debt increased substantially since the Great Recession in 2008 as a result of expansive fiscal policies, thus limiting fiscal space in the region to support economic growth. In 2013, the Caribbean economy is estimated to have expanded by 2.4 per cent, a slightly slower pace than in the past two years. However, the anticipated economic recovery in developed economies is expected to boost the tourism sector and have indirect spillover into other sectors, bringing the Caribbean GDP growth to 3.3 per cent and 3.8 per cent in 2014 and 2015, respectively.

A continued buoyant labour market in South America, with low unemployment rates, along with modest increases in real wages, maintained support for private consumption throughout 2013; further improvements, such as additional reductions in unemployment or faster job creation, will be more difficult to achieve in the years ahead, however. For the region as a whole, urban unemployment remains at similar levels to those recorded in 2012—about 6.2 per cent—although it has been relatively higher in several Central American and Caribbean countries. As in previous years, employment generation has been concentrated in the non-tradable sector, reflecting the role of domestic demand as the main driver of growth.

Low unemployment and higher real wages continue to support private consumption…

The outlook for inflation is fairly stable. Inflation increased slightly in 2013 as a result of higher food prices and accommodative monetary policies in some countries since the second half of 2012. In the second half of 2013, the median inflation rate was up slightly, bringing the overall regional inflation rate to about 6.7 per cent for the year. Despite relatively stable consumer prices for the region as a whole, inflation has been high in a number of countries. For instance, the Bolivarian Republic of Venezuela registered the highest inflation rate in the region in 2013, as a result of sharp currency devaluation and increased supply constraints in certain products. For the rest of the region, inflation is expected to remain relatively stable in 2014, while picking up moderately in Mexico and Central America.

…while inflation is expected to remain fairly stable throughout the forecast period

A wide range of monetary policies were adopted in 2013, both in inflation-targeting countries and countries with other monetary policy regimes. In 2012, several countries had modified their monetary stance with the goal of promoting economic activity that would close the output gap. But as inflationary pressures increased and nominal exchange rates depreciated (figure IV.10)—particularly following the May 2013 announcement by the Fed that it would gradually taper its QE programme—a tightening monetary policy cycle started in several countries, such as Brazil, the Dominican Republic and Guatemala. In a large number of countries, a relatively expansionary monetary policy stance in 2013 is expected to be gradually reversed throughout 2014 as inflationary pressures mount.

Several countries started to tighten their monetary policy, in the light of currency depreciations and inflation pressures

The impact of the Fed announcement also led to heightened volatility in the region's main stock markets and a decline in capital inflows to some countries. As the Fed pre-

Figure IV.10
Daily real effective exchange rate of selected Latin American currencies,
1 June 2012-1 November 2013

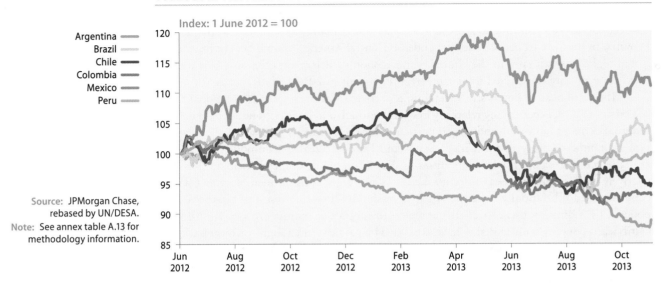

Argentina
Brazil
Chile
Colombia
Mexico
Peru

Index: 1 June 2012 = 100

Source: JPMorgan Chase, rebased by UN/DESA.
Note: See annex table A.13 for methodology information.

pares to exit from expansive monetary conditions, capital inflows from private creditors are expected to suffer particularly. As a result, less favourable financing for private investment, but also for countries with larger current-account deficits, such as Brazil, are potential challenges for the region. On a positive note, the region has accumulated abundant international reserves, providing monetary authorities with some room to deal with currency volatility. Although currency depreciations may cause imported inflation, they may also support the manufacturing sector in the medium term, particularly in Mexico and other Central American economies. However, structural reforms, such as the modernization of transportation and energy sectors, as well as easing the regulatory environment, are needed to increase productivity and to take advantage of additional export opportunities.

Lower commodity prices affected fiscal revenues in many countries, while fiscal reforms were implemented to broaden the tax base

Fiscal revenues in many countries in the region have been mainly hit by falling prices of export commodities, but also by lower economic activity and the drop in tourism, especially in the Caribbean. A great number of countries, such as Argentina, Chile, the Dominican Republic, Ecuador, El Salvador, Guatemala, Mexico, Panama and Peru, have implemented fiscal reforms in 2012-2103 in an attempt to broaden the tax base and to increase fiscal revenues. These reforms were crucial, but not yet sufficient. At the same time, public spending trended upwards during 2013, especially in South America, as a component of efforts to invigorate domestic demand. Expenditure rose above GDP growth rates in Argentina, Chile, Colombia, Ecuador, Peru, Paraguay, the Plurinational State of Bolivia and Uruguay. Despite important reforms in the tax system, fiscal balances are expected to deteriorate in 2013 (box IV.4) and some Governments may find it more difficult to provide stimulus if global economic conditions deteriorate further during the outlook period.

In the English-speaking Caribbean, public debt-to-GDP ratios are traditionally high, but since the Great Recession in 2008, several countries have increased public expenditure to support the economy, increasing new borrowing, which resulted in higher public debt. In 2013, fiscal deficits are expected to shrink, as serious efforts have been made to reduce spending (in Jamaica, for instance) and tax revenues should increase along with a better economic outlook.

Box IV.4
Twin deficits in Latin America and the Caribbean

The region of Latin America and the Caribbean is facing higher economic vulnerability as the current-account deficit, which is projected to widen in 2013 to more than 2 per cent of GDP, is now being coupled with greater fiscal deficits (figure IV.4.1). Slower GDP growth and a drop in commodity prices have hampered public revenues, narrowing the fiscal space in many countries. Under these circumstances, Governments are dealing with conflicting demands. On the one hand, market pressure will require strengthening fiscal accounts, while on the other hand, social pressure for better public services is growing, as witnessed by large-scale protests in some countries of the region.

Figure IV.4.1
Latin America and the Caribbean: overall budget balance, 2007-2013

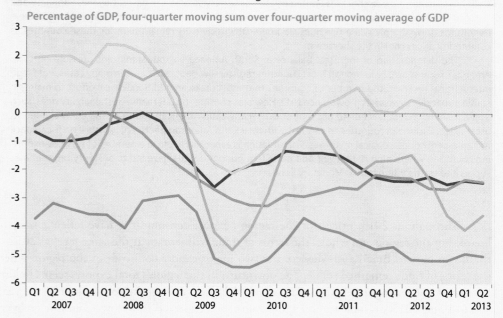

Percentage of GDP, four-quarter moving sum over four-quarter moving average of GDP

— Argentina, Brazil, Mexico
— Caribbean commodities exporters
— Caribbean services exporters (excluding St. Kitts and Nevis)
— Central America
— South America (excluding Argentina and Brazil)

Source: ECLAC.
Note: South America includes Bolivia (Plurinational State of), Chile, Colombia, Ecuador, Paraguay, Peru and Uruguay. Central America includes Costa Rica, Dominican Republic, El Salvador, Guatemala and Nicaragua. Caribbean commodities exporters includes Guyana, Suriname, Trinidad and Tobago. Caribbean services exporters includes Antigua and Barbuda, Bahamas, Barbados, Belize, Dominica, Grenada, Jamaica, St. Lucia and St. Vincent and the Grenadines. Data are for the central Government, except in the cases of Bolivia (Plurinational State of), Ecuador and Uruguay where data refer to the non-financial public sector.

The fiscal balance of the region's major economies—Argentina, Brazil and Mexico—deteriorated in the second half of 2011, an outcome that can be attributed to slower growth and the consequent impact of automatic stabilizers, as well as specific countercyclical measures adopted in Argentina and Brazil. Since then, the fiscal situation remained relatively stable in Brazil and Mexico, but it deteriorated further in Argentina in 2012 and 2013 (swinging from a slight surplus to a deficit of more than 2 per cent of GDP). This is becoming a matter of concern going forward, as Argentina has limited access to external sources of financing. In Brazil, the relative economic recovery in 2013 will likely soften the impact of any increases in public spending on the fiscal balance. In contrast, sharp cuts in public spending in Mexico have reigned in the deficit.

In the rest of South America (excluding Argentina and Brazil), higher deficits have largely come hand-in-hand with declining commodities prices. In Chile and Peru, fiscal conditions deteriorated in 2012 and 2013 as public expenditures grew rapidly, while corporate tax receipts, especially those in the mining sector, plummeted owing to higher production costs and lower global commodity prices. In some countries, such as Ecuador, the Plurinational State of Bolivia and Uruguay, strong growth in domestic demand partially offset lower public revenues from the trade sector.

In Central America, low levels of public revenues—on average 14.8 per cent of GDP, as compared to 27.4 per cent in South America[a]—coupled with persistent deficits, represent their greatest fiscal vulnerability. Nevertheless, recent tax reforms, which enlarged domestic tax bases increased public revenues in a number of countries, bolstering fiscal balances.

Box IV.4
Twin deficits in Latin America and the Caribbean (*continued*)

In the Caribbean, fiscal vulnerability and risks of debt distress are much more acute. In services-exporting countries, some efforts have been made to reduce deficits—including fiscal reforms that raised taxes and curtailed spending—but high public debt levels give little space to manoeuvre. The situation remains particularly grave in the Bahamas, Barbados, Dominica, and St. Lucia, each of which is expected to have a deficit of over 7 per cent of GDP in 2013 (according to preliminary data). The anticipated faster economic growth in the United States and a return to growth in Europe should bolster the fiscal situation in these countries, although recent tourist arrivals data suggests that this important sector has yet to recover before contributing more significantly to fiscal revenues.

Commodities-exporting countries in the Caribbean, like their Latin American counterparts, have also seen their fiscal balances affected by swings in global commodity prices. However, in contrast, their ability to withstand these shocks is limited by their relatively smaller tax bases. Guyana, Suriname and Trinidad and Tobago have all registered an increase in their budget deficits since mid-2012 as their expenditures grew sharply while revenues slumped. Downside risks remain high for these countries as commodity prices cool in the short-term.

The deterioration of the fiscal balance in South America has put significant pressure on Latin America's fiscal space. Even though most countries register low debt levels and, in many cases, hold high international reserves, the number of countries that must make an additional fiscal effort to maintain stable public debt levels has grown since 2012. However, considering alternative sustainability rules, such as maintaining a debt level of 40 per cent of GDP, many Latin American countries still enjoy significant fiscal space. Caribbean countries, in contrast with their Latin American peers, enjoy little if no fiscal space to implement countercyclical measures. The situation is especially acute in a number of services-exporting countries, where high debt levels and persistent budget deficits have led to austerity programmes supervised by the International Monetary Fund.

a This is a simple average of countries under review. See figure IV.4.1 for definitions and coverage of data.
Source: ECLAC.

The downturn in the region's exports seems to have bottomed out during 2013 and exports should benefit from the recovery in developed economies

Throughout 2013, prices for the region's export commodities have fallen across the board. For the region as a whole, the terms of trade will remain at the same level as 2012—thanks in part to Brazil and Mexico, the two major export countries in the region where the terms of trade remained stable. The downturn in the region's total exports seems to have bottomed out during 2013, as export values picked up during the second half of the year. In 2014 and 2015, an increase in export volumes is expected to follow economic recovery in developed economies. In addition, a price recovery of key commodities is anticipated for the region's exports, as international demand is expected to improve in 2014. However, despite anticipated improvement for the external sector in the near future, the deceleration of economic activity in China—the main commodity importer for the region—may reduce the annual trade gains of previous years. This could particularly affect several countries in South America.

The current-account deficit will widen slightly, mainly because of the deterioration in the trade balance

The current-account deficit is expected to have reached 2.0 per cent of GDP in 2013, up from 1.8 per cent in 2012. The widening of the current-account deficit is explained mainly by the deterioration of the balance of the trade in goods, as imports have increased faster than exports in the past few years and eroded the trade surplus. In addition, the sluggish performance of the inbound tourism market has worsened the deficit of the trade in services, particularly in the Caribbean countries. Furthermore, the surplus in the current transfers balance is expected to decline in 2013, as a result of the reduction in remittance flows to Mexico, despite the fact that remittance flows increased in most countries of the region. In 2014 and 2015, as developed economies are expected to perform better economically, demand for Latin American and Caribbean exports, including for the tourism sector, should generate higher revenues and narrow current-account deficits in the region.

As in 2012, the current-account deficit in 2013 was mainly funded by net foreign direct investment inflows, followed by net portfolio investment. Infrastructural investments, including in the commodity sector, should continue to attract FDI in the region during the forecast period, particularly in Brazil, Chile, Colombia, Peru and Guyana. Solid macroeconomic fundamentals and an expanding middle class should also reinforce the attractiveness of Latin America for international investors. However, FDI would need to be channelled towards non-commodity sectors in order to diversify the economies in the region. In 2013, the number of Latin American countries present in international debt markets increased with issuances of sovereign, corporate, and bank bonds by Guatemala, Honduras and the Plurinational State of Bolivia. The region reported slower growth in international reserves accumulation in a context of greater volatility in the international financial markets.

> The region will continue to attract FDI, funding a large part of the current-account deficit

This forecast is subject to various downside risks that are related to economic uncertainties in the economic prospects for the euro area and the United States, but also in China, which is now targeting slower growth than in previous years. Tighter monetary policy in the United States would lead to higher costs of external financing in a context of increasing fiscal and external imbalances in several economies in the region. In addition to external risks, domestic policies to support economic activity face a number of challenges. In the current context of high volatility of capital inflows and significant uncertainties in developed countries, the region will face the challenge of coordinating fiscal, monetary, and exchange-rate policies in order to preserve financial stability and stimulate economic growth. Some countries also face country-specific risks. A case in point is the Bolivarian Republic of Venezuela, where policymakers are challenged to deal with soaring inflation driven by supply constraints and currency devaluation.

> Serious risks on the downside are related to uncertainties in developed economies

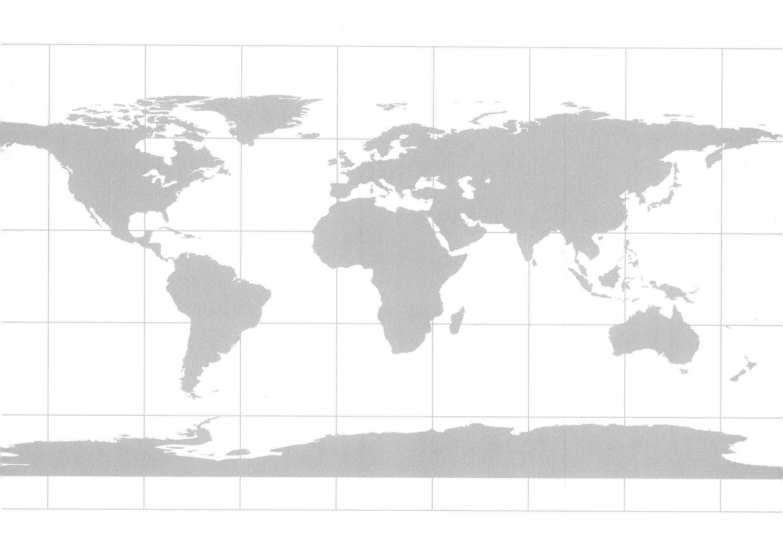

Statistical annex

Country classification

Data sources, country classifications and aggregation methodology

The statistical annex contains a set of data that the *World Economic Situation and Prospects (WESP)* employs to delineate trends in various dimensions of the world economy.

Data sources

The annex was prepared by the Development Policy and Analysis Division (DPAD) of the Department of Economic and Social Affairs of the United Nations Secretariat (UN/DESA). It is based on information obtained from the Statistics Division and the Population Division of UN/DESA, as well as from the five United Nations regional commissions, the United Nations Conference on Trade and Development (UNCTAD), the United Nations World Tourism Organization (UNWTO), the International Monetary Fund (IMF), the World Bank, the Organization for Economic Cooperation and Development (OECD), and national and private sources. Estimates for the most recent years were made by DPAD in consultation with the regional commissions, UNCTAD, UNWTO and participants in Project LINK, an international collaborative research group for econometric modelling coordinated jointly by DPAD and the University of Toronto. Forecasts for 2014 and 2015 are primarily based on the World Economic Forecasting Model of DPAD, with support from Project LINK.

Data presented in *WESP* may differ from those published by other organizations for a series of reasons, including differences in timing, sample composition and aggregation methods. Historical data may differ from those in previous editions of *WESP* because of updating and changes in the availability of data for individual countries.

Country classifications

For analytical purposes, *WESP* classifies all countries of the world into one of three broad categories: developed economies, economies in transition and developing economies. The composition of these groupings, specified in tables A, B and C, is intended to reflect basic economic country conditions. Several countries (in particular the economies in transition) have characteristics that could place them in more than one category; however, for purposes of analysis, the groupings have been made mutually exclusive. Within each broad category, some subgroups are defined based either on geographical location or on ad hoc criteria, such as the subgroup of "major developed economies", which is based on the membership of the Group of Seven. Geographical regions for developing economies are as follows: Africa, East Asia, South Asia, Western Asia, and Latin America and the Caribbean.[1]

---

[1] Names and composition of geographical areas follow those specified in the statistical paper entitled "Standard country or area codes for statistical use" (ST/ESA/STAT/SER.M/49/Rev. 4).

In parts of the analysis, a distinction is made between fuel exporters and fuel importers from among the economies in transition and the developing countries. An economy is classified as a fuel exporter if the share of fuel exports in its total merchandise exports is greater than 20 per cent and the level of fuel exports is at least 20 per cent higher than that of the country's fuel imports. This criterion is drawn from the share of fuel exports in the total value of world merchandise trade. Fuels include coal, oil and natural gas (table D).

For other parts of the analysis, countries have been classified by their level of development as measured by per capita gross national income (GNI). Accordingly, countries have been grouped as high-income, upper middle income, lower middle income and low-income (table E). To maintain compatibility with similar classifications used elsewhere, the threshold levels of GNI per capita are those established by the World Bank. Countries with less than $1,035 GNI per capita are classified as low-income countries, those with between $1,036 and $4,085 as lower middle income countries, those with between $4,086 and $12,615 as upper middle income countries, and those with incomes of more than $12,615 as high-income countries. GNI per capita in dollar terms is estimated using the World Bank Atlas method,[2] and the classification in table E is based on data for 2012.

The list of the least developed countries (LDCs) is decided upon by the United Nations Economic and Social Council and, ultimately, by the General Assembly, on the basis of recommendations made by the Committee for Development Policy. The basic criteria for inclusion require that certain thresholds be met with regard to per capita GNI, a human assets index and an economic vulnerability index.[3] As at 29 November 2013, there were 49 LDCs (table F).

WESP also makes reference to the group of heavily indebted poor countries (HIPCs), which are considered by the World Bank and IMF as part of their debt-relief initiative (the Enhanced HIPC Initiative).[4] In September 2013, there were 39 HIPCs (see table G).

Aggregation methodology

Aggregate data are either sums or weighted averages of individual country data. Unless otherwise indicated, multi-year averages of growth rates are expressed as compound annual percentage rates of change. The convention followed is to omit the base year in a multi-year growth rate. For example, the 10-year average growth rate for the decade of the 2000s would be identified as the average annual growth rate for the period from 2001 to 2010.

WESP utilizes exchange-rate conversions of national data in order to aggregate output of individual countries into regional and global totals. The growth of output in each group of countries is calculated from the sum of gross domestic product (GDP) of individual countries measured at 2005 prices and exchange rates. Data for GDP in

---

2   See http://data.worldbank.org/about/country-classifications.

3   *Handbook on the Least Developed Country Category: Inclusion, Graduation and Special Support Measures* (United Nations publication, Sales No. E.07.II.A.9). Available from http://www.un.org/esa/analysis/devplan/cdppublications/2008cdphandbook.pdf.

4   IMF, Debt Relief Under the Heavily Indebted Poor Countries (HIPC) Initiative Available from http://www.imf.org/external/np/exr/facts/pdf/hipc.pdf

2005 in national currencies were converted into dollars (with selected adjustments) and extended forwards and backwards in time using changes in real GDP for each country. This method supplies a reasonable set of aggregate growth rates for a period of about 15 years, centred on 2005.

The exchange-rate based method differs from the one mainly applied by the IMF and the World Bank for their estimates of world and regional economic growth, which is based on purchasing power parity (PPP) weights. Over the past two decades, the growth of world gross product (WGP) on the basis of the exchange-rate based approach has been below that based on PPP weights. This is because developing countries, in the aggregate, have seen significantly higher economic growth than the rest of the world in the 1990s and 2000s and the share in WGP of these countries is larger under PPP measurements than under market exchange rates.

Table A
Developed economies

Europe			Other countries	Major developed economies (G7)
European Union	New EU member States	Other Europe		
EU-15	Bulgaria	Iceland	Australia	Canada
Austria	Croatia	Norway	Canada	Japan
Belgium	Cyprus	Switzerland	Japan	France
Denmark	Czech Republic		New Zealand	Germany
Finland	Estonia		United States	Italy
France	Hungary			United Kingdom
Germany	Latvia			United States
Greece	Lithuania			
Ireland	Malta			
Italy	Poland			
Luxembourg	Romania			
Netherlands	Slovakia			
Portugal	Slovenia			
Spain				
Sweden				
United Kingdom				

Table B
Economies in transition

South-Eastern Europe	Commonwealth of Independent States and Georgia[a]	
Albania	Armenia	Republic of Moldova
Bosnia and Herzegovina	Azerbaijan	Russian Federation
Montenegro	Belarus	Tajikistan
Serbia	Georgia[a]	Turkmenistan
The former Yugoslav Republic of Macedonia	Kazakhstan	Ukraine
	Kyrgyzstan	Uzbekistan

a Georgia officially left the Commonwealth of Independent States on 18 August 2009. However, its performance is discussed in the context of this group of countries for reasons of geographic proximity and similarities in economic structure.

...mies by region[a]

		Asia	Latin America and the Caribbean
	Southern Africa	East Asia	Caribbean
	Angola	Brunei Darussalam	Barbados
	Botswana	China	Cuba
Libya[b]	Lesotho	Hong Kong SAR[c]	Dominican Republic
Mauritania	Malawi	Indonesia	Guyana
Morocco	Mauritius	Malaysia	Haiti
Sudan	Mozambique	Myanmar	Jamaica
Tunisia	Namibia	Papua New Guinea	Trinidad and Tobago
Central Africa	South Africa	Philippines	**Mexico and Central America**
	Zambia	Republic of Korea	
Cameroon	Zimbabwe	Singapore	Costa Rica
Central African Republic		Taiwan Province of China	El Salvador
Chad	**West Africa**	Thailand	Guatemala
Congo	Benin	Viet Nam	Honduras
Equatorial Guinea	Burkina Faso		Mexico
Gabon	Cabo Verde	**South Asia**	Nicaragua
Sao Tome and Prinicipe	Côte d'Ivoire	Bangladesh	Panama
East Africa	Gambia	India	**South America**
	Ghana	Iran (Islamic Republic of)	
Burundi	Guinea	Nepal	Argentina
Comoros	Guinea-Bissau	Pakistan	Bolivia (Plurinational State of)
Democratic Republic of the Congo	Liberia	Sri Lanka	Brazil
Djibouti	Mali	**Western Asia**	Chile
Eritrea	Niger	Bahrain	Colombia
Ethiopia	Nigeria	Iraq	Ecuador
Kenya	Senegal	Israel	Paraguay
Madagascar	Sierra Leone	Jordan	Peru
Rwanda	Togo	Kuwait	Uruguay
Somalia		Lebanon	Venezuela (Bolivarian Republic of)
Uganda		Oman	
United Republic of Tanzania		Qatar	
		Saudi Arabia	
		Syrian Arab Republic	
		Turkey	
		United Arab Emirates	
		Yemen	

a Economies systematically monitored by the Global Economic Monitoring Unit of DPAD.

b The name of the Libyan Arab Jamahiriya was officially changed to Libya on 16 September 2011.

c Special Administrative Region of China.

Table D
Fuel-exporting countries

Economies in transition	Developing countries				
	Latin America and the Caribbean	Africa	East Asia	South Asia	Western Asia
Azerbaijan	Bolivia (Plurinational State of)	Algeria	Brunei Darussalam	Iran (Islamic Republic of)	Bahrain
Kazakhstan		Angola	Indonesia		Iraq
Russian Federation	Colombia	Cameroon	Viet Nam		Kuwait
Turkmenistan	Ecuador	Chad			Oman
Uzbekistan	Trinidad and Tobago	Congo			Qatar
	Venezuela (Bolivarian Republic of)	Côte d'Ivoire			Saudi Arabia
		Egypt			United Arab Emirates
		Equatorial Guinea			Yemen
		Gabon			
		Libya			
		Nigeria			
		Sudan			

Table E
Economies by per capita GNI in 2012[a]

High-income		Upper middle income		Lower middle income	Low-income
Australia	Lithuania[b]	Albania[b]	Jordan	Armenia	Bangladesh
Austria	Luxembourg	Algeria	Kazakhstan	Bolivia	Benin
Bahrain	Malta	Angola	Lebanon	Cameroon	Burkina Faso
Barbados	Netherlands	Argentina	Libya	Cape Verde	Burundi
Belgium	New Zealand	Azerbaijan	Malaysia	Congo	Central African
Brunei	Norway	Belarus	Mauritius	Côte d'Ivoire	Republic
Darussalam	Oman	Bosnia and	Mexico	Djibouti	Chad
Canada	Poland	Herzegovina	Montenegro	Egypt	Comoros
Chile[b]	Portugal	Botswana	Namibia	El Salvador	Democratic Republic
Croatia	Qatar	Brazil	Panama	Georgia	of the Congo
Cyprus	Republic	Bulgaria	Peru	Ghana	Eritrea
Czech	of Korea	China	Romania	Guatemala	Ethiopia
Republic	Russian Federation[b]	Colombia	Serbia	Guyana	Gambia, The
Denmark	Saudi Arabia	Costa Rica	South Africa	Honduras	Guinea
Equatorial	Singapore	Cuba	Thailand	India	Guinea-Bissau
Guinea	Slovak	Dominican	The former	Indonesia	Haiti
Estonia	Republic	Republic	Yugoslav	Lesotho	Kenya
Finland	Slovenia	Ecuador	Republc of	Mauritania[b]	Kyrgyz Republic
France	Spain	Gabon	Macedonia	Moldova	Liberia
Germany	Sweden	Hungary[c]	Tunisia	Morocco	Madagascar
Greece	Switzerland	Iran, Islamic	Turkey	Nicaragua	Malawi
Hong Kong	Taiwan Province	Republic	Turkmenistan	Nigeria	Mali
SAR[d]	of China	Iraq[b]	Venezuela, RB	Pakistan	Mozambique
Iceland	Trinidad and	Jamaica		Papua New Guinea	Myanmar
Ireland	Tobago			Paraguay	Nepal
Israel	United Arab			Philippines	Niger
Italy	Emirates			São Tomé and	Rwanda
Japan	United Kingdom			Principe	Sierra Leone
Kuwait	United States			Senegal	Somalia
Latvia[b]	Uruguay[b]			Sri Lanka	Tajikistan
				Sudan	Tanzania
				Syrian Arab Republic	Togo
				Ukraine	Uganda
				Uzbekistan	Zimbabwe
				Vietnam	
				Yemen, Rep.	
				Zambia	

a Economies systematically monitored for the World Economic Situation and Prospects report and included in the United Nations' global economic forecast.
b Indicates the country has been shifted upward by one category from previous year's classification.
c Indicates the country has been shifted downward by one category from previous year's classification.
d Special Administrative Region of China.

Table F
Least developed countries (*as of November 2013*)

Africa		East Asia	South Asia	Western Asia	Latin America & the Caribbean
Angola	Madagascar	Cambodia[a]	Afghanistan[a]	Yemen	Haiti
Benin	Malawi	Kiribati[a]	Bangladesh		
Burkina Faso	Mali	Lao People's	Bhutan[a]		
Burundi	Mauritania	Democratic	Nepal		
Central African Republic	Mozambique	Republic[a]			
Chad	Niger	Myanmar			
Comoros	Rwanda	Samoa[a, b]			
Democratic Republic of the Congo	Sao Tome and Principe	Solomon Islands[a]			
Djibouti	Senegal	Timor Leste[a]			
Equatorial Guinea	Sierra Leone	Tuvalu[a]			
Eritrea	Somalia	Vanuatu[a]			
Ethiopia	South Sudan[a]				
Gambia	Sudan				
Guinea	Togo				
Guinea-Bissau	Uganda				
Lesotho	United Republic of Tanzania				
Liberia	Zambia				

a Not included in the WESP discussion because of insufficient data.
b Samoa will graduate from the list of the least developed countries in January 2014.

Table G
Heavily indebted poor countries (*as of September 2013*)

Post-completion point HIPCs[a]		Interim HIPCs[b]	Pre-decision point HIPCs[c]
Afghanistan	Honduras	Chad	Eritrea
Benin	Liberia	Comoros	Somalia
Bolivia	Madagascar		Sudan
Burkina Faso	Malawi		
Burundi	Mali		
Cameroon	Mauritania		
Central African Republic	Mozambique		
Congo	Nicaragua		
Côte D'Ivoire	Niger		
Democratic Republic of the Congo	Rwanda		
Ethiopia	Sao Tome and Principe		
Gambia	Senegal		
Ghana	Sierra Leone		
Guinea	Togo		
Guinea-Bissau	Uganda		
Guyana	United Republic of Tanzania		
Haiti	Zambia		

a Countries that have qualified for irrevocable debt relief under the HIPC Initiative.
b Countries that have qualified for assistance under the HIPC Initiative (that is to say, have reached decision point), but have not yet reached completion point.
c Countries that are potentially eligible and may wish to avail themselves of the HIPC Initiative or the Multilateral Debt Relief Initiative (MDRI).

Table H
Small island developing States

United Nations members		Non-UN Members/Associate Members of the Regional Commissions
Antigua and Barbuda	Marshall Islands	American Samoa
Bahamas	Mauritius	Anguilla
Bahrain	Nauru	Aruba
Barbados	Palau	Bermuda
Belize	Papua New Guinea	British Virgin Islands
Cabo Verde	Saint Kitts and Nevis	Cayman Islands
Comoros	Saint. Lucia	Commonwealth of Northern Marianas
Cuba	Saint Vincent and the Grenadines	Cook Islands
Dominica		Curacao
Dominican Republic	Samoa	
Federated States of Micronesia	São Tomé and Príncipe	French Polynesia
	Seychelles	Guadeloupe
Fiji	Singapore	Guam
Grenada	Solomon Islands	Martinique
Guinea-Bissau	Suriname	Montserrat
Guyana	Timor-Leste	New Caledonia
Haiti	Tonga	Niue
Jamaica	Trinidad and Tobago	Puerto Rico
Kiribati	Tuvalu	Turks and Caicos Islands
Maldives	Vanuatu	U.S. Virgin Islands

Table I
Landlocked developing countries

Landlocked developing countries		
Afghanistan	Lesotho	Mongolia
Armenia	Malawi	Nepal
Azerbaijan	American Samoa	Niger
Bhutan	Anguilla	Paraguay
Bolivia (Plurinational State of)	Aruba	Rwanda
Botswana	Bermuda	South Sudan
Burkina Faso	British Virgin Islands	Swaziland
Burundi	Cayman Islands	Tajikistan
Central African Republic	Commonwealth of Northern Marianas	The former Yugoslav Republic of Macedonia
Chad		
Ethiopia	Cook Islands	Turkmenistan
Kazakhstan	Curacao	Uganda
Kyrgystan	French Polynesia	Uzbekistan
Lao People's Democratic Republic	Mali	Zambia
	Republic of Moldova	Zimbabwe

Annex tables

Table A.1
Developed economies: rates of growth of real GDP, 2005-2015

Annual percentage change	2005-2012[a]	2005	2006	2007	2008	2009	2010	2011	2012	2013[b]	2014[c]	2015[c]
Developed economies	1.2	2.6	2.8	2.5	0.0	-3.7	2.6	1.5	1.3	1.0	1.9	2.4
United States	1.5	3.4	2.7	1.8	-0.3	-2.8	2.5	1.8	2.8	1.6	2.5	3.2
Canada	1.7	3.2	2.6	2.0	1.2	-2.7	3.4	2.5	1.7	1.6	2.4	2.8
Japan	0.5	1.3	1.7	2.2	-1.0	-5.5	4.7	-0.6	1.9	1.9	1.5	1.2
Australia	2.9	3.3	2.6	4.8	2.4	1.5	2.6	2.4	3.7	2.6	2.8	3.1
New Zealand	1.6	3.2	2.9	3.4	-0.8	-1.4	1.9	1.4	2.7	2.6	2.8	2.8
European Union	1.0	2.2	3.4	3.2	0.4	-4.5	2.0	1.7	-0.4	-0.1	1.4	1.9
EU-15	0.8	2.0	3.2	3.0	0.1	-4.6	2.0	1.5	-0.5	-0.1	1.4	1.8
Austria	1.6	2.4	3.7	3.7	1.4	-3.8	1.8	2.8	0.9	0.7	1.8	2.2
Belgium	1.2	1.8	2.7	2.9	1.0	-2.8	2.4	1.8	-0.3	-0.4	0.5	1.3
Denmark	0.4	2.4	3.4	1.6	-0.8	-5.7	1.6	1.1	-0.4	0.7	1.8	2.8
Finland	1.1	2.9	4.4	5.3	0.3	-8.5	3.4	2.7	-0.8	-0.8	0.7	1.4
France	0.9	1.8	2.5	2.3	-0.1	-3.1	1.7	2.0	0.0	0.1	0.8	1.1
Germany	1.4	0.7	3.7	3.3	1.1	-5.1	4.0	3.3	0.7	0.4	1.9	1.9
Greece	-1.4	2.3	5.5	3.5	-0.2	-3.1	-4.9	-7.1	-6.4	-4.5	-1.0	1.3
Ireland	1.1	6.1	5.5	5.0	-2.2	-6.4	-1.1	2.2	0.2	-0.3	1.2	2.2
Italy	-0.3	0.9	2.2	1.7	-1.2	-5.5	1.7	0.5	-2.5	-1.8	0.8	1.4
Luxembourg	1.8	5.3	4.9	6.6	-0.7	-5.6	3.1	1.9	-0.2	0.9	3.0	2.0
Netherlands	1.1	2.0	3.4	3.9	1.8	-3.7	1.5	0.9	-1.2	-1.2	0.5	1.2
Portugal	-0.1	0.8	1.4	2.4	0.0	-2.9	1.9	-1.3	-3.2	-2.1	0.1	1.3
Spain	0.8	3.6	4.1	3.5	0.9	-3.8	-0.2	0.0	-1.6	-1.2	0.9	2.1
Sweden	1.9	3.2	4.3	3.3	-0.6	-5.0	6.6	2.9	1.0	1.1	2.6	3.3
United Kingdom	0.8	3.2	2.8	3.4	-0.8	-5.2	1.7	1.1	0.1	1.4	2.2	2.4
New EU member States	2.8	4.8	6.4	6.0	4.0	-3.8	2.1	3.0	0.6	0.5	2.1	2.7
Bulgaria	2.8	6.4	6.5	6.4	6.2	-5.5	0.4	1.8	0.8	1.0	2.1	2.3
Croatia	0.6	4.3	4.9	5.1	2.1	-6.9	-2.3	0.0	-2.0	-0.9	1.0	2.0
Cyprus	1.7	3.9	4.1	5.1	3.6	-1.9	1.3	0.4	-2.4	-13.9	-4.2	-1.4
Czech Republic	2.6	6.8	7.0	5.7	3.1	-4.5	2.5	1.8	-1.0	-0.8	1.5	3.0
Estonia	2.7	8.9	10.1	7.5	-4.2	-14.1	2.6	9.6	3.9	1.5	2.9	3.0
Hungary	0.3	4.0	3.9	0.1	0.9	-6.8	1.1	1.6	-1.7	0.2	2.0	2.3
Latvia	2.0	10.1	11.0	10.0	-2.8	-17.7	-1.3	5.3	5.0	4.0	4.2	4.2
Lithuania	2.8	7.8	7.8	9.8	2.9	-14.8	1.6	6.0	3.7	3.2	3.5	3.5
Malta	2.2	3.6	2.6	4.1	3.9	-2.8	4.0	1.6	0.8	0.7	1.1	2.5
Poland	4.2	3.6	6.2	6.8	5.1	1.6	3.9	4.5	1.9	1.2	2.5	3.0
Romania	2.5	4.2	7.9	6.3	7.3	-6.6	-1.1	2.2	0.7	1.9	3.0	3.1
Slovakia	4.3	6.7	8.3	10.5	5.8	-4.9	4.4	3.0	1.8	0.9	2.0	2.2
Slovenia	1.4	4.0	5.9	7.0	3.4	-7.9	1.3	0.7	-2.5	-2.4	-0.2	1.0
Other Europe	1.7	2.7	3.1	3.4	1.3	-1.9	1.7	1.6	1.9	1.7	2.6	2.9
Iceland	1.5	7.2	4.7	6.0	1.2	-6.6	-4.1	2.7	1.4	2.0	2.4	2.5
Norway	1.3	2.6	2.3	2.7	0.1	-1.6	0.5	1.2	3.1	1.7	2.7	2.7
Switzerland	2.0	2.7	3.8	3.8	2.2	-1.9	3.0	1.8	1.0	1.6	2.5	3.0
Memorandum items												
North America	1.5	3.3	2.7	1.8	-0.2	-2.8	2.6	1.9	2.7	1.6	2.5	3.2
Western Europe	1.0	2.2	3.4	3.2	0.4	-4.4	2.0	1.7	-0.3	0.0	1.5	1.9
Asia and Oceania	0.9	1.6	1.8	2.6	-0.6	-4.4	4.3	-0.1	2.2	2.0	1.7	1.5
Major developed economies	1.1	2.4	2.6	2.2	-0.3	-3.9	2.9	1.5	1.6	1.2	2.0	2.4
Euro area	0.8	1.7	3.3	3.0	0.4	-4.4	2.0	1.6	-0.7	-0.5	1.1	1.6

Sources: UN/DESA, based on data of the United Nations Statistics Division and individual national sources.

Note: Country groups are calculated as a weighted average of individual country growth rates of gross domestic product (GDP), where weights are based on GDP in 2005 prices and exchange rates.

a Average percentage change.

b Partly estimated.

c Baseline scenario forecasts, based in part on Project LINK and UN/DESA World Economic Forecasting Model.

Table A.2
Economies in transition: rates of growth of real GDP, 2005-2015

Annual percentage change	2005-2012[a]	2005	2006	2007	2008	2009	2010	2011	2012	2013[b]	2014[c]	2015[c]
Economies in transition	4.3	6.6	8.5	8.7	5.3	-6.5	4.7	4.6	3.2	2.0	3.3	4.0
South-Eastern Europe	2.6	5.0	4.6	5.9	5.0	-2.1	1.7	1.9	-0.9	1.8	2.6	3.1
Albania	4.5	5.8	5.4	5.9	7.5	3.3	3.8	3.1	1.3	1.9	2.6	4.0
Bosnia and Herzegovina	2.4	3.9	5.5	6.0	5.6	-2.8	0.7	1.0	-0.7	0.8	2.0	2.5
Montenegro	3.3	4.2	8.6	10.7	6.9	-5.7	2.5	3.2	-2.5	1.9	2.5	3.0
Serbia	1.9	5.4	3.6	5.4	3.8	-3.5	1.0	1.6	-1.7	2.1	2.9	3.0
The former Yugoslav Republic of Macedonia	3.1	4.4	5.0	6.1	5.0	-0.9	2.9	2.8	-0.2	2.3	2.5	3.0
Commonwealth of Independent States and Georgia[d]	4.4	6.7	8.7	8.9	5.3	-6.8	4.9	4.8	3.4	2.0	3.4	4.1
Net fuel exporters	4.5	7.0	8.8	8.9	5.5	-6.3	4.9	4.7	3.7	2.2	3.5	4.1
Azerbaijan	13.4	28.0	34.5	25.5	10.6	9.4	4.6	-1.6	2.1	5.1	5.0	5.0
Kazakhstan	6.6	9.7	10.6	8.7	3.3	1.2	7.0	7.5	5.0	5.2	6.0	6.0
Russian Federation	4.0	6.4	8.2	8.5	5.2	-7.8	4.5	4.3	3.4	1.5	2.9	3.6
Turkmenistan	10.8	13.0	11.0	11.0	14.7	6.1	9.2	14.1	8.0	9.0	9.5	9.5
Uzbekistan	8.1	7.0	7.3	9.5	9.0	8.1	8.5	8.3	7.4	8.0	7.1	7.4
Net fuel importers	3.3	5.0	8.1	8.4	4.6	-9.8	5.2	5.4	1.2	1.0	2.8	3.8
Armenia	5.6	13.9	13.2	13.7	6.9	-14.2	2.2	4.7	7.2	4.0	5.5	5.0
Belarus	6.6	9.4	10.0	8.6	10.2	0.2	7.7	5.5	1.5	1.5	2.5	3.0
Georgia[d]	6.1	9.6	9.4	12.3	2.3	-3.8	6.3	7.2	6.1	2.1	5.0	5.0
Kyrgyzstan	3.4	-0.2	3.1	8.5	8.4	2.9	-0.5	6.0	-0.9	9.0	7.0	6.5
Republic of Moldova	3.7	7.5	4.8	3.0	7.8	-6.0	7.1	6.8	-0.8	4.2	4.5	4.5
Tajikistan	6.1	6.7	6.6	7.8	7.6	4.0	6.5	2.4	7.5	7.1	6.5	6.5
Ukraine	1.6	2.7	7.3	7.9	2.3	-14.8	4.2	5.2	0.2	-0.2	2.1	3.8

Sources: UN/DESA, based on data of the United Nations Statistics Division and individual national sources.

Note: Country groups are calculated as a weighted average of individual country growth rates of gross domestic product (GDP), where weights are based on GDP in 2005 prices and exchange rates.

a Average percentage change.

b Partly estimated.

c Baseline scenario forecasts, based in part on Project LINK and the UN/DESA World Economic Forecasting Model.

d Georgia officially left the Commonwealth of Independent States on 18 August 2009. However, its performance is discussed in the context of this group of countries for reasons of geographic proximity and similarities in economic structure.

Table A.3
Developing economies: rates of growth of real GDP, 2005-2015

Annual percentage change	2005-2012[a]	2005	2006	2007	2008	2009	2010	2011	2012	2013[b]	2014[c]	2015[c]
Developing countries[d]	6.1	6.8	7.6	7.9	5.4	2.7	7.7	5.9	4.7	4.6	5.1	5.3
Africa	4.7	6.0	6.0	6.3	5.6	2.6	4.6	0.8	5.7	4.0	4.7	5.0
North Africa	3.8	5.7	5.8	5.3	5.9	3.5	3.7	-6.1	7.2	2.3	3.3	4.3
East Africa	6.6	7.5	7.0	7.5	6.6	4.8	7.0	6.5	6.0	6.0	6.4	6.4
Central Africa	4.6	5.3	2.5	6.0	5.2	2.9	5.2	3.9	5.8	4.2	4.8	4.1
West Africa	5.9	5.8	5.1	5.6	5.9	5.5	6.9	6.1	6.7	6.7	6.9	6.8
Southern Africa	4.5	6.3	6.9	7.5	5.0	-0.5	3.7	4.0	3.5	3.6	4.2	4.4
Net fuel exporters	5.0	7.1	5.9	7.1	6.7	4.0	4.8	-2.8	7.7	3.9	4.8	5.2
Net fuel importers	4.4	5.1	6.0	5.5	4.6	1.2	4.5	4.5	3.9	4.1	4.6	4.9
East and South Asia	7.4	8.1	8.9	9.8	6.1	5.4	9.1	7.0	5.5	5.6	5.8	6.0
East Asia	7.6	8.1	9.1	10.2	6.4	5.2	9.3	7.1	5.9	6.0	6.1	6.1
South Asia	6.7	7.9	8.1	8.5	4.7	6.1	8.4	6.4	4.2	3.9	4.6	5.1
Net fuel exporters	5.3	6.1	5.8	6.9	4.8	4.2	5.9	5.4	3.6	3.0	4.0	4.6
Net fuel importers	7.7	8.3	9.3	10.1	6.2	5.5	9.4	7.1	5.6	5.8	6.0	6.1
Western Asia	5.1	7.0	7.4	5.5	4.7	-0.9	6.7	6.9	3.9	3.6	4.3	3.9
Net fuel exporters	5.8	6.7	8.3	5.9	7.2	0.5	5.8	6.8	5.2	4.3	4.7	4.9
Net fuel importers	4.4	7.4	6.4	5.1	1.9	-2.5	7.8	7.1	2.3	2.7	3.8	2.8
Latin America and the Caribbean	3.9	4.5	5.6	5.6	4.0	-1.5	5.8	4.4	3.0	2.6	3.6	4.1
South America	4.5	5.1	5.6	6.7	5.4	-0.2	6.4	4.6	2.5	3.2	3.4	4.1
Mexico and Central America	2.8	3.2	5.1	3.5	1.7	-4.2	5.0	4.1	4.0	1.5	4.0	4.2
Caribbean	4.7	8.0	10.3	6.4	3.7	0.6	3.2	2.7	2.8	2.4	3.3	3.8
Net fuel exporters	4.6	7.0	8.0	7.0	4.6	-0.7	1.5	5.4	4.7	2.7	3.5	3.8
Net fuel importers	3.8	4.1	5.3	5.3	3.9	-1.7	6.5	4.2	2.7	2.6	3.6	4.2
Memorandum items												
Least developed countries	6.5	8.0	8.0	9.0	7.7	5.0	5.8	3.6	4.9	5.4	5.7	5.7
East Asia (excluding China)	4.4	5.1	5.7	6.0	2.8	0.3	7.7	4.2	3.3	3.5	4.1	4.3
South Asia (excluding India)	4.6	5.9	6.0	6.1	3.5	3.5	4.8	4.4	2.3	1.7	3.0	3.8
Western Asia (excluding Israel and Turkey)	5.7	6.5	8.0	6.0	7.1	1.0	5.7	6.3	4.9	3.9	4.3	4.5
Arab States[e]	5.1	6.3	7.3	5.8	6.8	1.8	5.1	2.4	5.6	3.4	4.0	4.5
Landlocked developing economies	6.9	8.4	9.2	8.8	6.6	3.3	7.4	6.4	4.9	6.0	6.1	6.0
Small island developing economies	5.0	7.1	8.5	7.5	3.1	0.1	8.2	3.8	2.0	2.3	3.3	3.9
Major developing economies												
Argentina	6.7	9.2	8.5	8.7	6.8	0.8	9.2	8.9	1.9	5.0	3.0	3.0
Brazil	3.6	3.2	4.0	6.1	5.2	-0.3	7.5	2.7	0.9	2.5	3.0	4.2
Chile	4.5	6.2	5.7	5.2	3.3	-1.0	5.8	5.9	5.6	4.3	4.4	4.6
China	10.5	11.3	12.7	14.2	9.6	9.2	10.4	9.3	7.7	7.7	7.5	7.3
Colombia	4.8	4.7	6.7	6.9	3.5	1.7	4.0	6.6	4.0	3.7	4.2	4.5
Egypt	4.8	5.7	7.0	7.1	5.9	4.9	3.4	2.0	2.2	2.0	2.2	3.3
Hong Kong SAR[f]	4.2	7.4	7.0	6.5	2.1	-2.5	6.8	4.9	1.5	2.8	3.5	3.3
India	7.7	9.1	9.3	9.7	5.3	7.4	10.1	7.3	5.1	4.8	5.3	5.7
Indonesia	5.9	5.7	5.5	6.3	6.0	4.6	6.2	6.5	6.2	5.7	5.6	5.9
Iran, Islamic Republic of	4.2	5.2	5.9	7.8	3.1	3.5	5.4	3.6	-0.8	-2.0	0.8	1.7
Israel	4.3	4.9	5.8	5.9	4.1	1.1	5.0	4.6	3.2	3.2	2.2	3.3
Korea, Republic of	3.6	4.0	5.2	5.1	2.3	0.3	6.3	3.7	2.0	2.8	3.5	3.6

Table A.3
Developing economies: rates of growth of real GDP, 2005-2015 (*continued*)

Annual percentage change	2005-2012ᵃ	2005	2006	2007	2008	2009	2010	2011	2012	2013ᵇ	2014ᶜ	2015ᶜ
Malaysia	4.8	5.3	5.6	6.3	4.8	-1.5	7.4	5.1	5.6	4.4	4.8	5.0
Mexico	2.6	3.0	5.0	3.1	1.4	-4.7	5.1	4.0	3.9	1.2	4.0	4.2
Nigeria	6.7	6.5	6.0	6.5	6.3	6.9	7.8	6.8	6.5	6.5	6.9	6.7
Pakistan	3.7	6.9	5.5	3.2	2.3	2.2	2.2	3.4	4.0	3.6	3.2	4.3
Peru	7.0	6.8	7.7	8.9	9.8	0.9	8.8	6.9	6.3	5.3	6.1	6.3
Philippines	5.0	4.8	5.2	6.6	4.2	1.1	7.6	3.6	6.8	6.7	6.2	6.3
Saudi Arabia	6.3	7.3	5.6	6.0	8.4	1.8	7.4	8.6	5.1	4.0	5.1	5.0
Singapore	5.8	7.4	8.6	9.0	1.7	-0.8	14.8	5.2	1.3	3.6	3.7	4.0
South Africa	3.4	5.3	5.6	5.5	3.6	-1.5	3.1	3.5	2.5	2.7	3.3	3.7
Taiwan Province of China	3.8	4.7	5.4	6.0	0.7	-1.8	10.8	4.1	1.3	1.8	2.9	3.4
Thailand	3.6	4.2	4.9	5.4	1.7	-0.9	7.3	0.3	6.4	2.9	4.2	4.6
Turkey	4.4	8.4	6.9	4.7	0.7	-4.8	9.2	8.8	2.2	3.2	5.0	3.0
Venezuela, Bolivarian Republic of	4.8	10.3	9.9	8.8	5.3	-3.2	-1.5	4.2	5.5	1.2	2.5	2.9

Sources: UN/DESA, based on data of the United Nations Statistics Division and individual national sources.

Note: Country groups are calculated as a weighted average of individual country growth rates of gross domestic product (GDP), where weights are based on GDP in 2005 prices and exchange rates.

a Average percentage change.

b Partly estimated.

c Baseline scenario forecasts, based in part on Project LINK and the UN/DESA World Economic Forecasting Model.

d Covering countries that account for 98 per cent of the population of all developing countries.

e Currently includes data for Algeria, Bahrain, Comoros, Djibouti, Egypt, Iraq, Jordan, Kuwait, Lebanon, Libya, Mauritania, Morocco, Oman, Qatar, Saudi Arabia, Somalia, Sudan, Syrian Arab Republic, Tunisia, United Arab Emirates, and Yemen.

f Special Administrative Region of China.

Table A.4
Developed economies: consumer price inflation, 2005-2015

Annual percentage change[a]	2005	2006	2007	2008	2009	2010	2011	2012	2013[b]	2014[c]	2015[c]
Developed economies	2.4	2.3	2.1	3.5	-0.1	1.8	2.5	1.9	1.4	1.7	1.7
United States	3.7	3.2	2.6	4.3	-0.8	2.5	2.9	2.1	1.5	1.7	1.6
Canada	2.2	2.0	2.1	2.4	0.3	1.8	2.9	1.5	1.0	1.5	1.8
Japan	-0.3	0.2	0.1	1.4	-1.3	-0.7	-0.3	0.0	0.3	2.0	1.8
Australia	2.7	3.6	2.3	4.4	1.8	2.9	3.3	1.8	1.9	2.0	2.2
New Zealand	3.0	3.4	2.4	4.0	2.1	2.3	4.0	1.1	1.3	2.2	2.0
European Union	2.2	2.2	2.2	3.5	0.8	1.9	3.0	2.6	1.6	1.6	1.8
EU-15	2.1	2.2	2.1	3.3	0.7	1.9	3.0	2.5	1.6	1.6	1.7
Austria	2.1	1.7	2.2	3.2	0.4	1.7	3.5	2.6	2.0	2.0	2.0
Belgium	2.5	2.3	1.8	4.5	0.0	2.3	3.4	2.6	1.2	2.3	2.3
Denmark	1.7	1.9	1.7	3.6	1.1	2.2	2.7	2.4	1.3	1.6	1.9
Finland	0.8	1.3	1.6	3.9	1.6	1.7	3.3	3.2	2.3	1.9	2.0
France	1.9	1.9	1.6	3.2	0.1	1.7	2.3	2.2	1.0	1.6	1.8
Germany	1.9	1.8	2.3	2.8	0.2	1.1	2.5	2.1	1.7	1.6	1.7
Greece	3.5	3.3	3.0	4.2	1.4	4.7	3.1	1.0	-0.5	0.1	0.3
Ireland	2.2	2.7	2.9	3.1	-1.7	-1.6	1.2	1.9	0.5	0.5	1.2
Italy	2.2	2.2	2.0	3.5	0.8	1.6	2.9	3.3	1.4	1.8	1.7
Luxembourg	2.5	2.7	2.3	3.4	0.4	2.3	3.4	2.7	2.0	2.2	2.0
Netherlands	1.5	1.7	1.6	2.2	1.0	0.9	2.5	2.8	2.8	1.8	1.8
Portugal	2.1	3.0	2.4	2.7	-0.9	1.4	3.6	2.8	0.6	1.4	1.5
Spain	3.4	3.6	2.8	4.1	-0.2	2.0	3.1	2.4	1.6	0.8	1.5
Sweden	0.8	1.5	1.7	3.4	1.9	1.9	1.4	0.9	0.1	0.8	2.0
United Kingdom	2.1	2.3	2.3	3.6	2.2	3.3	4.5	2.8	2.6	1.8	1.7
New EU member States	3.4	3.1	4.1	6.1	3.1	2.8	3.7	3.7	1.8	2.2	2.4
Bulgaria	5.0	7.3	8.4	12.3	2.8	2.5	4.2	3.0	1.2	2.5	3.0
Croatia	3.3	3.2	2.9	6.0	2.4	1.0	2.3	3.4	2.7	3.0	3.0
Cyprus	2.6	2.5	2.3	4.7	0.4	2.4	3.3	2.4	0.5	1.9	2.2
Czech Republic	1.6	2.1	3.0	6.3	0.6	1.2	2.1	3.5	1.5	2.0	2.0
Estonia	4.1	4.5	6.7	10.6	0.2	2.7	5.1	4.2	3.5	3.5	3.5
Hungary	3.5	4.0	7.9	6.0	4.0	4.7	3.9	5.7	1.9	3.0	3.0
Latvia	6.7	6.5	10.1	15.4	3.5	-1.1	4.4	2.5	0.5	1.5	2.5
Lithuania	2.7	3.8	5.7	10.9	4.4	1.3	4.1	3.1	1.5	2.5	2.7
Malta	3.0	2.8	1.3	4.2	2.1	1.4	2.8	2.4	1.7	2.2	2.0
Poland	2.2	1.3	2.6	4.2	4.0	2.7	3.9	3.7	1.1	1.5	2.0
Romania	8.9	6.6	4.8	7.9	5.6	6.1	5.8	3.3	4.3	3.0	3.0
Slovakia	2.8	4.3	1.9	3.9	0.9	0.7	4.1	3.7	1.8	2.3	2.2
Slovenia	2.5	2.5	3.8	5.5	0.9	2.1	2.1	2.8	1.7	1.9	1.5
Other Europe	1.4	1.8	0.9	3.0	0.9	1.4	0.7	-0.1	0.7	1.0	1.4
Iceland	4.0	6.7	5.1	12.7	12.0	5.4	4.0	5.2	3.5	2.7	3.4
Norway	1.5	2.5	0.7	3.4	2.3	2.3	1.2	0.4	1.8	1.9	2.1
Switzerland	1.2	1.0	0.8	2.3	-0.7	0.6	0.1	-0.7	-0.3	0.3	0.8
Memorandum items											
North America	3.6	3.1	2.6	4.1	-0.7	2.4	2.9	2.1	1.5	1.7	1.6
Western Europe	2.1	2.2	2.2	3.5	0.8	1.9	2.9	2.4	1.6	1.6	1.7
Asia and Oceania	0.2	0.7	0.4	1.9	-0.8	-0.2	0.3	0.3	0.5	2.0	1.9
Major developed economies	2.4	2.3	2.0	3.4	-0.3	1.8	2.4	1.9	1.3	1.7	1.7
Euro area	2.2	2.2	2.1	3.3	0.3	1.5	2.7	2.5	1.5	1.6	1.7

Sources: UN/DESA, based on OECD, Main Economic Indicators; Eurostat; and individual national sources.
a Data for country groups are weighted averages, where weights for each year are based on 2005 GDP in United States dollars.
b Partly estimated.
c Baseline scenario forecasts, based in part on Project LINK and the UN/DESA World Economic Forecasting Model.

Table A.5
Economies in transition: consumer price inflation, 2005-2015

Annual percentage change[a]	2005	2006	2007	2008	2009	2010	2011	2012	2013[b]	2014[c]	2015[c]
Economies in transition	12.1	9.5	9.3	14.7	11.2	7.0	9.8	6.9	6.6	5.9	5.6
South-Eastern Europe	9.0	7.7	4.3	9.3	4.3	4.1	7.3	4.8	4.9	4.0	3.7
Albania	2.4	2.4	2.9	3.3	2.3	3.6	3.4	2.1	2.1	2.7	2.7
Bosnia and Herzegovina	3.7	6.1	1.5	7.4	-0.3	2.2	3.7	2.1	0.5	1.0	2.5
Montenegro	2.7	3.0	4.3	9.0	3.8	0.6	3.2	4.1	3.0	3.0	2.7
Serbia	16.1	11.7	6.4	12.4	8.2	6.1	11.2	7.3	8.4	6.0	5.0
The former Yugoslav Republic of Macedonia	0.5	3.2	2.3	8.4	-0.8	1.5	3.9	3.2	3.0	3.0	2.5
Commonwealth of Independent States and Georgia[d]	12.2	9.6	9.6	14.9	11.5	7.1	9.9	7.0	6.7	6.0	5.7
Net fuel exporters	12.0	9.8	9.2	14.3	11.1	6.8	8.5	5.1	6.8	5.8	5.6
Azerbaijan	-2.0	15.2	16.3	20.6	4.5	-0.9	8.0	1.8	2.5	5.0	4.5
Kazakhstan	7.5	8.6	10.8	17.1	7.3	7.1	8.3	5.1	6.0	6.4	6.1
Russian Federation	12.7	9.7	9.0	14.0	11.7	6.9	8.4	5.0	6.8	5.6	5.5
Turkmenistan	10.7	8.2	6.3	14.5	-2.7	4.4	12.0	8.2	10.2	10.0	8.0
Uzbekistan	10.0	14.2	12.3	12.7	14.1	9.4	12.8	11.5	10.0	11.0	8.8
Net fuel importers	13.3	8.7	11.7	19.0	14.3	9.4	18.6	19.0	6.1	7.0	6.2
Armenia	0.6	2.9	4.4	8.9	3.4	8.2	7.7	2.5	5.5	4.5	3.0
Belarus	9.8	7.0	8.7	14.5	12.6	7.9	51.4	60.0	21.0	12.0	8.3
Georgia[d]	8.2	9.2	9.2	10.1	1.7	7.1	8.6	-1.0	-0.5	3.0	3.0
Kyrgyzstan	4.4	5.6	10.1	24.5	6.9	8.0	16.4	2.7	7.4	6.0	5.0
Republic of Moldova	8.5	10.8	14.8	10.8	0.6	13.3	8.6	8.8	4.3	4.5	4.5
Tajikistan	6.3	18.5	19.2	32.9	6.5	6.4	27.3	6.0	5.8	5.5	5.5
Ukraine	16.2	9.3	13.1	21.6	17.4	10.1	8.7	8.2	1.4	5.9	6.0

Source: UN/DESA, based on data of the Economic Commission for Europe.

a Data for country groups are weighted averages, where weights for each year are based on 2005 GDP in United States dollars.

b Partly estimated.

c Baseline scenario forecasts, based in part on Project LINK and the UN/DESA World Economic Forecasting Model.

d Georgia officially left the Commonwealth of Independent States on 18 August 2009. However, its performance is discussed in the context of this group of countries for reasons of geographic proximity and similarities in economic structure.

Table A.6
Developing economies: consumer price inflation, 2005-2015

Annual percentage change[a]	2005	2006	2007	2008	2009	2010	2011	2012	2013[b]	2014[c]	2015[c]
Developing countries by region	4.9	5.3	19.2	8.1	4.6	5.4	6.3	5.5	5.7	5.6	5.3
Africa	8.2	12.4	156.1	10.9	12.8	7.0	7.9	8.2	8.0	7.8	7.2
North Africa	3.2	4.4	5.6	9.8	6.5	6.3	7.8	9.1	10.6	10.0	8.6
East Africa	11.1	10.9	10.7	21.7	79.4	13.2	16.5	12.6	6.9	6.7	6.9
Central Africa	3.9	4.3	1.1	6.6	4.3	2.4	2.0	4.4	3.9	3.3	3.3
West Africa	14.2	7.3	5.4	11.2	9.3	10.1	8.9	9.3	7.3	7.5	7.6
Southern Africa	10.7	25.8	469.6	10.2	7.8	5.3	6.2	6.2	6.2	6.2	6.1
Net fuel exporters	8.3	5.9	6.0	11.1	8.6	8.8	9.4	10.4	10.6	10.2	9.1
Net fuel importers	8.2	18.4	298.1	10.8	16.7	5.3	6.4	6.2	5.5	5.5	5.4
East and South Asia	3.6	3.6	4.9	7.4	2.8	4.9	6.2	4.8	4.9	4.8	4.5
East Asia	2.8	2.7	3.9	6.0	0.6	3.1	4.9	2.8	2.5	3.1	3.2
South Asia	6.5	7.1	8.6	12.6	11.2	11.6	11.1	12.4	13.9	11.3	9.4
Net fuel exporters	11.2	11.8	10.4	16.9	7.9	7.2	12.2	13.0	18.2	12.9	10.0
Net fuel importers	2.8	2.8	4.3	6.4	2.3	4.7	5.6	4.0	3.6	4.0	4.0
Western Asia	5.7	7.7	7.4	10.2	4.1	5.6	5.9	5.5	5.7	5.3	6.1
Net fuel exporters	5.1	7.4	8.1	10.7	2.9	4.2	5.9	2.8	3.2	3.4	4.1
Net fuel importers	6.4	8.0	6.7	9.6	5.3	7.1	5.9	8.5	8.4	7.3	8.3
Latin America and the Caribbean	6.1	5.0	5.1	7.6	5.9	5.9	6.3	5.9	6.7	6.6	5.9
South America	7.2	5.6	5.6	8.6	6.5	7.0	8.0	7.1	8.4	8.2	7.1
Mexico and Central America	4.4	3.9	4.3	5.7	5.1	4.2	3.6	4.1	4.0	4.4	4.2
Caribbean	4.6	5.1	4.4	8.0	2.5	5.0	4.7	3.5	3.5	2.9	3.2
Net fuel exporters	9.8	7.8	9.9	16.8	13.7	13.3	13.0	11.0	17.5	16.5	13.4
Net fuel importers	5.6	4.5	4.3	6.1	4.7	4.8	5.3	5.1	5.0	5.1	4.8
Memorandum items											
Least developed countries	10.6	9.0	9.4	13.6	24.8	10.4	11.7	12.5	10.3	8.8	7.9
East Asia (excluding China)	3.9	3.9	3.1	6.1	1.9	3.0	4.3	2.9	2.6	3.0	3.1
South Asia (excluding India)	10.9	9.7	12.8	20.9	11.6	10.7	15.4	17.6	22.0	15.6	11.8
Western Asia (excluding Israel and Turkey)	5.0	7.4	7.8	11.0	2.8	4.2	5.9	4.2	5.3	4.0	4.4
Arab States[d]	4.4	6.5	7.1	10.6	4.1	4.9	6.5	5.7	7.0	5.9	5.7
Landlocked developing economies	15.9	39.5	698.0	15.6	6.5	5.4	10.0	7.2	6.3	6.5	6.0
Small island developing economies	2.5	3.0	3.2	6.9	1.6	3.6	4.7	3.8	2.8	2.9	2.9
Major developing economies											
Argentina	9.6	10.9	8.8	8.6	6.3	10.8	9.5	10.0	10.5	11.4	10.8
Brazil	6.8	4.2	3.6	5.6	4.9	5.0	6.7	5.8	5.7	5.4	4.8
Chile	3.1	3.4	4.4	8.7	0.3	1.4	3.3	3.0	1.8	2.5	3.1
China	1.8	1.5	4.7	5.9	-0.7	3.3	5.5	2.6	2.5	3.1	3.3
Colombia	5.0	4.3	5.5	7.0	4.2	2.3	3.4	3.2	2.5	4.3	3.9
Egypt	4.9	7.6	9.3	18.3	11.8	11.3	10.1	7.1	9.1	10.2	8.5
Hong Kong SAR[e]	0.9	2.1	2.0	4.3	0.6	2.3	5.3	4.1	4.3	3.9	3.8
India	4.2	5.8	6.4	8.3	10.9	12.0	8.9	9.7	9.7	9.0	8.1
Indonesia	10.5	13.1	6.5	10.2	4.4	5.1	5.4	4.3	6.9	6.3	5.5
Iran, Islamic Republic of	13.4	11.9	17.2	25.5	13.5	10.1	20.6	27.3	38.5	24.8	17.6
Israel	1.3	2.1	0.5	4.6	3.3	2.7	3.5	1.7	1.6	1.3	1.7
Korea, Republic of	2.8	2.2	2.5	4.7	2.8	2.9	4.0	2.2	1.3	2.1	2.5

Table A.6
Developing economies: consumer price inflation, 2005-2015 (*continued*)

Annual percentage change	2005	2006	2007	2008	2009	2010	2011	2012	2013[b]	2014	2015[c]
Major developing economies (*continued*)											
Malaysia	3.0	3.6	2.0	5.4	0.6	1.7	3.2	1.7	1.9	2.8	3.2
Mexico	4.0	3.6	4.0	5.1	5.3	4.2	3.4	4.1	4.0	4.4	4.2
Nigeria	17.9	8.2	5.4	11.6	11.5	13.7	10.8	12.2	9.1	9.5	9.6
Pakistan	9.1	7.9	7.6	20.3	13.6	13.9	11.9	9.7	7.5	7.9	7.0
Peru	1.6	2.0	1.8	5.8	2.9	1.5	3.4	3.7	2.8	2.5	2.0
Philippines	6.5	5.5	2.9	8.3	4.1	3.9	4.6	3.2	2.9	3.5	3.7
Saudi Arabia	0.7	2.2	4.2	9.9	5.1	5.3	5.8	2.9	3.8	3.3	4.3
Singapore	0.4	1.0	2.1	6.5	0.6	2.8	5.3	4.5	2.5	2.9	2.7
South Africa	2.0	3.2	6.2	10.0	7.3	4.0	5.1	5.8	5.8	5.9	5.7
Taiwan Province of China	2.3	0.6	1.8	3.5	-0.9	1.0	1.4	1.9	1.0	1.8	1.8
Thailand	4.5	4.6	2.2	5.5	-0.8	3.3	3.8	3.0	2.2	2.6	3.0
Turkey	8.2	9.6	8.8	10.4	6.3	8.6	6.5	8.9	7.5	8.5	10.2
Venezuela, Bolivarian Republic of	17.4	12.8	16.9	29.9	27.1	28.2	26.1	21.1	39.0	34.4	27.1

Source: UN/DESA, based on IMF, International Financial Statistics.

a Data for country groups are weighted averages, where weights are based on GDP in 2005 prices and exchange rates.

b Partly estimated.

c Baseline scenario forecasts, based in part on Project LINK and the UN/DESA World Economic Forecasting Model.

d Currently includes data for Algeria, Bahrain, Comoros, Djibouti, Egypt, Iraq, Jordan, Kuwait, Lebanon, Libya, Mauritania, Morocco, Oman, Qatar, Saudi Arabia, Somalia, Sudan, Syrian Arab Republic, Tunisia, United Arab Emirates and Yemen.

e Special Administrative Region of China.

Table A.7
Developed economies: unemployment rates,[a, b] 2005-2015

Percentage of labour force	2005	2006	2007	2008	2009	2010	2011	2012	2013[c]	2014[d]	2015[d]
Developed economies	6.9	6.3	5.8	6.1	8.4	8.8	8.5	8.5	8.6	8.4	8.1
United States	5.1	4.6	4.6	5.8	9.3	9.6	8.9	8.1	7.5	7.1	6.5
Canada	6.8	6.3	6.0	6.1	8.3	8.0	7.5	7.3	7.1	7.0	6.8
Japan	4.4	4.1	3.8	4.0	5.1	5.1	4.6	4.4	3.9	3.7	4.0
Australia	5.0	4.8	4.4	4.2	5.6	5.2	5.1	5.2	5.4	5.8	6.1
New Zealand	3.8	3.9	3.7	4.2	6.1	6.5	6.5	7.3	6.6	6.8	6.4
European Union	9.1	8.3	7.2	7.0	9.0	9.6	9.7	10.4	11.0	11.0	10.6
EU-15	8.3	7.8	7.1	7.2	9.1	9.6	9.6	10.6	11.1	11.1	10.8
Austria	5.2	4.8	4.4	3.8	4.8	4.4	4.1	4.4	5.0	4.9	4.8
Belgium	8.4	8.3	7.5	7.0	7.9	8.3	7.2	7.6	8.3	8.3	7.9
Denmark	4.8	3.9	3.8	3.4	6.0	7.5	7.6	8.0	8.1	8.0	7.7
Finland	8.4	7.7	6.9	6.4	8.2	8.4	7.8	7.8	8.5	8.6	8.3
France	9.3	9.2	8.4	7.8	9.5	9.7	9.6	10.3	10.9	11.1	10.9
Germany	11.3	10.3	8.7	7.5	7.8	7.1	6.0	5.5	5.3	5.2	5.0
Greece	9.9	8.9	8.3	7.7	9.5	12.6	17.7	24.3	27.3	28.4	28.7
Ireland	4.4	4.5	4.7	6.4	12.0	13.9	14.7	14.8	13.7	13.3	12.9
Italy	7.7	6.8	6.1	6.7	7.8	8.4	8.4	10.7	12.1	12.3	12.0
Luxembourg	4.4	4.8	4.2	5.0	5.1	4.2	4.6	5.3	4.9	4.7	4.5
Netherlands	5.3	4.3	3.6	3.1	3.7	4.5	4.5	5.3	6.7	7.5	7.0
Portugal	7.7	7.8	8.1	7.7	9.6	11.0	12.9	15.9	17.0	17.3	17.2
Spain	9.2	8.5	8.3	11.3	18.0	20.1	21.6	25.1	26.5	26.4	25.3
Sweden	7.6	7.0	6.1	6.2	8.3	8.6	7.8	8.0	7.9	7.8	7.5
United Kingdom	4.8	5.4	5.3	5.7	7.6	7.8	8.0	7.9	7.5	7.3	7.2
New EU member States	11.9	10.0	7.7	6.5	8.4	9.9	9.8	9.4	10.8	10.4	10.0
Bulgaria	10.1	8.9	6.9	5.6	6.8	10.2	11.2	12.3	12.6	12.0	11.4
Croatia	12.6	11.1	9.6	8.4	9.1	11.8	13.4	14.9	16.8	16.0	15.5
Cyprus	5.3	4.5	4.0	3.6	5.4	6.2	7.7	11.1	19.1	21.2	21.7
Czech Republic	7.9	7.1	5.3	4.4	6.7	7.3	6.7	6.8	7.3	7.1	7.0
Estonia	7.9	5.9	4.6	5.6	13.8	16.9	12.6	11.5	11.0	10.5	10.3
Hungary	7.2	7.5	7.4	7.8	10.0	11.2	11.0	10.9	10.5	10.2	9.9
Latvia	9.0	6.8	6.0	7.4	17.1	18.7	15.3	15.1	14.5	14.0	12.5
Lithuania	8.3	5.6	4.3	5.8	13.7	17.8	15.4	13.2	12.6	11.7	11.0
Malta	7.2	7.1	6.4	5.7	6.8	6.6	6.5	6.5	6.5	6.5	6.5
Poland	17.9	14.0	9.6	7.0	8.1	9.7	9.7	10.5	12.0	11.6	11.0
Romania	7.2	7.3	6.4	5.8	6.9	7.3	7.4	7.1	7.0	6.8	6.5
Slovakia	16.4	13.5	11.2	9.6	12.1	14.5	13.7	13.9	14.2	13.9	13.8
Slovenia	6.5	6.0	4.9	4.4	5.9	7.3	8.2	8.9	9.1	9.0	8.6
Other Europe	4.4	3.7	3.2	3.1	4.0	4.2	3.8	3.8	4.0	4.2	4.3
Iceland[e]	2.9	2.8	2.2	2.7	7.0	7.4	7.4	6.7	5.0	4.6	4.5
Norway	4.5	3.4	2.5	2.6	3.2	3.6	3.3	3.2	3.6	3.5	3.5
Switzerland	4.3	3.9	3.6	3.3	4.3	4.4	3.9	4.1	4.2	4.6	4.8
Memorandum items											
Major developed economies	6.3	5.9	5.5	5.9	8.1	8.2	7.7	7.4	7.2	7.0	6.7
Euro area	9.2	8.5	7.6	7.6	9.5	10.1	10.1	11.3	12.0	12.1	11.8

Source: UN/DESA, based on data of the OECD and Eurostat.

a Unemployment data are standardized by the OECD and Eurostat for comparability among countries and over time, in conformity with the definitions of the International Labour Organization (see OECD, Standardized Unemployment Rates: Sources and Methods (Paris, 1985)).

b Data for country groups are weighted averages, where labour force is used for weights.

c Partly estimated.

d Baseline scenario forecasts, based in part on Project LINK and the UN/DESA World Economic Forecasting Model.

e Not standardized.

Table A.8
Economies in transition and developing economies: unemployment rates,[a] 2004-2013

Percentage of labour force	2004	2005	2006	2007	2008	2009	2010	2011	2012	2013[b]
South-Eastern Europe										
Albania[c]	14.4	14.1	13.8	13.2	12.5	13.6	13.5	13.3	13.1	12.8
Bosnia and Herzegovina	..	..	31.1	29.0	23.4	24.1	27.2	27.6	28.0	27.5
Montenegro	31.1	30.3	29.6	19.4	16.8	19.1	19.7	19.7	19.7	20.3
Serbia	18.5	20.8	20.9	18.1	13.6	16.1	19.2	23.0	23.9	24.5
The former Yugoslav Republic of Macedonia	37.2	37.3	36.0	34.9	33.8	32.2	32.0	31.4	31.0	28.6
Commonwealth of Independent States and Georgia[d]										
Armenia	31.6	31.2	27.8	28.7	16.4	18.7	19.0	18.4	17.3	16.5
Azerbaijan	8.4	7.6	6.8	6.5	6.0	5.9	5.6	5.4	5.4	5.5
Belarus[c]	1.9	1.5	1.1	1.0	0.8	0.9	0.7	0.6	0.5	0.5
Georgia[d]	12.6	13.8	13.6	13.3	16.5	16.9	16.3	15.1	15.0	15.0
Kazakhstan	8.4	8.1	7.8	7.3	6.6	6.6	5.8	5.4	5.3	5.2
Kyrgyzstan	2.9	3.3	3.5	3.3	2.8	2.8	2.5	2.6	2.5	2.5
Republic of Moldova	8.1	7.3	7.4	5.1	4.0	6.4	7.4	6.7	5.6	6.0
Russian Federation	7.8	7.2	7.2	6.1	6.4	8.4	7.5	6.6	5.5	5.6
Tajikistan[c]	2.0	2.1	2.3	2.5	2.1	2.1	2.2	2.1	2.6	2.5
Turkmenistan[c]	..	3.7	..	3.6	2.5	2.2	2.0	2.3	2.1	2.0
Ukraine	8.6	7.2	7.4	6.6	6.4	8.8	8.1	8.0	7.7	8.2
Uzbekistan[c]	0.4	0.3	0.3	0.2	0.2	0.2	0.2	0.2	0.2	0.2
Africa										
Algeria	17.7	15.3	12.3	13.8	11.3	10.2	10.0	10.0	10.4	10.2
Botswana	..	..	17.6	20.2	..	..	17.8	..	..	..
Egypt	10.3	11.2	10.7	8.9	8.7	9.4	9.0	12.0	12.5	13.1
Mauritius	8.4	9.6	9.1	8.5	7.2	7.3	7.8	7.9	8.0	8.3
Morocco	10.8	11.1	9.7	9.8	9.6	9.1	9.1	8.9	9.0	9.1
South Africa	27.0	26.6	25.5	23.3	22.9	24.0	24.9	24.9	25.1	25.2
Tunisia[e]	..	12.9	12.5	12.4	12.4	13.3	13.0	18.3	17.4	17.0
Developing America										
Argentina[f]	13.6	11.6	10.2	8.5	7.9	8.7	7.7	7.2	7.3	7.6
Barbados	9.6	9.1	8.7	7.4	8.1	10.0	10.8	11.2	11.6	11.0
Bolivia[f]	6.2	8.1	8.0	7.7	6.7	7.9	6.1	5.8	..	..
Brazil[h, g]	11.5	9.8	10.0	9.3	7.9	8.1	6.7	6.0	5.5	5.6
Chile	10.0	9.2	7.8	7.1	7.8	9.7	8.2	7.2	6.4	6.1
Colombia[h]	15.3	13.9	12.9	11.4	11.5	13.0	12.4	11.5	11.2	11.6
Costa Rica	6.7	6.9	6.0	4.8	4.8	8.5	7.1	7.7	7.8	..
Dominican Republic	18.4	17.9	16.2	15.6	14.1	14.9	14.3	14.6	14.7	15.0
Ecuador[i]	9.7	8.5	8.1	7.3	6.9	8.5	7.6	6.0	4.9	4.7
El Salvador	6.5	7.3	5.7	5.8	5.5	7.3	7.0	6.6	6.2	..
Guatemala	4.4	..	..	..	..	..	4.8	3.1	4.0	..
Honduras	8.0	6.1	4.6	3.9	4.2	4.9	6.4	6.8	5.6	..
Jamaica	11.4	11.2	10.3	9.8	10.6	11.4	12.4	12.6	13.9	15.9
Mexico	5.3	4.7	4.6	4.8	4.9	6.6	6.4	6.0	5.9	5.6
Nicaragua	8.6	7.0	7.0	6.9	8.0	10.5	9.7	..	..	..
Panama	14.1	12.1	10.4	7.8	6.5	7.9	7.7	5.4	4.8	5.1

Percentage of labour force	2004	2005	2006	2007	2008	2009	2010	2011	2012	2013[b]
Paraguay[f]	10.0	7.6	8.9	7.2	7.4	8.2	7.0	6.5	6.1	8.2
Peru[f, j]	9.4	9.6	8.5	8.4	8.4	8.4	7.9	7.7	7.5	
Trinidad and Tobago	8.3	8.0	6.2	5.5	4.6	5.3	5.9	5.1	5.2	..
Uruguay[f]	13.1	12.2	10.8	9.4	8.0	7.7	7.2	6.3	6.5	6.7
Venezuela, Bolivarian Republic of	15.3	12.3	10.6	8.4	7.3	7.9	8.7	8.3	8.1	8.1
Developing Asia										
China	4.2	4.2	4.1	4.0	4.2	4.3	4.1	4.1	4.1	4.1
Hong Kong SAR[k]	6.8	5.6	4.8	4.0	3.5	5.3	4.3	3.4	3.3	3.4
India[l]	5.0	..	..	..	..	9.4	..	3.8	4.7	..
Indonesia	9.9	11.2	10.3	9.1	8.4	7.9	7.1	6.8	6.2	6.1
Iran, Islamic Republic of	10.3	11.5	..	10.5	10.3	11.5	13.5	12.3	12.2	..
Israel	10.4	9.0	8.4	7.3	6.1	7.6	6.6	5.6	6.9	6.5
Jordan	12.5	14.8	14.0	13.1	12.7	12.8	12.5	12.9	12.2	13.1
Korea, Republic of	3.7	3.7	3.5	3.2	3.2	3.6	3.7	3.4	3.2	3.2
Malaysia	3.5	3.5	3.3	3.2	3.3	3.6	3.3	3.1	3.0	3.1
Pakistan	7.7	7.7	6.2	5.3	5.2	5.5	5.8	6.0	6.2	6.1
Philippines[m, n]	11.8	9.8	7.9	7.3	7.4	7.5	7.4	7.0	7.0	7.3
Saudi Arabia	5.8	6.1	6.3	6.1	6.3	6.3	6.2	5.9	5.6	5.7
Singapore	3.4	3.1	2.7	2.1	2.2	3.0	2.2	2.0	2.0	1.9
Sri Lanka[o]	8.1	7.2	6.5	6.0	5.2	5.7	4.9	4.0	4.0	4.5
Taiwan Province of China	4.4	4.1	3.9	3.9	4.1	5.9	5.2	4.4	4.2	4.2
Thailand	2.1	1.8	1.5	1.4	1.4	1.5	1.1	0.7	0.7	0.8
Turkey	9.0	9.2	8.8	8.9	9.7	12.6	10.7	9.8	9.1	9.8
Viet Nam[f]	5.6	5.3	4.8	4.6	4.7	3.3	1.8	1.6	2.0	2.2

Sources: UN/DESA, based on data of the Economic Commission for Europe (ECE); ILO LABORSTAT database and KILM 7th edition; Economic Commission for Latin America and the Caribbean (ECLAC); and national sources.

a   As a percentage of labour force. Reflects national definitions and coverage. Not comparable across economies.

b   Partly estimated.

c   End-of-period registered unemployment data (as a percentage of labour force).

d   Georgia officially left the Commonwealth of Independent States on 18 August 2009. However, its performance is discussed in the context of this group of countries for reasons of geographic proximity and similarities in economic structure.

e   New methodology starting in 2005.

f   Urban areas.

g   Six main cities.

h   Thirteen main cities.

i   Covers Quito, Guayaquil and Cuenca.

j   Metropolitan Lima.

k   Special Administrative Region of China.

l   Data for 2011 and 2012 refer to the fiscal year.

m   Partly adopts the ILO definition; that is to say, it does not include one ILO criterion, namely, "currently available for work".

n   Break in series: new methodology starting in 2005.

o   Excluding Northern and Eastern provinces.

Table A.9
Major developed economies: quarterly indicators of growth, unemployment and inflation, 2011-2013

Percentage	2011				2012				2013		
	I	II	III	IV	I	II	III	IV	I	II	III
Growth of gross domestic product[a] (*percentage change in seasonally adjusted data from preceding quarter*)											
Canada	2.2	-0.6	6.2	1.9	0.8	1.6	0.8	0.9	2.2	1.8	2.7
France	4.5	-0.2	1.0	0.7	0.1	-1.4	0.7	-0.7	-0.2	2.2	-0.6
Germany	6.3	0.4	1.7	0.4	2.7	-0.3	0.8	-1.8	0.0	2.9	1.3
Italy	0.3	1.0	-0.6	-2.9	-4.4	-2.4	-1.7	-3.7	-2.3	-1.1	-0.5
Japan	-7.7	-3.0	10.7	1.0	5.1	-0.8	-3.7	0.6	4.3	3.8	1.9
United Kingdom	1.9	0.4	2.4	-0.4	0.0	-1.8	2.5	-1.2	1.5	2.7	3.2
United States	-1.3	3.2	1.4	4.9	3.7	1.2	2.8	0.1	1.1	2.5	2.8
Major developed economies[b]	-0.7	1.1	3.0	2.4	2.6	0.1	1.0	-0.4	1.3	2.5	2.1
Euro area	3.1	0.3	0.3	-0.8	-0.4	-1.2	-0.5	-2.0	-0.9	1.1	0.4
Unemployment rate[c] (*percentage of total labour force*)											
Canada	7.7	7.5	7.3	7.4	7.4	7.3	7.3	7.2	7.1	7.1	7.1
France	9.6	9.5	9.6	9.8	9.9	10.2	10.3	10.6	10.8	10.8	11.0
Germany	6.3	6.0	5.8	5.6	5.5	5.5	5.4	5.4	5.4	5.3	5.3
Italy	7.9	7.9	8.6	9.2	10.0	10.6	10.8	11.4	11.9	12.1	12.3
Japan	4.7	4.7	4.5	4.5	4.5	4.4	4.3	4.2	4.2	4.0	4.0
United Kingdom	7.7	7.9	8.2	8.3	8.2	7.9	7.8	7.7	7.8	7.7	
United States	9.0	9.0	9.0	8.7	8.3	8.2	8.0	7.8	7.7	7.6	7.3
Major developed economies[d]	7.7	7.7	7.7	7.6	7.5	7.4	7.4	7.3	7.3	7.2	
Euro area	9.9	9.9	10.2	10.6	10.9	11.3	11.5	11.8	12.0	12.1	12.2
Change in consumer prices (*percentage change from one year ago*)											
Canada	2.6	3.4	3.0	2.7	2.3	1.6	1.2	0.9	0.9	0.8	1.2
France	2.0	2.2	2.3	2.6	2.6	2.3	2.3	1.7	1.2	0.9	1.1
Germany	2.2	2.5	2.6	2.6	2.4	2.1	2.1	2.0	1.8	1.5	1.7
Italy	2.3	2.9	2.7	3.7	3.6	3.6	3.4	2.6	2.1	1.3	1.1
Japan	-0.5	-0.4	0.1	-0.3	0.3	0.2	-0.4	-0.2	-0.6	-0.3	0.9
United Kingdom	4.1	4.4	4.7	4.7	3.5	2.7	2.4	2.7	2.8	2.7	2.7
United States	2.1	3.4	3.8	3.3	2.8	1.9	1.7	1.9	1.7	1.4	1.6
Major developed economies[b]	1.9	2.7	2.9	2.7	2.4	1.8	1.6	1.6	1.4	1.2	1.5
Euro area	2.5	2.8	2.7	2.9	2.7	2.5	2.5	2.3	1.9	1.4	1.3

Source: UN/DESA, based on Eurostat, OECD and national sources.
a Expressed as an annualized rate.
b Calculated as a weighted average, where weights are based on 2005 GDP in United States dollars.
c Seasonally adjusted data as standardized by OECD.
d Calculated as a weighted average, where weights are based on labour force.

Table A.10

Selected economies in transition: quarterly indicators of growth and inflation, 2011-2013

Percentage	2011				2012				2013		
	I	II	III	IV	I	II	III	IV	I	II	III
Rates of growth of gross domestic product[a]											
Armenia	1.9	3.1	6.7	5.2	5.4	7.1	9.1	6.2	7.5	0.6	..
Azerbaijan[b]	1.6	0.9	0.5	0.1	0.5	1.5	1.1	2.2	3.1	5.0	5.4
Belarus	10.6	11.2	1.7	0.3	3.0	2.5	2.6	-2.0	4.0	-0.5	..
Georgia	5.8	6.0	7.9	8.5	6.7	8.2	7.5	2.8	2.4	1.5	..
Kazakhstan[b]	6.8	7.0	7.2	7.5	5.6	5.6	5.2	5.0	4.7	5.1	..
Kyrgyzstan[b]	0.6	4.9	8.3	5.7	-8.4	-6.9	-5.6	-0.9	7.6	7.9	9.2
Republic of Moldova	6.9	7.1	6.9	6.7	1.0	0.6	-1.7	-2.5	3.5	6.1	..
Russian Federation	3.5	3.4	5.0	5.1	4.8	4.3	3.0	2.1	1.6	1.2	1.2
The former Yugoslav Republic of Macedonia	6.4	3.7	1.2	0.9	-1.3	-0.9	0.4	1.0	2.9	3.9	..
Ukraine	5.4	3.9	6.5	4.7	2.2	3.0	-1.3	-2.5	-1.1	-1.3	-1.5
Change in consumer prices[a]											
Armenia	11.1	8.8	5.8	5.1	3.3	1.0	2.4	3.4	3.0	5.2	..
Azerbaijan	8.9	8.5	7.6	6.1	3.0	1.2	0.0	-0.2	1.1	2.7	..
Belarus	12.6	31.7	63.1	102.4	107.8	82.4	52.3	24.8	22.6	19.4	16.0
Bosnia and Herzegovina	3.5	4.1	3.9	3.2	2.3	2.1	1.8	2.0	0.8	0.4	0.0
Georgia	13.3	12.6	6.7	2.1	-1.3	-1.9	0.0	-0.6	-1.9	-0.5	..
Kazakhstan	8.5	8.4	8.9	7.7	5.1	4.9	4.8	5.7	6.8	6.1	..
Kyrgyzstan	20.5	22.5	16.9	7.2	1.9	-0.3	2.1	7.1	7.7	7.2	..
Republic of Moldova	6.2	7.3	8.9	8.6	6.2	4.2	4.4	4.0	4.3	5.1	..
Russian Federation	9.5	9.5	8.1	6.7	3.9	3.8	6.0	6.5	7.1	7.2	6.4
The former Yugoslav Republic of Macedonia	3.9	4.7	3.7	3.3	2.4	2.2	3.7	4.9	3.4	3.6	2.8
Ukraine	7.7	10.8	8.4	5.0	3.8	2.2	2.6	2.4	1.2	-0.4	-0.3

Source: UN/DESA, based on data of the Economic Commission for Europe, European Bank for Reconstruction and Development and national sources.

a Percentage change from the corresponding period of the preceding year.

b Data reflect growth rate of cumulative GDP from the beginning of the year.

Table A.11
Major developing economies: quarterly indicators of growth, unemployment and inflation, 2011-2013

Percentage	2011				2012				2013		
	I	II	III	IV	I	II	III	IV	I	II	III
Rates of growth of gross domestic product[a]											
Argentina	9.9	9.1	9.3	7.3	5.2	0.0	0.7	2.1	3.0	8.3	..
Brazil	4.2	3.3	2.1	1.4	0.8	0.5	0.9	1.4	1.9	3.3	..
Chile	9.8	5.8	3.2	5.0	5.1	5.7	5.8	5.7	4.7	4.0	4.7
China	9.8	9.7	9.5	9.3	8.1	7.8	7.7	7.8	7.7	7.5	7.8
Colombia	5.6	6.5	8.0	6.5	5.9	4.8	2.9	3.3	2.7	4.2	..
Ecuador	7.7	8.5	8.7	6.4	6.6	5.5	4.3	4.1	3.5	3.5	..
Hong Kong SAR[b]	7.6	5.1	4.0	3.0	0.7	0.9	1.5	2.8	2.9	3.2	2.9
India	9.9	7.5	6.5	6.0	5.1	5.4	5.2	4.7	4.8	4.4	4.8
Indonesia	6.5	6.5	6.5	6.5	6.3	6.4	6.2	6.1	6.0	5.8	5.6
Israel	5.0	4.1	5.8	3.4	3.9	2.9	3.2	3.1	2.9	4.9	..
Korea, Republic of	4.2	3.5	3.6	3.3	2.8	2.3	1.6	1.5	1.5	2.3	3.3
Malaysia	5.2	4.3	5.7	5.3	5.1	4.9	5.4	6.5	4.1	4.3	5.0
Mexico	4.4	3.2	4.1	4.2	4.8	4.4	3.1	3.3	0.6	1.6	1.3
Philippines	4.9	3.6	3.2	4.0	6.5	6.3	7.3	7.1	7.7	7.5	7.0
Singapore	9.1	1.8	5.7	3.6	1.5	2.3	0.0	1.5	0.3	4.2	5.1
South Africa	3.8	3.6	3.3	3.7	2.7	2.9	2.2	2.1	1.6	2.3	1.8
Taiwan Province of China	7.4	4.6	3.5	1.2	0.6	-0.1	0.7	4.0	1.6	2.5	1.6
Thailand	3.2	2.7	3.7	-8.9	0.4	4.4	3.1	19.1	5.4	2.9	2.7
Turkey	12.4	9.3	8.7	5.3	3.1	2.8	1.5	1.4	2.9	4.4	..
Venezuela, Bolivarian Republic of	4.8	2.6	4.4	4.9	5.9	5.6	5.5	5.5	0.6	2.6	1.1
Unemployment rate[c]											
Argentina	7.4	7.3	7.2	6.7	7.1	7.2	7.6	6.9	7.9	7.2	6.8
Brazil	6.3	6.3	6.0	5.3	5.8	5.9	5.4	4.9	5.6	5.9	5.4
Chile	7.3	7.1	7.4	7.0	6.5	6.6	6.5	6.3	6.2	6.2	5.7
Colombia	12.4	11.1	10.4	9.3	11.6	10.5	10.2	9.2	11.4	9.6	9.4
Ecuador	7.0	6.4	5.5	5.1	4.9	5.2	4.6	5.0	4.6	4.9	4.5
Hong Kong SAR[b]	3.4	3.7	3.4	3.1	3.3	3.3	3.5	3.1	3.4	3.4	3.5
Israel	5.7	5.2	6.1	6.8	6.9	6.9	6.8	6.8	6.6	6.8	6.1
Korea, Republic of	4.2	3.4	3.1	2.9	3.9	3.3	3.0	2.8	3.6	3.1	2.9
Malaysia	3.1	3.0	3.1	3.0	3.0	3.0	3.0	3.1	3.1	3.0	..
Mexico	5.1	5.2	5.7	4.8	5.0	4.8	5.1	4.9	4.9	5.0	5.2
Philippines	7.4	7.2	7.1	6.4	7.2	6.9	7.0	6.8	7.1	7.5	7.3
Singapore	1.9	2.1	2.0	2.0	2.1	2.0	1.9	1.8	1.9	2.1	1.8
South Africa	25.0	25.7	25.0	23.9	25.2	24.9	25.5	24.9	25.2	25.6	24.7
Taiwan Province of China	4.6	4.3	4.4	4.2	4.2	4.1	4.3	4.3	4.2	4.1	4.3
Thailand	0.8	0.6	0.6	0.6	0.7	0.9	0.6	0.5	0.7	0.7	..
Turkey	10.3	10.2	9.6	9.2	9.2	9.0	9.2	9.4	9.4	9.6	..
Uruguay	6.7	6.5	6.3	5.8	6.1	6.8	6.6	6.0	6.9	6.7	6.4
Venezuela, Bolivarian Republic of	9.3	8.4	8.2	7.0	9.1	8.0	7.7	6.5	8.2	7.5	7.8

Percentage	2011				2012				2013		
	I	II	III	IV	I	II	III	IV	I	II	III
Change in consumer prices[a]											
Argentina	11.0	9.7	9.0	9.5	8.9	9.9	10.0	10.6	10.8	10.4	10.5
Brazil	6.1	6.6	7.1	6.7	5.8	5.0	5.2	5.6	6.2	6.5	6.2
Chile	2.9	3.3	3.1	4.0	4.1	3.1	2.6	2.2	1.5	1.3	2.1
China	5.1	5.7	6.3	4.6	3.8	2.9	1.9	2.1	2.4	2.4	2.8
Colombia	3.3	3.0	3.5	3.9	3.5	3.4	3.1	2.8	1.9	2.1	2.2
Ecuador	3.4	4.1	4.9	5.5	5.6	5.1	5.1	4.6	3.5	2.9	2.1
Hong Kong SAR[b]	3.8	5.1	6.5	5.7	5.2	4.2	3.0	3.7	3.7	4.0	5.3
India[d]	..	..	..	..	8.7	10.2	9.9	10.1	10.7	9.5	9.7
Indonesia	6.8	5.9	4.7	4.1	3.7	4.5	4.5	4.4	5.3	5.6	8.6
Israel	4.0	4.1	3.3	2.5	1.8	1.6	1.8	1.6	1.4	1.2	1.6
Korea, Republic of	3.8	4.0	4.3	4.0	3.0	2.4	1.6	1.7	1.4	1.1	1.2
Malaysia	2.8	3.3	3.4	3.2	2.3	1.7	1.4	1.3	1.5	1.8	2.2
Mexico	3.5	3.3	3.4	3.5	3.9	3.9	4.6	4.1	3.7	4.6	3.4
Philippines	4.5	4.9	4.7	4.7	3.1	2.9	3.5	2.9	3.2	2.7	2.4
Singapore	5.1	4.7	5.5	5.5	4.9	5.3	4.2	4.0	4.0	1.6	1.8
South Africa	3.8	4.6	5.4	6.1	6.1	5.8	5.1	5.6	5.7	5.7	6.2
Taiwan Province of China	1.3	1.6	1.4	1.4	1.3	1.6	2.9	1.8	1.8	0.8	0.0
Thailand	3.0	4.1	4.1	4.0	3.4	2.5	2.9	3.2	3.1	2.3	1.7
Turkey	4.3	5.9	6.4	9.2	10.5	9.4	9.0	6.8	7.2	7.0	8.3
Venezuela, Bolivarian Republic of	28.2	23.1	25.8	27.4	25.3	22.6	18.5	18.7	19.4	29.9	37.6

Sources: IMF, International Financial Statistics, and national sources.

a Percentage change from the corresponding quarter of the previous year.

b Special Administrative Region of China.

c Reflects national definitions and coverage. Not comparable across economies.

d Data based on a new statistics available from 2011 onward.

Table A.12
Major developed economies: financial indicators, 2004-2013

Percentage	2004	2005	2006	2007	2008	2009	2010	2011	2012	2013[a]
Short-term interest rates[b]										
Canada	2.3	2.8	4.2	4.6	3.4	0.7	0.8	1.2	1.2	1.2
France[c]	2.1	2.2	3.1	4.3	4.6	1.2	0.8	1.4	0.6	0.2
Germany[c]	2.1	2.2	3.1	4.3	4.6	1.2	0.8	1.4	0.6	0.2
Italy[c]	2.1	2.2	3.1	4.3	4.6	1.2	0.8	1.4	0.6	0.2
Japan	0.1	0.1	0.3	0.7	0.8	0.6	0.4	0.3	0.3	0.2
United Kingdom	4.6	4.7	4.8	6.0	5.5	1.2	0.7	0.9	0.8	0.5
United States	1.6	3.5	5.2	5.3	3.0	0.6	0.3	0.3	0.3	0.2
Long-term interest rates[d]										
Canada	4.6	4.1	4.2	4.3	3.6	3.2	3.3	2.8	1.9	2.1
France	4.1	3.4	3.8	4.3	4.2	3.6	3.1	3.3	2.5	2.2
Germany	4.0	3.4	3.8	4.2	4.0	3.2	2.7	2.6	1.5	1.5
Italy	4.3	3.6	4.0	4.5	4.7	4.3	4.0	5.4	5.5	4.4
Japan	1.5	1.4	1.7	1.7	1.5	1.3	1.1	1.1	0.8	0.7
United Kingdom	4.9	4.4	4.5	5.0	4.6	3.6	3.6	3.1	1.9	2.4
United States	4.3	4.3	4.8	4.6	3.7	3.3	3.2	2.8	1.8	2.3
General government financial balances[e]										
Canada	1.0	1.7	1.8	1.5	-0.3	-4.5	-4.9	-3.7	-3.4	-3.0
France	-3.6	-3.0	-2.4	-2.7	-3.3	-7.6	-7.1	-5.3	-4.8	-4.2
Germany	-3.8	-3.3	-1.7	0.2	-0.1	-3.1	-4.2	-0.8	0.1	0.1
Italy	-3.6	-4.5	-3.4	-1.6	-2.7	-5.4	-4.3	-3.7	-2.9	-3.0
Japan	-5.9	-4.8	-1.3	-2.1	-1.9	-8.8	-8.3	-8.9	-9.5	-10.0
United Kingdom	-3.5	-3.4	-2.9	-3.0	-5.1	-11.2	-10.0	-7.9	-6.2	-6.9
United States	-5.5	-4.2	-3.1	-3.7	-7.2	-12.8	-12.2	-10.7	-9.3	-6.5

Sources: UN/DESA, based on OECD, Economic Outlook; OECD, Main Economic Indicators and Eurostat.

a Average for the first nine months for short- and long-term interest rates.

b Three-month Interbank Rate.

c Three-month Euro Interbank Offered Rate (EURIBOR).

d Yield on long-term government bonds.

e Surplus (+) or deficit (-) as a percentage of nominal GDP. Estimates for 2013.

Table A.13
Selected economies: real effective exchange rates, broad measurement,[a, b] 2004-2013

	2004	2005	2006	2007	2008	2009	2010	2011	2012	2013[c]
Developed economies										
Australia	120.8	127.8	133.1	142.2	141.2	129.8	145.9	155.7	157.6	153.6
Bulgaria	113.1	116.3	126.3	133.0	143.1	139.6	142.7	150.4	151.6	151.9
Canada	104.5	108.0	111.6	112.4	103.2	95.0	101.6	100.1	97.8	95.3
Croatia	113.8	114.8	115.7	116.9	124.8	127.3	127.2	127.1	129.4	131.6
Czech Republic	121.5	129.5	133.6	139.2	157.2	149.2	149.7	155.5	150.4	150.1
Denmark	114.5	112.1	109.9	109.9	110.8	117.4	112.2	109.6	107.6	110.5
Euro area	120.8	119.5	120.6	125.3	130.7	125.4	117.7	119.8	114.5	119.5
Hungary	118.8	119.0	115.4	119.6	122.1	118.8	118.5	116.7	113.7	114.2
Japan	83.4	79.1	72.1	67.2	73.7	83.5	83.6	85.3	84.1	69.1
New Zealand	140.1	147.0	135.6	145.9	134.4	127.2	139.3	145.1	152.3	161.4
Norway	110.4	117.0	122.8	131.8	134.3	129.2	139.3	145.7	145.6	143.4
Poland	102.0	111.3	113.5	117.5	126.2	109.4	114.3	114.0	112.4	112.4
Romania	125.3	151.7	169.2	188.5	179.1	171.3	172.9	174.4	165.4	176.7
Slovakia	116.8	117.0	118.3	128.5	131.9	141.0	129.7	124.5	121.8	124.0
Sweden	96.4	93.4	94.3	97.7	92.0	89.3	92.2	92.1	90.2	91.1
Switzerland	110.2	106.1	101.5	96.6	98.7	106.9	109.7	117.8	113.5	113.0
United Kingdom	99.9	97.5	97.3	99.3	87.5	80.1	80.9	81.4	85.7	85.2
United States	91.9	89.2	86.7	82.6	79.3	87.8	83.3	78.3	82.2	85.6
Economies in transition										
Russian Federation	139.6	153.7	169.3	178.9	191.6	181.1	197.2	203.0	208.5	217.6
Developing economies										
Argentina	60.9	60.1	58.5	57.8	59.0	57.1	57.6	56.0	59.6	57.5
Brazil	105.5	129.2	140.3	155.0	174.5	167.5	192.0	206.7	189.0	188.6
Chile	99.9	111.5	117.7	116.9	122.4	126.6	126.0	127.3	132.0	129.1
China	96.0	98.2	101.0	103.3	112.2	112.4	113.5	116.4	119.3	125.7
Colombia	94.6	104.6	102.5	110.1	114.0	107.5	123.8	123.3	126.3	121.6
Ecuador	113.2	119.5	128.9	124.2	134.7	109.5	126.3	139.4	141.0	145.1
Egypt	66.3	72.2	74.3	76.6	86.8	85.5	92.4	92.5	96.0	87.1
Hong Kong SAR[d]	90.1	86.6	84.3	80.2	75.9	80.7	77.8	74.4	77.3	79.5
India	99.0	101.2	99.0	106.1	99.2	94.0	100.3	97.7	91.6	87.7
Indonesia	113.4	113.7	141.8	149.1	162.5	163.0	183.8	183.5	181.6	180.7
Israel	85.5	86.4	87.0	88.0	98.2	97.7	102.9	103.2	99.0	106.8
Korea, Republic of	95.8	105.7	110.7	108.5	91.5	79.7	86.5	88.8	88.6	92.6
Kuwait	95.0	96.4	95.3	93.3	97.3	96.5	98.1	96.2	98.7	102.5
Malaysia	100.7	103.3	107.0	112.7	115.7	113.1	124.4	131.0	131.8	131.1
Mexico	98.8	104.3	107.7	108.4	109.7	93.8	102.1	105.3	103.4	108.2
Morocco	97.4	94.9	94.8	93.8	94.4	100.1	96.0	92.0	91.0	93.9
Nigeria	110.6	126.2	134.6	132.2	143.6	137.3	149.7	147.2	166.8	180.7
Pakistan	99.6	101.4	105.0	104.8	105.2	107.1	117.1	127.4	128.2	129.0
Peru	99.5	99.3	99.3	99.6	106.5	105.5	109.9	110.9	118.8	118.8
Philippines	100.4	106.7	129.0	135.4	130.2	128.9	118.3	110.0	111.9	107.2

Table A.13

Selected economies: real effective exchange rates, broad measurement,[a, b] **2004-2013** (*continued*)

	2004	2005	2006	2007	2008	2009	2010	2011	2012	2013[c]
Developing economies (*continued*)										
Saudi Arabia	87.8	85.1	84.2	82.0	83.4	92.2	93.2	91.1	95.4	101.0
Singapore	102.2	106.8	112.1	119.5	125.3	114.4	116.4	118.6	116.2	118.0
South Africa	114.9	117.3	113.2	109.0	99.9	104.7	118.0	115.6	108.8	97.4
Taiwan Province of China	90.7	89.1	88.9	87.7	84.6	76.6	79.6	79.7	78.6	79.4
Thailand	99.8	102.4	111.3	124.5	120.8	111.9	122.6	125.6	125.7	133.7
Turkey	115.6	124.0	120.0	127.3	125.6	115.4	120.1	108.8	108.5	106.9
Venezuela, Bolivarian Republic of	98.3	98.7	107.3	119.0	137.7	188.3	116.6	132.6	155.6	145.9

Source: JPMorgan Chase.

a Year 2000=100.

b Indices based on a "broad" measure currency basket of 46 currencies (including the euro). The real effective exchange rate, which adjusts the nominal index for relative price changes, gauges the effect on international price competitiveness of the country's manufactures owing to currency changes and inflation differentials. A rise in the index implies a fall in competitiveness and vice versa. The relative price changes are based on indices most closely measuring the prices of domestically produced finished manufactured goods, excluding food and energy, at the first stage of manufacturing. The weights for currency indices are derived from 2000 bilateral trade patterns of the corresponding countries.

c Average for the first ten months.

d Special Administrative Region of China.

Table A.14
Indices of prices of primary commodities, 2004-2013

Index: Year 2000=100	Non-fuel commodities					Combined index		Manufactured export prices	Real prices of non-fuel commodities[a]	Crude petroleum[b]
	Food	Tropical beverages	Vegetable oilseeds and oils	Agricultural raw materials	Minerals and metals	Dollar	SDR			
2004	119	100	155	125	137	126	112	117	108	130.6
2005	127	126	141	129	173	140	126	120	117	183.5
2006	151	134	148	147	278	183	164	123	149	221.3
2007	164	148	226	164	313	207	178	133	155	250.4
2008	234	178	298	198	332	256	213	142	180	342.2
2009	220	181	213	163	232	213	182	134	159	221.2
2010	230	213	262	226	327	256	222	136	188	280.6
2011	265	270	333	289	375	302	253	148	204	389.3
2012	270	212	307	223	322	277	239	145	191	396.6
2010										
I	232	198	234	210	310	248	212	134	185	273.2
II	205	201	233	209	319	237	211	132	180	277.5
III	225	220	258	216	314	249	217	135	185	267.3
IV	257	233	322	268	366	290	247	141	206	303.5
2011										
I	274	278	364	315	406	321	271	144	223	365.9
II	261	283	345	303	393	308	255	150	205	407.1
III	270	274	324	290	382	306	254	150	204	393.2
IV	255	247	299	248	319	274	232	146	187	391.0
2012										
I	257	232	316	246	342	280	241	147	191	425
II	264	208	318	229	323	275	238	144	191	387
III	285	211	318	205	306	278	242	144	193	386
IV	276	198	277	211	319	274	236	147	187	389
2013										
I	266	186	280	216	332	273	237	147	186	396.7
II	260	176	262	202	297	259	228	147	176	365.6
III	251	169	258	202	296	252	221	...	...	387.4

Sources: UNCTAD, Monthly Commodity Price Bulletin; United Nations, Monthly Bulletin of Statistics; and data from the Organization of the Petroleum Exporting Countries (OPEC) website, available from http://www.opec.org.

a Combined index of non-fuel commodity prices in dollars, deflated by manufactured export price index.

b The new OPEC reference basket, introduced on 16 June 2005, currently has 12 crudes.

Table A.15
World oil supply and demand, 2005-2014

	2005	2006	2007	2008	2009	2010	2011	2012	2013[a]	2014[b]
World oil supply[c, d] *(millions of barrels per day)*	84.3	85.0	84.7	86.6	85.4	87.4	88.7	91.0	91.5	93.2
Developed economies	16.5	16.3	16.0	16.8	17.0	17.2	17.4	18.3	19.4	20.5
Economies in transition	12.0	12.4	12.9	12.9	13.3	13.5	13.6	13.6	13.8	13.9
Developing economies	54.0	54.4	53.6	54.9	53.1	54.6	55.6	57.0	56.1	56.6
OPEC[e]	34.2	34.3	34.6	36.1	34.0	34.7	35.8	37.6	36.8	36.8
Non-OPEC	19.8	20.1	19.0	18.8	19.1	19.9	19.8	19.4	19.3	19.8
Processing gains[f]	1.9	1.9	2.2	2.0	2.0	2.1	2.1	2.1	2.2	2.2
World total demand[g]	83.8	85.1	86.5	86.5	85.4	88.4	89.0	90.0	91.0	92.1
Oil prices *(dollars per barrel)*										
OPEC basket[h]	50.6	61.1	69.1	94.5	61.1	77.5	107.5	109.5	105.7	105.2
Brent oil	54.4	65.4	72.7	97.6	61.9	79.6	111.6	112.0	108.5	108.0

Sources: United Nations, World Bank, International Energy Agency, U.S. Energy Information Administration, and OPEC.

a Partly estimated.

b Baseline scenario forecasts.

c Including global biofuels, crude oil, condensates, natural gas liquids (NGLs), oil from non-conventional sources and other sources of supply.

d Totals may not add up because of rounding.

e Includes Angola as of January 2007 and Ecuador as of December 2007.

f Net volume gains and losses in the refining process (excluding net gain/loss in the economies in transition and China) and marine transportation losses.

g Including deliveries from refineries/primary stocks and marine bunkers, and refinery fuel and non-conventional oils.

h The new OPEC reference basket, introduced on 16 June 2005, currently has 12 crudes.

Table A.16
World trade:[a] changes in value and volume of exports and imports, by major country group, 2005-2015

Annual percentage change	2005	2006	2007	2008	2009	2010	2011	2012[b]	2013[c]	2014[c]	2015[c]
Dollar value of exports											
World	13.8	15.2	16.1	14.1	-19.7	19.5	18.1	2.6	2.0	5.8	7.1
Developed economies	9.4	12.6	15.3	11.1	-19.7	13.8	15.2	-1.7	1.7	3.3	4.8
North America	11.3	11.6	11.5	9.6	-16.9	17.2	14.5	3.6	1.9	5.4	6.5
EU plus other Europe	9.0	13.5	17.1	11.2	-20.0	10.5	16.0	-3.4	2.8	2.5	3.9
Developed Asia	8.4	8.6	11.2	13.9	-23.4	30.9	11.5	-1.9	-6.4	3.9	6.7
Economies in transition	28.0	24.9	21.7	31.6	-33.0	27.8	31.6	10.7	2.7	4.0	5.3
South-Eastern Europe	18.5	25.6	30.5	22.2	-20.3	12.8	21.3	-1.4	10.5	5.5	5.0
Commonwealth of Independent States	28.4	24.8	21.4	32.0	-33.5	28.5	32.1	11.1	2.4	3.9	5.3
Developing economies	21.2	19.0	16.9	17.3	-18.3	27.7	20.9	7.6	2.5	8.9	10.0
Latin America and the Caribbean	20.2	18.6	12.8	15.3	-20.7	31.0	17.8	5.1	0.4	8.3	10.0
Africa	29.5	23.4	12.7	27.6	-26.4	28.5	20.4	21.2	-3.6	3.5	5.8
Western Asia	30.2	18.1	15.7	28.7	-26.3	20.8	29.1	6.5	1.2	5.0	6.4
East and South Asia	18.5	18.8	18.6	13.8	-14.5	28.5	20.0	6.7	4.0	10.6	11.3
Dollar value of imports											
World	13.3	14.5	15.9	14.4	-20.1	19.0	18.0	2.0	1.7	6.1	7.5
Developed economies	11.2	12.9	13.4	11.4	-22.0	14.4	15.8	-1.9	-0.2	3.9	5.4
North America	13.0	10.8	6.5	7.6	-22.1	19.9	13.2	2.7	1.9	6.5	7.4
EU plus other Europe	10.2	14.4	16.9	11.6	-21.6	11.0	15.7	-5.1	0.0	2.7	4.4
Developed Asia	12.8	9.7	10.5	20.7	-24.8	23.9	23.1	6.2	-6.8	4.0	5.1
Economies in transition	20.6	24.5	34.9	29.1	-29.9	22.0	28.2	8.9	7.8	4.9	5.8
South-Eastern Europe	8.1	16.7	39.6	26.3	-27.6	3.0	19.3	0.1	7.4	5.2	5.9
Commonwealth of Independent States	22.1	25.3	34.5	29.4	-30.1	23.9	28.9	9.6	7.8	4.9	5.8
Developing economies	17.6	17.0	19.6	19.1	-15.4	26.7	20.8	7.2	3.9	9.0	10.3
Latin America and the Caribbean	18.6	18.1	19.3	20.8	-20.2	28.3	19.3	4.7	2.6	7.2	8.4
Africa	21.4	18.0	27.3	25.0	-11.7	10.7	16.6	5.6	7.1	10.6	11.8
Western Asia	21.4	18.4	28.8	21.8	-17.5	14.9	18.9	7.4	9.5	10.5	12.0
East and South Asia	16.2	16.4	16.9	17.3	-14.3	31.2	21.9	7.9	2.7	8.8	10.1
Volume of exports											
World	7.6	9.5	6.9	2.8	-9.3	12.7	6.5	3.1	2.2	4.6	5.2
Developed economies	5.6	8.7	6.2	1.9	-11.7	11.3	5.5	2.4	1.6	3.9	4.7
North America	5.0	6.7	6.9	3.2	-10.0	10.5	6.6	3.1	2.0	4.3	4.9
EU plus other Europe	5.8	9.4	5.8	1.6	-11.4	10.6	6.0	2.2	1.2	3.6	4.6
Developed Asia	5.2	8.0	7.2	1.8	-17.1	18.0	-0.4	1.6	3.8	4.8	4.9
Economies in transition	3.5	6.6	7.3	1.8	-7.4	6.6	3.0	1.1	0.7	3.5	4.5
South-Eastern Europe	16.5	13.6	7.9	4.4	-10.3	19.6	6.6	3.4	6.8	6.2	5.3
Commonwealth of Independent States	3.1	6.3	7.3	1.7	-7.3	6.2	2.9	1.0	0.4	3.4	4.4
Developing economies	11.6	11.0	7.9	4.2	-6.0	15.4	8.4	4.3	3.2	5.7	5.8
Latin America and the Caribbean	7.6	6.2	4.7	1.6	-9.6	9.6	6.5	2.4	2.5	4.5	5.1
Africa	10.4	11.8	3.3	7.9	-14.4	9.1	-3.4	11.6	-0.9	5.9	5.1
Western Asia	9.2	7.7	5.1	3.5	-8.3	6.7	7.6	5.0	-0.4	4.1	4.0
East and South Asia	13.9	13.4	10.4	4.4	-2.9	20.0	10.7	3.6	4.7	6.3	6.4

Table A.16
World trade a: changes in value and volume of exports and imports, by major country group, 2005-2015 (*continued*)

Annual percentage change	2005	2006	2007	2008	2009	2010	2011	2012	2013	2014	2015
Volume of imports											
World	8.2	9.5	7.7	2.8	-10.5	13.6	6.9	2.6	2.4	4.8	5.3
Developed economies	6.1	8.1	5.0	0.4	-12.2	10.8	4.7	1.0	0.5	4.0	4.5
North America	6.3	6.0	2.8	-2.1	-13.4	12.9	5.0	2.4	1.4	4.8	5.0
EU plus other Europe	6.2	9.6	6.0	1.1	-11.4	9.9	4.1	-0.2	-0.0	3.4	4.4
Developed Asia	5.0	4.7	4.5	2.5	-14.2	11.8	7.0	5.5	1.6	5.4	3.7
Economies in transition	11.1	15.9	22.7	11.7	-26.1	16.6	16.2	7.3	6.6	4.6	5.0
South-Eastern Europe	6.0	7.5	16.1	7.1	-19.0	8.8	5.1	1.7	4.4	5.4	6.0
Commonwealth of Independent States	11.7	16.8	23.4	12.1	-26.7	17.3	17.1	7.7	6.8	4.6	4.9
Developing economies	12.7	11.8	11.8	6.4	-5.8	18.1	9.7	4.6	4.6	5.9	6.3
Latin America and the Caribbean	10.9	14.1	13.0	8.1	-14.8	21.6	10.5	4.9	3.5	5.3	4.7
Africa	11.6	11.0	18.4	9.1	-5.7	7.5	7.3	4.5	5.6	6.6	6.9
Western Asia	16.3	10.0	18.8	7.7	-13.8	8.8	9.0	4.1	4.6	4.8	6.0
East and South Asia	12.6	11.7	9.2	5.3	-1.6	20.7	10.0	4.6	4.8	6.2	6.6

Source: UN/DESA.
a Includes goods and non-factor services.
b Partly estimated.
c Baseline scenario forecasts, based in part on Project LINK.

Table A.17

Balance of payments on current accounts, by country or country group, summary table, 2004-2012

Billions of dollars	2004	2005	2006	2007	2008	2009	2010	2011	2012
Developed economies	-332.0	-493.9	-578.6	-537.3	-671.6	-221.3	-194.3	-238.4	-212.4
Japan	172.1	166.1	170.9	212.1	159.9	146.6	204.0	119.3	60.4
United States	-629.3	-739.8	-798.5	-713.4	-681.3	-381.6	-449.5	-457.7	-440.4
Europe[a]	147.5	108.8	81.5	21.8	-93.5	98.9	149.7	189.7	295.3
EU-15	114.9	51.3	35.6	43.7	-52.4	40.3	63.3	112.0	180.2
New EU member States	-47.4	-42.4	-63.8	-106.6	-119.7	-38.2	-43.6	-43.3	-25.9
Economies in transition[b]	57.8	82.4	88.7	54.1	90.2	35.6	63.1	101.0	68.6
South-Eastern Europe	-5.8	-5.1	-5.3	-11.5	-18.5	-7.3	-5.9	-8.4	-8.2
Commonwealth of Independent States[c]	63.5	87.5	94.0	65.6	108.7	42.9	69.0	109.4	76.7
Developing economies	274.5	449.2	699.7	765.9	775.0	385.5	445.8	500.1	495.3
Net fuel exporters	123.7	263.5	381.9	334.7	435.2	75.7	220.9	491.6	471.6
Net fuel importers	150.8	185.7	317.8	431.2	339.9	309.8	224.9	8.5	23.7
Latin America and the Caribbean	21.4	34.6	48.9	8.7	-36.9	-28.4	-61.2	-76.2	-102.3
Net fuel exporters	16.1	28.2	33.8	18.6	37.6	-0.0	3.3	17.5	3.7
Net fuel importers	5.3	6.4	15.1	-9.8	-74.5	-28.3	-64.5	-93.6	-106.1
Africa	11.6	37.4	84.3	68.3	60.9	-33.5	-0.0	-14.2	-31.1
Net fuel exporters	24.6	55.2	106.0	102.4	114.0	5.9	39.5	43.6	48.6
Net fuel importers	-13.0	-17.8	-21.7	-34.1	-53.1	-39.4	-39.5	-57.9	-79.7
Western Asia	59.0	136.0	179.8	139.3	221.9	41.7	99.3	283.7	339.9
Net fuel exporters[d]	75.1	159.2	206.4	175.5	264.3	51.6	144.3	363.8	399.2
Net fuel importers	-16.2	-23.2	-26.7	-36.2	-42.4	-9.8	-45.1	-80.2	-59.3
East and South Asia	182.5	241.2	386.7	549.6	529.2	405.6	407.8	306.8	288.8
Net fuel exporters	7.9	20.9	35.7	38.3	19.2	18.3	33.8	66.6	20.0
Net fuel importers	174.6	220.3	351.0	511.3	509.9	387.3	373.9	240.2	268.8
World residual[e]	0.2	37.7	209.8	282.7	193.6	199.8	314.7	362.8	351.5

Sources: International Monetary Fund (IMF), World Economic Outlook, October 2013; and IMF, Balance of Payments Statistics.

a Europe consists of the EU-15, the new EU member States and Iceland, Norway and Switzerland.

b Includes Georgia.

c Excludes Georgia, which left the Commonwealth of Independent States on 18 August 2009.

d Data for Iraq not available prior to 2005.

e Statistical discrepancy.

Table A.18
Balance of payments on current accounts, by country or country group, 2004-2012

Billions of dollars	2004	2005	2006	2007	2008	2009	2010	2011	2012
Developed economies									
Trade balance	-434.5	-652.0	-797.0	-799.9	-932.5	-488.2	-598.1	-798.8	-767.9
Services, net	175.5	231.1	297.8	405.2	445.6	389.0	447.1	544.9	543.5
Income, net	129.4	165.6	159.6	153.6	141.9	197.1	297.1	371.3	362.4
Current transfers, net	-202.4	-238.6	-238.9	-296.2	-326.7	-319.3	-340.3	-355.8	-350.4
Current-account balance	-332.0	-493.9	-578.6	-537.3	-671.6	-221.3	-194.3	-238.4	-212.4
Japan									
Trade balance	128.5	93.9	81.1	105.1	38.5	43.3	91.0	-20.6	-73.2
Services, net	-34.3	-24.1	-18.2	-21.2	-20.8	-20.4	-16.1	-22.2	-31.2
Income, net	85.7	103.9	118.7	139.8	155.3	135.9	141.5	176.0	179.1
Current transfers, net	-7.9	-7.6	-10.7	-11.5	-13.1	-12.3	-12.4	-13.8	-14.2
Current-account balance	172.1	166.1	170.9	212.1	159.9	146.6	204.0	119.3	60.4
United States									
Trade balance	-666.4	-784.1	-838.8	-822.7	-834.0	-510.5	-650.2	-744.1	-741.5
Services, net	61.5	76.2	86.4	123.7	131.7	126.9	150.8	187.3	206.8
Income, net	64.1	67.6	43.3	100.6	146.1	123.6	177.7	232.7	223.9
Current transfers, net	-88.6	-99.5	-89.4	-114.9	-125.2	-121.6	-127.8	-133.5	-129.7
Current-account balance	-629.3	-739.8	-798.5	-713.4	-681.3	-381.6	-449.5	-457.7	-440.4
Europe[a]									
Trade balance	73.1	4.1	-69.6	-105.3	-172.0	-14.2	-49.2	-65.8	63.1
Services, net	151.8	183.3	234.9	313.1	353.7	297.7	338.1	412.3	404.7
Income, net	28.3	51.3	53.4	-18.2	-87.0	-2.0	56.4	46.4	28.5
Current transfers, net	-105.7	-129.9	-137.1	-168.0	-188.3	-182.7	-195.6	-203.2	-201.1
Current-account balance	147.5	108.8	81.5	21.8	-93.5	98.9	149.7	189.7	295.3
EU-15									
Trade balance	78.6	2.0	-65.1	-73.0	-147.2	-39.1	-74.8	-109.2	0.6
Services, net	110.0	134.5	178.7	243.9	270.4	222.5	257.4	324.0	323.6
Income, net	32.1	41.5	58.8	40.6	10.1	35.6	74.6	99.8	54.9
Current transfers, net	-105.7	-126.6	-136.7	-167.9	-185.7	-178.7	-193.9	-202.6	-198.8
Current-account balance	114.9	51.4	35.6	43.7	-52.4	40.3	63.3	112.0	180.2
New EU member States									
Trade balance	-43.0	-45.7	-62.3	-92.1	-116.8	-36.4	-38.0	-39.9	-22.9
Services, net	15.5	19.9	23.0	31.6	37.1	31.5	33.3	39.4	39.2
Income, net	-29.0	-27.1	-36.4	-59.0	-54.2	-45.8	-54.2	-60.7	-57.7
Current transfers, net	9.1	10.4	11.9	12.9	14.2	12.5	15.3	17.9	15.6
Current-account balance	-47.4	-42.4	-63.8	-106.6	-119.7	-38.2	-43.6	-43.3	-25.9
Economies in transition[b]									
Trade balance	79.5	113.6	133.9	114.6	177.4	106.0	156.2	224.6	214.1
Services, net	-16.5	-16.6	-15.9	-24.2	-28.5	-24.5	-31.8	-37.8	-52.6
Income, net	-16.2	-26.8	-42.0	-48.3	-72.7	-59.4	-74.7	-100.2	-104.3
Current transfers, net	10.8	12.1	12.7	12.0	14.0	13.6	13.4	14.4	11.3
Current-account balance	57.8	82.4	88.7	54.1	90.2	35.6	63.1	101.0	68.6

Billions of dollars	2004	2005	2006	2007	2008	2009	2010	2011	2012
Economies in transition[b] (continued)									
South-Eastern Europe									
Trade balance	-14.3	-13.8	-15.1	-22.0	-28.7	-18.8	-16.7	-19.8	-18.3
Services, net	0.7	0.6	0.8	1.1	1.4	1.6	1.7	2.1	2.0
Income, net	0.5	0.0	0.2	-0.2	-0.7	-0.4	-0.9	-1.0	-1.3
Current transfers, net	7.3	8.1	8.8	9.6	9.6	10.3	9.9	10.3	9.5
Current-account balance	-5.8	-5.1	-5.3	-11.5	-18.5	-7.3	-5.9	-8.4	-8.2
Commonwealth of Independent States[c]									
Trade balance	93.8	127.4	149.0	136.6	206.1	124.8	172.9	244.4	232.4
Services, net	-17.1	-17.2	-16.7	-25.3	-29.9	-26.0	-33.5	-39.9	-54.6
Income, net	-16.7	-26.8	-42.2	-48.1	-72.0	-59.1	-73.8	-99.2	-103.0
Current transfers, net	3.6	4.1	3.9	2.4	4.4	3.2	3.5	4.2	1.9
Current-account balance	63.5	87.5	94.0	65.6	108.7	42.9	69.0	109.4	76.7
Developing economies									
Trade balance	363.8	574.5	770.3	824.2	864.0	534.3	672.5	857.7	870.1
Services, net	-56.5	-76.1	-89.5	-104.3	-143.1	-164.6	-165.2	-212.6	-248.0
Income, net	-151.7	-198.6	-168.7	-166.5	-180.6	-193.0	-280.4	-361.6	-329.1
Current transfers, net	120.2	150.6	189.1	214.4	236.9	210.1	220.8	223.2	204.1
Current-account balance	274.5	449.2	699.7	765.9	775.0	385.5	445.8	500.1	495.3
Net fuel exporters									
Trade balance	257.6	410.7	521.5	526.8	709.3	338.4	539.1	878.7	880.9
Services, net	-75.8	-88.6	-114.7	-156.1	-212.3	-204.4	-208.4	-240.7	-272.5
Income, net	-51.5	-62.9	-37.5	-41.0	-64.6	-49.1	-94.6	-119.7	-110.8
Current transfers, net	-5.2	5.5	14.3	6.9	4.9	-8.0	-13.2	-20.3	-24.3
Current-account balance	123.7	263.5	381.9	334.7	435.2	75.7	220.9	491.6	471.6
Net fuel importers									
Trade balance	106.2	163.8	248.9	297.3	154.7	195.9	133.4	-21.0	-10.8
Services, net	19.3	12.5	25.2	51.8	69.2	39.8	43.2	28.1	24.4
Income, net	-100.2	-135.7	-131.1	-125.4	-116.0	-143.9	-185.8	-241.9	-218.3
Current transfers, net	125.5	145.1	174.8	207.5	232.0	218.1	234.1	243.4	228.4
Current-account balance	150.8	185.7	317.8	431.2	339.9	309.8	224.9	8.5	23.7
Latin America and the Caribbean									
Trade balance	60.8	83.9	101.7	72.9	43.8	54.5	51.4	75.7	49.6
Services, net	-15.1	-19.1	-21.2	-28.6	-37.8	-51.9	-54.2	-68.1	-88.8
Income, net	-69.2	-83.4	-95.7	-102.5	-110.0	-88.5	-118.8	-146.6	-124.8
Current transfers, net	45.0	53.2	64.0	66.9	67.1	57.5	60.4	62.8	61.6
Current-account balance	21.4	34.6	48.9	8.7	-36.9	-28.4	-61.2	-76.2	-102.3
Africa									
Trade balance	33.4	67.6	93.4	95.5	113.7	-0.0	50.7	59.9	44.1
Services, net	-10.9	-15.0	-21.7	-33.6	-55.3	-48.3	-53.3	-64.3	-69.2
Income, net	-34.5	-44.9	-36.3	-49.3	-61.5	-46.5	-63.8	-76.7	-82.7
Current transfers, net	24.9	30.8	50.5	57.7	66.1	62.5	68.2	73.4	78.4
Current-account balance	11.6	37.4	84.3	68.3	60.9	-33.5	-0.0	-14.2	-31.1

Table A.18
Balance of payments on current accounts, by country or country group, 2004-2012 (*continued*)

Billions of dollars	2004	2005	2006	2007	2008	2009	2010	2011	2012
Developing economies (*continued*)									
Western Asia[d]									
Trade balance	110.6	184.9	236.2	222.2	343.2	169.1	253.1	466.7	537.4
Services, net	-25.5	-26.8	-44.3	-64.6	-86.5	-76.1	-88.4	-107.2	-113.5
Income, net	-17.1	-13.9	2.0	7.8	-5.0	-12.1	-17.4	-17.3	-16.0
Current transfers, net	-9.1	-8.2	-14.1	-26.1	-29.8	-39.1	-48.0	-58.5	-68.0
Current-account balance	59.0	136.0	179.8	139.3	221.9	41.7	99.3	283.7	339.9
East Asia									
Trade balance	194.9	280.2	391.1	505.4	479.9	433.2	438.6	412.4	440.7
Services, net	-14.0	-28.7	-20.4	-2.6	0.6	-9.5	-3.9	-24.1	-31.1
Income, net	-22.7	-46.7	-27.4	-13.3	7.9	-31.9	-58.2	-100.5	-78.2
Current transfers, net	24.7	32.9	38.0	50.9	62.1	48.8	54.7	43.9	25.2
Current-account balance	182.9	237.7	381.3	540.4	550.5	440.6	431.3	331.7	356.7
South Asia									
Trade balance	-36.0	-42.1	-52.1	-71.8	-116.6	-122.5	-121.2	-157.0	-201.8
Services, net	9.0	13.5	18.1	25.1	35.9	21.2	34.5	51.1	54.6
Income, net	-8.1	-9.8	-11.3	-9.2	-12.0	-14.1	-22.2	-20.5	-27.5
Current transfers, net	34.7	41.9	50.8	65.0	71.4	80.5	85.4	101.5	106.8
Current-account balance	-0.4	3.5	5.5	9.2	-21.3	-35.0	-23.5	-24.9	-67.8
World residual[e]									
Trade balance	8.8	36.2	107.2	138.8	108.9	152.1	230.6	283.5	316.3
Services, net	102.6	138.4	192.4	276.7	274.0	199.9	250.1	294.5	242.8
Income, net	-38.5	-59.8	-51.1	-61.1	-111.4	-55.4	-58.0	-90.5	-70.9
Current transfers, net	-71.4	-75.9	-37.2	-69.8	-75.9	-95.7	-106.1	-118.2	-135.0
Current-account balance	0.2	37.7	209.9	282.7	193.6	199.8	314.7	362.8	351.5

Sources: International Monetary Fund (IMF), World Economic Outlook, October 2013; and IMF, Balance of Payments Statistics.
a Europe consists of EU-15, new EU member States plus Iceland, Norway and Switzerland.
b Includes Georgia.
c Excludes Georgia, which left the Commonwealth of Independent States on 18 August 2009.
d Data for Iraq not available prior to 2005.
e Statistical discrepancy.

Table A.19
Net ODA from major sources, by type, 1991-2012

| Donor group or country | Growth rate of ODA (2011 prices and exchange rates) | | | | | ODA as a percentage of GNI | Total ODA (millions of dollars) | Percentage distribution of ODA by type, 2012 | | | |
	1991-2001	2001-2009	2010	2011	2012	2012	2012	Bilateral Total	Multilateral Total (United Nations & Other)	United Nations	Other
Total DAC countries	-0.5	5.0	5.9	-2.2	-3.9	0.29	126384	70.9	29.1	5.2	23.9
Total EU	-0.4	5.6	5.9	-3.0	-7.2	0.40	64505	63.1	36.9	5.5	31.4
Austria	7.7	7.5	9.3	-14.2	6.1	0.28	1112	48.4	51.6	2.7	48.9
Belgium	-0.0	6.3	18.6	-12.7	-13.0	0.47	2303	62.0	38.0	7.8	30.1
Denmark	4.2	-1.1	3.2	-3.3	-1.8	0.83	2693	71.4	28.6	10.7	17.9
Finland	-5.0	7.6	8.2	-2.5	-0.4	0.53	1320	60.5	39.5	11.7	27.9
France[a]	-3.5	4.3	6.6	-5.4	-0.8	0.46	12106	66.2	33.8	2.0	31.9
Germany	-1.5	5.8	12.0	2.5	-0.7	0.38	13108	66.6	33.4	2.6	30.9
Greece	...	5.8	-13.1	-21.1	-17.0	0.13	324	27.3	72.7	7.7	65.0
Ireland	14.9	12.6	-4.3	-2.9	-5.8	0.48	809	66.3	33.7	11.6	22.2
Italy	-6.7	4.5	-4.8	35.8	-34.7	0.13	2639	18.8	81.2	7.0	74.3
Luxembourg	15.6	6.6	-5.1	-7.9	9.8	1.00	399	69.3	30.7	13.0	17.6
Netherlands	2.3	2.1	2.9	-6.1	-6.6	0.71	5524	70.7	29.3	9.8	19.5
Portugal	4.0	0.9	31.7	3.2	-13.1	0.28	581	68.4	31.6	1.9	29.7
Spain	5.6	10.3	-5.4	-33.8	-49.7	0.15	1948	43.3	56.7	3.4	53.3
Sweden	0.2	7.4	-7.0	10.3	-3.4	0.99	5242	69.5	30.5	12.7	17.8
United Kingdom	2.7	8.1	13.9	-0.6	-2.2	0.56	13659	65.2	34.8	4.7	30.1
Australia	0.6	5.6	11.7	9.9	10.4	0.36	5440	85.3	14.7	4.2	10.4
Canada	-3.0	5.4	14.1	-2.6	4.1	0.32	5678	75.8	24.2	3.3	21.0
Japan	-0.1	-3.3	11.8	-8.8	-2.1	0.17	10494	65.5	34.5	5.4	29.1
New Zealand	3.2	5.1	-7.6	9.7	3.0	0.28	455	81.4	18.6	10.6	8.1
Norway	1.6	4.6	-3.0	-5.1	0.4	0.93	4754	74.9	25.1	13.1	12.0
Switzerland	2.2	3.8	-4.7	12.6	4.5	0.45	3022	80.9	19.1	6.8	12.4
United States	-2.0	9.5	3.9	-0.7	-2.8	0.19	30460	83.9	16.1	3.5	12.7

Source: UN/DESA, based on OECD/DAC online database, available from http://www.oecd-ilibrary.org/statistics.

a Excluding flows from France to the Overseas Departments, namely Guadeloupe, French Guiana, Martinique and Réunion.

Table A.20
Total net ODA flows from OECD Development Assistance Committee countries, by type, 2003-2012

	Net disbursements at current prices and exchange rates (billions of dollars)									
	2003	2004	2005	2006	2007	2008	2009	2010	2011	2012
Official Development Assistance	69.6	80.1	108.3	105.4	104.9	122.7	120.5	129.0	134.4	126.4
Bilateral official development assistance	50.1	54.8	83.1	77.5	73.7	87.1	83.9	91.0	94.3	89.6
in the form of:										
Technical cooperation	18.4	18.7	20.8	22.4	15.1	17.3	17.6	18.0	17.8	0.2
Humanitarian aid	4.4	5.2	7.2	6.8	6.5	8.8	8.6	9.3	9.7	8.2
Debt forgiveness	9.8	8.0	26.2	18.9	9.7	11.1	2.0	4.2	6.3	0.0
Bilateral loans	-1.0	-2.8	-0.8	-2.4	-2.2	-1.1	2.5	3.3	1.7	...
Contributions to multilateral institutions[a]	19.5	25.4	25.2	27.9	31.2	35.6	36.6	38.0	40.1	36.7
of which are:										
UN agencies	4.9	5.2	5.5	5.3	5.9	5.9	6.2	6.5	6.6	...
EU institutions	6.9	9.0	9.4	10.1	12.0	13.5	14.2	13.6	13.6	...
World Bank	3.6	6.4	5.3	7.2	6.2	8.6	7.6	9.1	10.1	...
Regional development banks	1.8	2.3	2.2	2.5	2.4	3.2	3.1	3.2	4.1	...
Others	2.3	2.5	2.7	2.7	4.6	4.4	5.4	5.7	5.7	...
Memorandum item										
Bilateral ODA to least developed countries	16.5	16.0	15.9	17.3	19.7	23.4	24.3	28.5	29.7	...

Source: UN/DESA, based on OECD/DAC online database, available from http://www.oecd.org/dac/stats/idsonline.

a Grants and capital subscriptions. Does not include concessional lending to multilateral agencies.